W9-BRZ-926

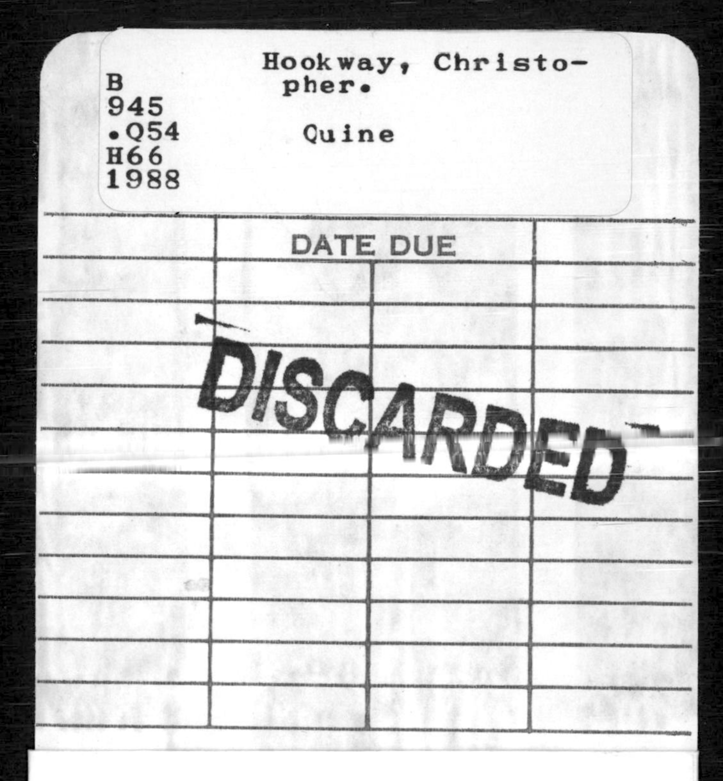
Hookway, Christopher.
Quine
DATE DUE
DISCARDED

Quine

Quine

Language, Experience and Reality

Christopher Hookway

Stanford University Press
Stanford, California
1988

Stanford University Press
Stanford, California

Originating publisher: Polity Press, Cambridge
in association with Basil Blackwell, Oxford
First published in the U.S.A. by
Stanford University Press, 1988
Printed in Great Britain
Cloth ISBN 0-8047-1386-3
Paper ISBN 0-8047-1475-4
LC 87-62782

Contents

For my mother and father

Preface

This volume examines the views of the most influential American philosopher of the post-war period, Willard van Orman Quine. His views are interesting and important in their own right, but they are of value too in providing the background to much recent analytical philosophy. Many philosophers who do not agree with Quine consciously develop their views in response to his, and I hope that the book will help with understanding these developments. In line with the aims of the series, I have tried to make the book accessible to non-philosophers and to students. To this end, there is little discussion of technical issues in logic and the philosophy of mathematics, and I have tried to explain all of the logical notation that I have used.

Writing about a contemporary philosopher calls for a balance between exposition and critical evaluation. A compromise is needed between a careful exposition which risks suggesting that the subject cannot provide a clear statement of his own views, and an extended critical engagement which may leave the reader uncertain why the author thinks his subject's views are important. Quine's writings are not easily understood: he is a systematic philosopher, and the systematic underpinnings of his positions are not always apparent. Hence, the early chapters are weighted more heavily towards exegesis, and towards placing Quine's views within this wider context, but the amount of critical evaluation grows as the volume proceeds.

I am grateful to Jonathan Dancy for comments upon an early draft, which led to many improvements of style and substance, to Harold Noonan, whose comments on part of the text saved me from several mistakes, and to Michael Bryon for helpful discussions of Quine and Carnap. My greatest debt is to my wife, Jo, who provided indispensable personal support during the writing, and technical support in coping with a recalcitrant word processor, and even found time to improve my English after reading the final draft.

C. H.

Note on References

Works cited in the text are listed in the References (pp. 221–4). This list is in two main parts, the first covering works by Quine and subdivided into 'Books', and 'Articles which are not reprinted in any of the books'. In each case the list is given in date order of first publication, and an abbreviation is shown by which the work is referred to in the text as source for quotations. For ease of reference book initials are given in parentheses after first mention of articles that appear in the books.

The second part of the References, 'Other References', lists works by other writers. It is arranged alphabetically and, for authors with more than one entry, in date order of first publication; where applicable, however, page references in the text are to the subsequent edition cited. Works in this part are referred to in the text by author/date.

Introduction

Quine was born in 1908. He studied as a graduate student at Harvard, and apart from short visits to Oxford, Paris and other centres of learning, he stayed there as a philosophy teacher until his retirement in the mid-1970s. No contemporary thinker can equal the influence he has upon recent analytical philosophy, through both his teaching and his extensive publications.

These publications include at least fifteen books together with numerous articles. Many of these, including most of the early ones, are concerned with formal logic. The works with the greatest philosophical impact are *From a Logical Point of View*, published in 1953, and *Word and Object*, from 1960. A number of monographs and collections have appeared since then, and his philosophical views have been clarified and developed in many ways. However, the core of his position is present in these relatively early works. The former is a collection of papers, including two classics, 'On what there is' and 'Two dogmas of empiricism'. These contain trenchant criticisms of many of the assumptions of twentieth-century empiricism, and advocate what is described as a kind of pragmatism.

Word and Object is an extended treatise on philosophy of language. Many themes from the earlier book remain, but they are systematically developed and related to a naturalistic perspective which had not been evident in 1953. This naturalism involves stressing continuities between philosophy and empirical science, and approaching philosophical issues from the point of view of an austere, somewhat behaviourist standpoint. It leads to one of Quine's most famous, and most controversial, doctrines, the indeterminacy of translation.

Particularly because he avowed 'pragmatism' in 1953, and because he is linked to John Dewey by his defence of 'naturalism', some people are tempted to view Quine as a distinctively American philosopher. He is seen as continuing the pragmatist tradition of Peirce, William James, Dewey, Mead and others. While he was influenced by his Harvard teacher C. I. Lewis, who belonged to that tradition, such an interpretation would be highly misleading. It encourages a distorted reading of the work of the earlier pragmatists, who would have found many of Quine's views uncongenial, and, more important, it can prevent our appreciating Quine's relations to the logical empiricist or logical positivist movement. While in his early twenties Quine had visited the Vienna Circle, the home of logical positivism, and this seems to have shaped his philosophical outlook. His views cannot be understood other than as a response to the positions defended by Rudolf Carnap and the other positivists. The force of his critical arguments is missed when it is not appreciated that he is arguing against the form of empiricism which he encountered in the work of Carnap. And the reader will fail to understand his positive views if it is not seen that he remained faithful to the underlying spirit of positivism.

The outlook of the Viennese positivists involved several related components. Most important was a commitment to scientism: scientific knowledge serves as a paradigm for all knowledge; and philosophy can be a respectable activity only if it can itself be pursued as a science. In most cases, this was coupled with the claim that all of the sciences could be unified into a single body of knowledge grounded in physics, and with the view that physics tells the whole story about the fundamental character of reality. This led to a repudiation of areas of discourse that did not meet scientific standards. Metaphysics, religious claims, ethical and aesthetic propositions were rejected as meaningless. These views were grounded semantically, employing the empiricist view that the meaning of a word or sentence somehow involved a connection with experience. If we do not know what experience would show that a proposition was true, we do not understand the proposition. Philosophers could employ logical analysis to clarify the meanings of troublesome words and sentences – or to reveal that they had no meaning.

In 'Two dogmas of empiricism' (FLPV), Quine attacked the semantic doctrines of the positivists. He denied that we can talk sensibly about the links between particular propositions and experience, rejected the positivists' ideal of philosophical analysis, challenged their reductionist assumptions, and insisted upon the holistic character of the relations between our beliefs and our experience. He concluded that philosophers' use of the notion of meaning was indefensible, and thus challenged the whole idea of philosophical analysis.

However, his commitment to other positivist dogmas remained. He never rejected empiricism, and he continued to believe that philosophy must be scientific. This is the source of his naturalism; and his austere behaviourist approach reflects his continuing loyalty to the view that reality is a *physical* system. His greatest philosophical contribution has probably been to develop, in a consistent and rigorous fashion, the consequences of a set of assumptions whose appeal cannot be denied even by those philosophers who reject them. All our knowledge of external reality comes through the senses; the only real knowledge is scientific knowledge; and the universe is, fundamentally, a physical system. Above all, Quine is a systematic philosopher who has articulated this empiricist, physicalist vision of knowledge and reality with great clarity.

This volume is divided into four parts. The first of these examines the views defended in *From a Logical Point of View*, and introduces the sources of Quine's naturalism. The second part explains the metaphysical and logical doctrines which determine the character of many of his views, and which come to the fore in *Word and Object*. We here consider his physicalism and his view that an adequate language for science is 'extensional'. In the third part, we examine the indeterminacy of translation, and compare Quine's views with those of a philosopher much influenced by him, Donald Davidson. Davidson exploits Quine's insights about language while rejecting some of the underlying commitments which link him to the positivist movement. This enables us, in the final part, to begin to evaluate Quine's physicalist naturalism and his empiricism. By the end of this part, we shall unravel some of the complexities of Quine's position and see how it is possible to dissent from it.

Part I

The Evolution of Empiricism

1

Language and the World

1.1 INTRODUCTION

In 'Five milestones of empiricism', reprinted in *Theories and Things*, Quine describes 'five points where empiricism has taken a turn for the better' (TT, p. 67) since the seventeenth century. He sees his own work as the culmination of this process of improvement. Examining these five 'milestones' will enable us to introduce some of the doctrines for which he is best known, and will also help us to see how Quine himself views the historical context of his philosophical position. This will occupy us for the first three chapters.

We do not require a precise definition of 'empiricism': it is enough that empiricists take seriously the claims of the sciences to provide our best knowledge of reality, and hold that this knowledge is grounded in sensory experience. When we raise the philosophical question of how such knowledge of reality is possible at all, we tend to focus first upon questions of evidential support: how does experience enable us to sort our beliefs into those that are true and those that are false? But there is a prior question about how thoughts and utterances can be about the world at all: what is it for a sound, an inscription on paper or a blackboard, or a state of someone's mind, to represent some external state of affairs? What is involved in understanding a thought or utterance, in knowing what it means? These questions raise a host of issues about representation, meaning and reference which have been fundamental for twentieth-century analytical philosophy.

It is an assumption of much twentieth-century philosophy that we naturally fall victim to certain deeply mistaken pictures of how thought and language relate to the world. They tend to be uncritically accepted, but seriously distort our philosophical thinking; indeed, these false pictures often give rise to apparent philosophical problems, which can be dismissed once the pictures that produce them are rejected. For many analytical philosophers, all of the traditional 'problems of philosophy' result from this kind of distortion. The 'milestones' to which Quine refers all involve developments in our philosophical understanding of representation: they promise philosophical enlightenment by overthrowing entrenched, but mistaken, conceptions of how thought and language work.

We can pass over the first milestone rapidly. It is 'the shift of attention from ideas to words'; focusing the analysis of representation upon linguistic expressions or utterances rather than upon thoughts or ideas. The merit of this shift was that attention could turn from shadowy objects of introspection to more easily examined public representations. My concern in this chapter is with the second milestone, 'the shift of semantic focus from terms to sentences'. This introduces some of the most important foundational doctrines for contemporary philosophy of language. Examining these will help us to explain Quine's approach to issues of what he calls 'ontology', in his classic paper 'On what there is' (FLPV).

1.2 MEANING AND NAMING

A natural starting point for an explanation of how language works is that words stand for things; we understand a word when we know what thing it stands for. Thus, I understand the word 'London' when I know which city it refers to or denotes, and I understand 'Quine' when I know which person it names. A sentence can then be looked on as a sequence or arrangement of words, and our understanding of the sentence is built out of our knowledge of what the words stand for. Finally, we can say that a sentence is true when the arrangement of words in the sentence corresponds, in some fashion, to the arrangement in reality of the things that those words stand for. This is only a vague sketch of a possible theory – the notion of arrangement conceals a host of problems – but it will do as a stalking horse for our present discussion; it cannot be denied that it has considerable initial plausibility. In this section, I shall introduce some problems faced by any theory of this general shape. We can then investigate how Quine's second milestone enables us to move beyond this theory and respond to these problems.

By way of preparation, we must labour the obvious point that a language such as English contains expressions of different kinds. Consider the sentence:

Quine is American.

The name 'Quine' functions as a subject expression which purports to pick out a unique individual: we shall call it a singular term. 'London' is also a singular term, and it is clear too that a more complex phrase, a 'definite description' such as 'The author of *Word and Object*', can also be used to pick out a single individual. The expression 'is American' does not purport to pick out a single individual, but rather expresses a general characteristic which can be applied to many things: such expressions can be called predicates. The sentence inset above is formally analogous to

London is populous.

Each employs a singular term together with a predicate which is used to apply some characteristic to the individual that the singular term refers to. Using upper case letters 'F', 'G' etc. to mark the places occupied by predicates, and lower cases letters 'a', 'b', etc. to mark the places of singular terms, we can express this common form:

Fa (It is a logician's convention that the predicate is written first.)

A sentence such as:

Brutus killed Caesar

contains two singular terms (two subject expressions), 'Brutus' and 'Caesar', together with a predicate expression that expresses a relation between two persons, that of killing. Using 'R' etc. to mark the places of relational predicates, we can express the form of this sentence:

Rab.

The sentence

London is south of Birmingham

is also of this form: it concerns a relation between two things.

There is one other kind of expression to which I want to draw attention here. In a sentence like

It is not the case that Quine is German,

the expression 'it is not the case that' is attached to the complete sentence 'Quine is German'. Similarly, two complete sentences are conjoined by 'and' in:

Quine is American and Frege is German.

Following logician's practice, I shall use '~' to express 'it is not the case that' (negation) and '&' to express 'and' (conjunction). The forms of our last two sentences can be expressed:

~Fa

Fa & Gb.

These expressions which attach to, or connect, complete sentences will be called connectives or operators. 'Or' (disjunction), formally expressed by 'v', functions analogously to 'and'.

Thus, we have three kinds of expressions: singular terms, including names; predicates including relational expressions; and various operators. There is no suggestion that this exhausts the resources of a natural language, nor that it accounts for all occurrences of the expressions that we have mentioned. But it provides us with a useful account of a fragment of most natural languages, and contains just enough complexity to enable us to understand some important philosophical doctrines: we can formulate difficulties for our plausible account of language.

Let us begin by looking at how predicates work. It seems easy enough to find the things that singular terms stand for: 'Quine' stands for a man, 'London' for a city, and these are comfortably concrete observable objects. But what of an expression like 'is red', 'is American' or 'killed'? These do not stand for concrete observable objects. 'Red' cannot stand for any particular red object for it could not then be used to say truly of any other object that it is red. The only candidate for the referent of 'is red' is that it stands for the attribute or general character of redness or of being-red. This does not seem to be a concrete or observable thing: I can see particular red things, but I cannot see the general character of redness. We seem to be committed by our account of representation to the view that there are such general characters, that we are aware of them, and that we only understand predicates by somehow associating them with such general objects.

A parallel problem arises from the use of operators or connectives: what do 'not' and 'and' stand for? There does not seem to be anything in our experience to serve as the meanings of these expressions, yet the theory of meaning under discussion requires that there be such objects and that understanding the expressions involves associating them with these objects. Once we extend the fragment of language with which we are dealing, it looks as if we shall be led into such absurdities as the claim that there is something, viz. nothing, which the expression 'nothing' stands for.

Finally, let us consider the expressions for which the referential theory of meaning seems best suited, names and other singular terms. We all of us, including Quine, presumably understand the two sentences below:

Hamlet killed Laertes
Pegasus was a winged horse

It does not matter for the present whether we think those sentences are true or false. It is enough that we can understand them, for they contain names – 'Hamlet', 'Laertes', and 'Pegasus' – for creatures from fiction or mythology. Although we can observe actors portraying Hamlet, we cannot see the Prince of Denmark himself. He stands in no causal relations to other concrete objects, and he has no location in space and time. Like Pegasus, he seems to be a non-existent object. If the views about names described above are correct, then our understanding of the names employed in these sentences shows that there are – and that we can talk about – real things which do not exist.

Even if this is accepted, there is scope for considerable disagreement about just what these names refer to. Some hold – implausibly – that Hamlet is an idea in someone's mind; others claim that he is a merely possible object; others that he is a *sui generis* fictional entity. We do not need to get involved in these debates, since Quine does not consider that these examples raise a serious problem for the referential theory. Adopting a view that was anticipated by Frege, and has subsequently been developed in much more detail by John Searle and Gareth Evans, Quine suggests that talk of Pegasus, Hamlet and their properties is not serious factual discourse. We 'frivolously' *pretend* to make assertions about winged horses, and to talk about the goings-on in Elsinore, whenever our idiom deviates from talk of such concrete objects as texts and the inscriptions that they contain. Hence, I only pretend to use 'Hamlet' as an ordinary proper name, so my usage does not show that I recognize the reality of Hamlet (FLPV, p. 103).

However, as my last sentence indicates, I can use names for characters of fiction in what are plainly serious assertions. For example, I may truly say:

Hamlet did not really exist

Pegasus did not really exist

I understand those sentences and think that they are true. If I only understand the names they contain by knowing who or what the expressions name, then I must know that both 'Hamlet' and 'Pegasus' refer to something non-existent. So, Quine – and all of us – must agree that there are non-existent objects. Unless the names referred to things, the two sentences could not be true; and since the sentences are true, those referents must be non-existent. Hence, the theory of meaning we are considering suggests that there are non-existent objects.

These problems do not refute the theory of language from which we started, but they point towards philosophical problems that become very pressing once the theory is accepted. What are these objects? How do we know about them? What are their properties? It is easy to find the resulting view of the world very embarrassing. The world seems to contain far more objects than are explicitly discussed in the sciences. And our grasp of our familiar language appears to involve an acquaintance with objects which are not evident to our senses. For a philosopher who is sympathetic to empiricism, the burgeoning population of abstract objects is something to be avoided. Empiricists often prize their down-to-earth common sense, but the common-sense view of the world does not seem to find room for these curious abstractions.

A prejudice in favour of the concrete is commonly found among philosophers who take science seriously, or who believe that our knowledge derives primarily from the senses. They show no reluctance to admit that the world contains objects which are visible; and invisible objects like protons are accepted because they stand in causal relations to other objects and are causally implicated in our ways of coming to knowledge about them. But abstract objects – things like numbers, classes, attributes, non-existent or fictional entities, which do not enter into the causal structures studied by the physical sciences, and have no location in space and time – are treated with suspicion. That Quine shares this prejudice is evident from the first paragraph of a paper jointly written with Nelson Goodman in 1947, 'Steps towards a constructive nominalism'. This reads:

> We do not believe in abstract entities. No one supposes that abstract entities – classes, relations, properties, etc. – exist in space–time; but we mean more than this. We renounce them altogether.
>
> (Goodman 1972, p. 173)

Although Quine subsequently came to acknowledge some abstract entities, and described this passage as expressing merely the hypothetical basis for the investigations occupying the rest of the paper, it is plain that he sympathizes with the mistrust of abstract entities here expressed.

In their 1947 paper, Quine and Goodman attribute some of this suspicion of the abstract to the belief that it is not possible to make sense of at least one sort of abstract object – the classes studied in set theory – without either running into contradiction or relying upon *ad hoc* and unnatural analyses. But, fundamentally, their refusal to admit the abstract objects with which mathematicians and others seem to deal 'is based on a philosophical intuition that cannot be justified by appeal to anything more ultimate' (p. 174).

In 'On what there is', Quine raises a question about the reality of attributes and considers it in relation to some of the assumptions about language that we are examining:

> There are red houses, red roses, red sunsets; this much is prephilosophical common sense in which we all must agree. These houses, roses and sunsets, then, must have something in common; and this which they have in common is . . . the attribute of redness.
>
> (FLPV, p. 10)

When he asks why we should admit that there is this abstract entity – the attribute, property, or 'universal', redness – the arguments he considers have the following basic strategy. When I make an assertion such as

The rose is red,

I employ a predicate expression – 'red' or 'is red'. This expression is plainly meaningful; I understand it. If an expression is meaningful, then there is something it stands for, it has a meaning. The meaning of our predicate is this abstract entity, the attribute of redness. By granting that general terms are meaningful, we admit the reality of some abstract entities – their meanings. Universals are the *meanings* of general terms. If the referential theory of meaning is adopted, this seems hard to resist.

Thus, each of the three classes of expressions we have considered presents philosophical problems if our natural theory of meaning is adopted. At different times, some philosophers have been prepared to bite the bullet, accepting that there are far more things around than the sciences would have us believe. In different ways, around the turn of the century, Moore, Russell and Meinong were prepared to take a strongly realist view of many of these strange objects. The problems they raise are primarily of two kinds. The first, already alluded to, is epistemological: in order to account for our understanding of language, we must show that we are in cognitive contact with these things. It seems easiest to do that by positing a faculty for intellectual acquaintance with them which will grate with the prejudices of an empiricist.

The second problem is metaphysical: it is often claimed that we understand the nature of objects of a particular kind, and we can talk about them intelligibly, only when we can understand identity statements involving terms referring to the object. We may say such things as

> There is a number that is prime
>
> There is number which is the sum of two and seven

But we do not know what numbers are until, as well as using numerals to refer to them, we understand what is involved in saying

> Nine *is the same number as* the sum of two and seven.

We know when two singular terms stand for the same number. It is a condition of our treating persons as objects that we know how to answer questions about whether two terms refer to the same person, and so on. Hence, one basis for questioning the reality of abstract objects concerns whether a clear sense has been attached to the appropriate statements of identity or sameness. (See FLPV, p. 4, where Quine uses just such an argument against the claim that there are possible objects – recall the claim in the joint paper with Goodman that reference to abstract entities is likely to bring paradox and unclarity with it.)

1.3. WORDS AND SENTENCES

The second milestone of empiricism was a doctrine introduced, and used to great effect, by Bentham; it was also embraced by Frege and Russell (TT, pp. 68–70). It involves a 'shift of attention from words to sentences': the primary vehicle of meaning is seen no longer as the word but as the sentence' (TT, pp. 68–9); 'the meanings of words are abstractions from the truth conditions of sentences that contain them' (TT, p. 69).

Verbal behaviour primarily involves uttering *sentences*. These are the shortest units of language which can actually be used to perform linguistic actions. Unless a specific conversational context is provided, we can make no sense of the utterance of a single word. Our grasp of the meaning of a word enables us to use and understand the sentences in which it occurs. It is a natural corollary of this that an account of how language works is adequate if it makes sense of what we do with sentences: words are best viewed simply as recurrent features of sentences. Focusing on individual words in abstraction from a wider sentential context can then appear as a source of philosophical illusion. Thus, Hume asked what idea or impression we associate with any given word, assuming that if we cannot provide one, then the word has no meaning. We may now suspect that this challenge has no force: if I can use and understand all of the sentences in which a word appears, that shows that I understand it; it is beside the point that I associate no image or impression with the word alone. An empiricist who thinks that our grasp of our language involves linking it to experience need claim only that we understand an expression when we know how to test the sentences in which it occurs against experience. He need not match experiences to individual words.

If this is correct, we should be wary of assuming that every word corresponds to some thing or idea – its meaning. So long as we can explain how the presence of a word is reflected in what can be done with the sentences that contain it, we have all the account we need of its meaning. Hence, Frege insisted in his early writings that we should not ask after the meaning of a name in isolation, but only in the context of a sentence: once we know how the name functions in sentences, we know its meaning.

This insight can be applied in a number of different ways. For example, it can liberate us from the urge to look for some object which functions as the 'meaning' of a predicate. We can focus, instead, upon the roles of predicates in sentences, and upon the kinds of claims about meanings that are actually made in ordinary talk about talk. Thus, in 'On what there is', Quine writes:

> The useful ways in which people ordinarily talk or seem to talk about meanings boil down to two: the *having* of meanings, which is significance, and *sameness* of meaning, or synonymy. What is called *giving* the meaning of an utterance is simply the uttering of a synonym, couched, ordinarily, in clearer language than the original. If we are allergic to meanings as such, we can speak directly of utterances as significant or insignificant, and as synonymous or heteronymous one with another. The problem of explaining these adjectives . . . is as difficult as it is important. But the explanatory value of special and irreducible intermediary entities called meanings is surely illusory.
>
> (FLPV, pp. 11–12)

The point being made is that we should be able to explain what is involved in expressions being meaningful, to account for what we do when we learn or explain meanings, and to explain what is involved when expressions mean the same, without introducing meanings as abstract objects. Ordinary talk of meaning does not force this way of thinking upon us; and we should not assume that an expression is meaningful only if there is some meaning that it has. Positing objects like meanings need not be part of the best explanatory theory of how we are able to speak a language.

In the previous section, we also raised a problem about the meaning of connectives: what do 'and' and 'not' stand for? It was one of the fundamental thoughts of Wittgenstein's *Tractatus Logico-Philosophicus* that these expressions (called the 'logical constants' because of their fundamental role in inference) 'do not represent'. Exploring what this might involve will offer a further illustration of the primacy of sentence meaning. The idea is that these expressions are truth functional. Consider the following three assertions:

Quine is American

Frege is German

Quine is American and Frege is German

The third does not report some additional fact about or feature of the world which is not captured in the two previous claims. Rather, I understand the word 'and', in uses of these kinds, when I grasp that the conjunction of two sentences is true when both are true, and that otherwise it is false. I do not need acquaintance with some abstract entity conjunction, and there are not features of the world which can only be described in a language which contains 'and'. Once I know this rule for determining the truth values of conjunctive sentences on the basis of the truth values of the parts, then I understand 'and', and can sensibly use conjunctive sentences. Similarly, I understand 'it is not the case that' when I see that the complex sentence formed by prefixing that operator to another sentence is true when the prefixed sentence is false, and false when it is true. The connectives are 'truth functional' because the truth values of the sentences we construct with their aid are functions of (depend upon) the truth values of their parts. The primacy of sentence meaning enables us to avoid the problem of accounting for our acquaintance with the abstract objects conjunction and negation.

There is another way to apply the insight, which appears to involve a wholly different strategy. Quine often links the primacy of sentence meaning to the use, by Bentham and Russell, of the method of paraphrase or *contextual definition* (TT, pp. 60–70, 73). As we have seen, one argument for the existence of attributes exploits the fact that we appear to refer to them with singular terms. Thus

Redness is a colour.

We might try to remove the illusion that 'redness' was a singular term standing for some mysterious abstract entity by paraphrasing this sentence as

Anything red is coloured.

This does not yield an analysis of the word 'redness'. There is no part of the second sentence which means the same as 'redness'. Rather, it suggests a method for paraphrasing every sentence that contains the word 'redness' into a clearer one that lacks this term. We offer, not an account of the word 'redness', but an account of all of the sentences in which that word occurs. In Quine's view, only the primacy of sentence meaning can explain why such analyses seem satisfactory. A familiar example of the same strategy involves sentences like:

The average car owner drives 200 miles each week.

This appears to ascribe a property to a curious abstract object, the 'average car owner'. Anyone possessed of ontological scruples may complain that there is no such thing. The quoted sentence provides a misleading expression of a thought whose structure is more perspicuously revealed by the paraphrase:

If you divide the number of miles driven by cars each week by the number of drivers, the answer is 200.

The apparent reference to 'the average car owner' has vanished.

Our two applications of this second 'milestone' are importantly different. The first forces us to refocus our sense of what has to be explained when we account for our ability to use language. By turning our attention away from words to sentences, it enables us to see that there need not be an object (its meaning) for which each word stands. However, it does not direct our attention away from the task of explaining our understanding of an ordinary natural language. The paraphrase technique, on the other hand, simply provides another sentence which, supposedly, 'reveals' the content that it shares with the first. Rather than offering insight into how a natural language works, we see a suspicion of natural languages as vehicles for the perspicuous representation of thoughts: we must always be on the lookout for deceptive formulations.

It is important to see how this second application is related to the primacy of sentence meaning. If word meaning is primary, we can only clarify the meaning of a sentence by clarifying the meanings of the words that it contains. A revealing paraphrase would have to contain paraphrases or analyses of the more troublesome terms in the sentence. Quine holds that the primacy of sentence meaning frees us of this requirement. A perspicuous paraphrase of a puzzling sentence may contain no constituent corresponding to some word or phrase in the sentence it paraphrases. No portion of our paraphrases captured the meaning of 'the average driver' or 'redness'. However, we can feel confident that we have understood the original sentences because we have a recipe for constructing paraphrases of any sentences in which these expressions occur. Only a prejudice that the meaning of each word must be separately captured in our analysis could lead us to be dissatisfied with this, according to Quine.

Problems emerge when we ask for a fuller account of the relation between the original sentences and their paraphrases. One position is that the paraphrases provide 'analyses' of the original sentences: they characterize the structure of the 'thoughts' which were clothed in potentially misleading linguistic garb for communicative purposes; or they elucidate some underlying logical or grammatical structure 'present in' the original sentences. As we shall subsequently see, Quine, unlike Russell, is unhappy with this sort of account of what is going on. He would favour a weaker claim, that the two can 'serve the same purpose', and that the paraphrases are preferable, probably because they are clearer. He is likely to insist that our expressive capacities would not be limited if we revised our language, using only the long-winded paraphrases and banning the more familiar idioms. While such a change might interfere with rhetorical or conversational aspects of language use, it would not leave us unable to describe states of affairs which we could previously discuss. Moreover, in using this clumsy, awkward language we should escape the misleading surface features of English which deceive us into being puzzled by unreal philosophical problems.

The claim is not that we should actually speak this revised form of English. Rather, we should restrict our attention to it when our interests are philosophical. Looking at the paraphrases in this way enables us to obtain their philosophical benefits without believing in hidden structures which guide our thought but are disguised by the surface forms of English. (For a fuller discussion, see chapter 5 below.)

1.4. OBJECTS AND ONTOLOGY

When we return to the problems about names for fictional entities and other 'non-existent' objects, we may think that the primacy of sentence meaning promises a straightforward solution. A name may be meaningful even if it fails to refer, so long as we understand the sentences in which it occurs: it is only prejudice that makes us suppose that a name cannot be meaningful unless it refers. However, Quine does not rest with that observation, and it is important that we should understand why.

First, note that names typically do refer to objects. It is a natural objection to the referential theory of meaning that it takes a model of meaning which applies to names and generalizes it to cover expressions of all kinds. Thus, we should not be overhasty in ignoring the referents of names and other singular terms. Secondly, there are philosophical reasons for being wary. We naturally view the world as composed of *objects* which have different characteristics. Theories differ in what objects they take the world to contain. Quine speaks of the set of objects which a speaker takes to exist as his 'ontology': an assertion 'ontologically commits' its author to objects of a certain kind if the assertion would only be true if objects of that kind existed. If we are to retain this view of the world, then two problems require attention. First, we need a philosophical elucidation of the concept of an object: just what is it for something to be an *object*? Secondly, we need an explanation of how we establish which objects a given theory or theorist is 'committed' to. How do we establish whether, for example, elementary arithmetic is true only if there are such abstract objects as numbers?

Perhaps the fact that names typically refer to objects provides the key to the solution of these problems. Some philosophers have claimed that we can only elucidate the concept of an object through the concept of a name or singular term: all we can say about objects is that they are the the things that singular terms refer to. If that were so, then we might undermine our concept of an object by blithely rejecting a referential account of the functioning of names, brandishing the slogan that the sentence is the unit of meaning. Moreover, it is desirable that there be a way of telling from a theory or assertion just what its ontological commitments are: we would like a *criterion* of ontological commitment. It is natural to suppose that a theory is committed to there being objects of a certain kind if it makes claims which involve names or singular terms for objects of that kind. Unless singular terms stand for objects, how are we to establish what objects a given theory says there are? Names appear to be intimately related to objects, and it would be wrong to lose sight of this.

In 'On what there is' (FLPV), Quine pursues this question: are there any forms of linguistic behaviour through which we do unambiguously commit ourselves to the existence of objects of different kinds? This prompts a search for a criterion of ontological commitment: a rule that we can apply to a body of assertions in order to determine what ontology must be accepted by anyone who is willing to make all those assertions. As Alonzo Church has remarked, Quine was the first philosopher to take seriously the search for such a criterion (Church 1958). 'On what there is' contains the results of this search. The remainder of this chapter provides an informal introduction to these views.

1.5 RUSSELL'S THEORY OF DESCRIPTIONS AND QUINE'S CRITERION OF ONTOLOGICAL COMMITMENT

We begin with Russell's theory of descriptions. Quine looks upon this as the paradigm use of paraphrase in philosophical analysis and, as we shall see, his views about ontological commitment serve as a kind of corollary to it.

In early work, Russell had accepted that every meaningful expression of a language stands for something. This led him to what Quine calls his 'intolerably indiscriminate ontology' (TT p. 74): alongside existents, were such entities as 'numbers, the Homeric gods, relations, chimeras, and four-dimensional spaces' (Russell, 1903 p. 449; quoted in TT p. 74). By the time he wrote his classic 1905 paper 'On denoting', Russell wished to avoid these excesses. His account of definite descriptions provides one of his means towards achieving this.

Russell claimed that neither of these two sentences

The King of France is bald

The King of France does not exist

has the logical structure that we have represented

Fa.

Neither is really of subject–predicate form. Hence, it is not a precondition of either making sense that there 'is' (in some sense) a King of France. The surface appearance of each sentence conceals an underlying logical structure according to which neither sentence contains a singular term. Their structures can be represented more perspicuously thus:

There is one, and only one King of France, and he is bald

It is not the case that there is a King of France

Although these sentences do involve the predicate expression 'is a King of France', they do not contain *singular terms* which purport to refer to him. If there is no King of France, the first is straightforwardly false, and the second is true; neither contains a name or other singular term which fails to refer. Hence, ordinary definite descriptions are not genuine singular terms; so, arguments which urge the reality of different kinds of objects by assuming that definite descriptions *are* singular terms fail. We are fooled because the surface appearance of sentences of our language can conceal their underlying logical structure.

Russell's theory provides a tool which enables us to escape the seductive force of the surface structure of our language. We do not commit ourselves to the existence of objects whenever we use a definite description. The paraphrases enable us to identify those descriptions which do commit us to the existence of objects; they are the ones which are paraphrased as saying that 'there are' objects of the appropriate kinds. Neither sentence requires there to be a King of France for it to be meaningful. Only the first requires that there be a King of France for it to be true. So, while the sincere assertor of

The King of France is bald

must believe that there is a King of France, the utterer of

The King of France does not exist

need not.

One of the merits of Russell's theory of descriptions is that it enables us to simplify and clarify our ways of referring to objects. Some, but not all, expressions of the form 'the F' purport to refer to objects. When sentences containing them are paraphrased in accordance with Russell's theory, the referential function is consigned to a form of expression which *always* serves to allude to objects the speaker takes to exist – the idiom 'there is —.' Eliminating definite descriptions from our language rids us of a form of expression which only sometimes serves to refer to an object. We take a step towards a language where our ontological commitments are all manifested in constructions which can only be used when the speaker is prepared to acknowledge that there are objects of a certain kind.

Since we use ordinary proper names for objects whose existence we deny, we have some distance to go before we reach such a language. Can Russell's theory help us with the next step? It is not surprising that Quine – and in this he follows Russell – advocates a similar use of paraphrase to eliminate names from a philosophically illuminating language. He claims that we should look on ordinary names as, in effect, disguised definite descriptions, and paraphrase sentences containing them in a parallel fashion.

At first glance, this is unpromising. Application of Russell's technique to definite descriptions depended upon their having syntactic structure and containing general terms such as '— is a King of France'. Since names are typically unstructured, how can a parallel analysis be developed? One possibility, advocated by Russell, is to look on a name as an abbreviated description: what we mean by 'Pegasus', for example, might be 'the winged horse of Bellerophon'. But Quine is content to adopt a more straightforward strategy. He introduces into the language new primitive general terms, each true of just one thing, expressing the property of being-pegasus, or of pegasizing. The name 'Pegasus' can then be paraphrased as 'the pegasizer' and the two sentences that have interested us can be reformulated:

> There is one and only one thing that pegasizes and it has wings
>
> It is not the case that something pegasizes

The effect of thus regimenting our discourse is that we move closer to the stage at which all of our ontological commitments are carried by constructions which invariably express the ontological assumptions of those who employ them in serious assertions.

To see the force of Quine's 'criterion of ontological commitment' we, fortunately, do not have to decide whether purging a language of names is a real possibility. We can grant that it is a logical consequence of

> Pegasus has wings

that

> There is something which is Pegasus and has wings.

And Quine's fundamental claim is that we can discern someone's ontology – find out what objects he takes to make up the furniture of the world – by attending to the sentences of this second form that he is prepared to assent to.

You find out what someone thinks there is by establishing what he is prepared to say that there is. This may seem a less than riveting conclusion. Quine himself has commented on its 'triviality' and lamented that so many critics have supposed that 'there is more afoot than meets the eye, despite my protests' (TT, p. 73). The point of stressing it, he observes, is simply to guard against the sorts of errors that have been exposed in this chapter. It disarms the assumptions about names, definite descriptions, and meaning that we have seen at work. There is more to Quine's ontological position than this criterion, and in Parts II and III we shall be able to examine how he puts it to work to arrive at his answer to the question: what is there?

When we ask what bearing the primacy of sentence meaning has upon these ontological matters, two contrasting morals suggest themselves. One will be evident from our examination of sentences about redness and average drivers. Through paraphrase we can eliminate apparent reference to abstract or non-existent objects from our discourse. But the claim that such paraphrase dispels philosophical illusion is controversial: an objection to this kind of use of the method of paraphrase was introduced in Alston (1958), and has been revived by Crispin Wright (1983). Suppose we grant that the two sentences being discussed mean the same. Quine draws the moral that the sentence containing 'redness' does not really deal with the properties of an abstract entity: its content is more perspicuously captured by the paraphrase. Somebody could reject this, claiming that the second sentence is really about the abstract object redness: the existence of the paraphrase relation shows that, appearances to the contrary, the claim is about the fact that redness is a colour. In other words, if the paraphrase relation holds, how are we to decide which statement is a more revealing or perspicuous description of reality?

So long as we agree that abstract entities are to be treated with suspicion, our sympathies may lie with Quine: if we can possibly resist accepting that there are such things, we should do so. But accepting the primacy of sentence meaning removes one important reason for suspicion of abstract entities. If we think that the word is the unit of meaning, then we are likely to believe that we learn the meaning of a name by confronting, or standing in some causal relation with, its bearer. It is hard to see how objects that do not exist in space and time can engage with the mechanisms whereby we learn language. We can form impressions of concrete objects, but not of abstract ones. Once we leave the word behind as the unit of meaning, the position is radically changed. All that is involved in understanding a name, on that view, is understanding the sentences which contain it. So if, for example, I use the language of arithmetic which contains numerals (names for numbers), and if I know how to find out the truth values of any of the sentences which contain numerals, that is all that is involved in accepting numbers as objects. There is no requirement that I be able to see numbers, or stand in causal relations with them. Consequently, one effect of the second milestone of empiricism may be a recognition that abstract entities provide less of a threat to our ordinary ways of thinking than had previously been supposed. All that is at issue, when we ask whether numbers exist, is whether sentences which contain singular terms for numbers are true.

It follows from this that when we accept the primacy of sentence meaning, our 'prejudice in favour of the concrete' may need to be re-assessed. Scepticism about whether objects of a certain kind are real should be grounded upon finding incoherence in our claims about them, or upon claiming that reference to them is explanatorily redundant. As we shall explain in Part II, Quine himself holds to a form of physicalism: the only objects that exist are those that are underwritten by physical theory. This provides a basis for a prejudice in favour of the concrete which is independent of these claims about words and sentences.

Two further glances ahead are appropriate here. First, for all his castigation of theories which propose incoherent or profligate ontologies, Quine's considered view involves the doctrine of 'ontological relativity' which entails that, in absolute terms, there is no fact of the matter concerning what the ontological commitments of a theory or theorist are. The question 'What objects is X talking about?' has no determinate answer. Section 8.5, returns to these issues.

Secondly, Quine usually states his criterion in modal terms: a theory is committed to those objects which *must* exist if it is true. As we shall note in chapter 2, and discuss more fully in chapter 7, Quine rejects the kind of notion of necessity which seems to be expressed by this 'must'. Hence, it is sometimes objected that Quine's views on ontological commitment conflict with his other philosophical views. I suspect that there is no inconsistency here, although the objection does direct us to the limited application that Quine's criterion has. I shall not be able to explain this until the final chapter (section 12.3).

2

Rules and Rationality

2.1 MEANING, RATIONALITY AND THE *A PRIORI*

As we have noted, Quine's work must be understood against the background of logical empiricism, in particular the views of Rudolf Carnap. In this chapter, we shall introduce some of Carnap's ideas, and begin to examine Quine's response to them. The most important of these is an account of language which emphasizes the notion of a *linguistic rule*. Since Carnap's views about linguistic rules developed, I shall be selective in my exposition, concentrating upon aspects of his position which illuminate Quine's views. As preparation for a discussion of one of Quine's most famous papers 'Two dogmas of empiricism' (FLPV), we shall begin by considering the uses to which this notion was put by the logical empiricists.

The first of these uses emerges from our criticisms of the referential account of meaning. If the simple referential theory of language is abandoned, the question arises of how to explain the functioning of language. What is involved in understanding and using words and sentences? When do different expressions mean the same? It is plausible to respond to these questions by stressing that there are conventionally accepted rules which fix the uses of words. I understand an expression when I know the rule which governs its use and use it in accordance with that rule; misunderstanding follows from failing to know the rule or misapplying it For example, the rule governing the use of the word 'vixen' may be that it applies to something if, and only if, that thing is a female fox; the truth functional account of connectives, encountered in the previous chapter, formulates the rules for using those expressions. Talk of rules promises a satisfying model of what understanding a word or sentence involves.

A second issue concerns rationality. The logical empiricists were impressed by science because it appeared to employ rational procedures which ensured consensus among scientists about the merits of their theories. Scientific results – unlike metaphysical claims or those made in ethical debates – were testable: any investigator should agree about the bearing of observations or experiments upon controversial theories; debates were not endless. An important task was to explain this 'fact' (if fact it was): what is the source of the standards that ensure this agreement and underlie scientific rationality?

The rules that were introduced to account for meaning and understanding were helpful here too. Anyone who understood the word 'vixen' would agree about the bearing of information about the gender and species of an animal on the claim that it is a vixen. If all the terms employed in scientific theories are governed by rules which determine the experiential circumstances under which they apply to something, then we can appeal to their shared mastery of these rules to explain why scientists agree about the bearing of observations and experiments upon hypotheses. Scientific rationality involves accepting the verdicts of observations in ways that are fixed by the conventional meanings of the terms used in formulating their theories. Hence, an account of the rules governing scientific language would lead towards the desired account of scientific rationality.

As was pointed out above, empiricists hold that all of our substantive knowledge about the world comes through the senses. Science employs precise, disciplined procedures for testing theories against experience. However, we seem to know many things – and to be very certain of them – without the benefit of such empirical tests. For example – a rather trivial one – we know that vixens are female foxes. That knowledge is not confirmed by experience: we seem to know in advance that no experience could refute it. If something we took to be a vixen proved to be male, we would revise our opinion that it was a vixen rather than abandon the claim that all vixens are female foxes. Similarly, consider the arithmetical claim that 17+54=71. Having satisfied ourselves that this is true by calculation, we shall not allow experience or experiment to cast doubt upon it. If we find 60 or 72 objects when we put together 17 and 54, we conclude that some have vanished or more appeared, some have coalesced or others divided: we show no inclination to doubt the arithmetic certainty. These knowledge claims seem to be *a priori*: they do not risk empirical refutation, and do not need empirical support. It is a potential embarrassment for an empiricist that we can know such things.

Once again, appeal to linguistic rules promises assistance. That vixens are female foxes, it is suggested, is straightforwardly a product of the rule or convention that determines the meaning of 'vixen': the statement is true by convention or definition and makes no substantive claim about the world. Such statements are called analytic: analysis of their meanings is all that is required in order to see that they are true. In similar vein, the truth of fundamental logical principles can be discovered by reflecting upon the meanings of the connectives they contain. The hope, then, is to show that the truths of mathematics are all likewise determined by the rules fixing the meanings of arithmetical terms. All putative *a priori* knowledge is analytic: an empty reflection of the rules governing the meanings of the expressions of our language. All respectable synthetic (non-analytic) truths can be known only through experiment and observation.

The term 'analytic' was used by Kant. He claimed that a proposition was analytic when the concept of the predicate was contained in the concept of the subject: the concept female is thus contained in the concept vixen. The underlying thought that such propositions are empty or trivial has a much longer history. In fact, Kant's definition is unsatisfactory: its metaphorical talk of 'containment' needs clarification and it does not apply to relational propositions which do not divide straightforwardly into subject and predicate. However, as Quine admits, its intent is easily grasped: 'a statement is analytic when it is true by virtue of meaning and independently of fact' (FLPV, p. 21). Carnap's talk of linguistic rules offers an explanation of what is involved in a statement being 'true by virtue of meaning'. And Quine's attack on the 'dogma' of the analytic/synthetic distinction is primarily directed at the sort of picture of language which Carnap defends.

2.2 CLASSICAL ANALYSIS

We start with a simple version of such a theory. It is the view of thought and reality which the logical positivists thought that they found in Wittgenstein's *Tractatus Logico-Philosophicus*, and which appeared in the first of Carnap's major works, *Logical Structure of the World*.

Everyone accepts the same set of fundamental logical principles; these reflect a universal conception of a valid argument. In consequence, all languages contain the same fundamental logical framework: they differ only in the symbols they use to express these logical relations and in the names and predicates they contain. This logical vocabulary is composed of truth functional connectives: the logical laws are determined simply by the fact that every statement is either true or false; and all of the laws of logic are tautologous.

The second 'fixed point' for investigation is experience. All knowledge grows out of experience, which is simply 'given' to us, and does not reflect our own constructive activity. Our most primitive vocabulary contains terms for describing and classifying our experience. Since all investigators experience the world in the same way, all languages contain a similar range of terms for describing and classifying experience. If we restrict attention to sentences containing only these logical connectives and the primitive experiential vocabulary, only misunderstanding can prevent people agreeing about the bearing of any particular experience upon any statement. They will agree that, in the light of that experience, the statement is shown to be true, or to be false, or it is still open what truth value it has. If investigators employed languages which contained only this restricted vocabulary, it would be easy to explain how they reach agreement so readily. All questions would be resoluble.

Of course, we do not speak such a language. We use many terms which are neither truth functional connectives nor predicates which apply to elements of experience. However, the view we are considering holds that these other meaningful expressions can be understood as abbreviations of expressions which could be cast in a more primitive language of this sort. Just as 'vixen' is introduced to abbreviate 'female fox', so all non-observational predicates abbreviate observational expressions which are probably very complicated. In principle, every factual claim *could* be expressed in the more primitive language. In practice, we should find ourselves using absurdly long and complex sentences: hence the value of non-observational terms – we acquire an elegant language which offers short simple abbreviations of long clumsy expressions.

One role for philosophy is then reductive analysis: we articulate the principles exploited when we translate a sentence of ordinary language into the more primitive observational one. The philosopher formulates analytic truths involving defined and primitive expressions. Moreover, if a statement is analytic, then, when we translate into the primitive segment of the language, exploiting definitions and synonyms, it turns into a logical truth or tautology. Thus, the primitive sentence corresponding to

Vixens are foxes

is

Female foxes are foxes.

This model of language is bound to be attractive to an empiricist who has learned the lessons about the primacy of sentence meaning – one who has passed the second milestone. Our grasp of the meanings of the expressions of our language involves accepting a system of rules determining the meanings of the sentences that contain them. Each sentence has a determinate meaning: there is a fixed set of experiences that will confirm it, and another set that will disconfirm it. Logical analysis reveals how each sentence of ordinary English abbreviates a very complex sentence employing only the experiential vocabulary. The philosopher's task is to describe the rules that govern linguistic behaviour and trace the rule-governed connections between language and experience.

Moreover, it explains how we proceed rationally in evaluating empirical statements. Since the meanings of such statements reflect rules linking them to reports of sensory experience, they yield criteria to be followed in evaluating the statements against experience. It promises an explanation of what so impressed Carnap in his book *The Logical Syntax of Language*: the fact that the scientific method is so very efficient at producing agreement upon scientific results. These shared rules determine which experiences refute, and which confirm, the claims made by scientists. Science is largely constituted by a body of rules for securing rational agreement upon the truth values of scientific propositions. Thus, since all use the same system of analytic rules, all will agree that the fact that litmus paper fails to turn red settles that the liquid in the flask is not acid.

2.3 CARNAP'S VIEWS

This reductive model of language soon failed. First, the belief that Frege, Russell and Wittgenstein had developed the one true logic which formed the common skeleton of all languages was challenged when rival logics developed. The most important of these was intuitionist logic, due to Brouwer. Secondly, the project of analysing terms of ordinary language and science in simple sensory terms gradually ran into the ground. Carnap's attempt to carry out this project simply emphasized the difficulties it faced; by the 1930s, few philosophers believed it was possible.

Carnap moved to a more complex, although related, position. He envisaged a plurality of languages or linguistic frameworks. Each embodied a system of logical principles, and the terms employed in each were given meaning by analytic principles or 'meaning postulates' linking claims employing them, directly or indirectly, to observational claims, expressed in 'protocol sentences'. These analytic principles do not provide us with expressions cast in observational terms which are equivalent to the terms whose meanings they determine. But they set up logical relations that connect experience to sentences other than protocol sentences. For example, one of the meaning postulates determining the meaning of 'soluble' might be

> If a substance is placed in water at normal temperature and pressure, then, if it is soluble, it dissolves.

Guided by this rule, we deny that a substance is soluble when it fails to dissolve when placed in water in such circumstances. Similarly, our rule linking the property of being an acid with turning blue litmus red can be retained even if there is no possibility of fully unpacking the meaning of 'acid' in observational terms.

In Carnap's work, this development leads to a kind of relativism. Relative to a framework, observation or calculation can lead to objective answers to questions. So long as all inquirers share a framework, questions may be rationally resoluble. But disputes about which framework to employ cannot be settled in this straightforward manner. Most philosophers assume that before we accept a framework, we must satisfy ourselves that reality genuinely contains the sorts of things with which it deals: we should adopt a framework only if we believe that it is true to the nature of reality. Carnap rejects this assumption. When we decide which frameworks to use, then, we are not concerned with their truth, but with 'pragmatic considerations'.

> The acceptance cannot be judged as being either true or false because it is not an assertion. It can only be judged as being more or less expedient, fruitful, conducive to the aim for which the language is intended.
>
> (Carnap 1956, p. 214)

So pragmatic considerations of simplicity and usefulness are relevant to the adoption of frameworks. Our preference for simple frameworks does not reflect the belief that reality is simple, for choice of framework does not rest upon the belief that it corresponds to reality.

This feature of choice of framework is reflected in Carnap's 'Principle of Tolerance' (1937, pp. 51–2; 1956, p. 221) – also called the principle of 'the conventionality of language forms' (Schilpp 1963, p. 55).

> *In logic there are no morals*. Everyone is at liberty to build up his own logic, i.e. his own form of language, as he wishes.
>
> (1937, p. 52)

> Let us be cautious in making assertions and critical in examining them, but let us be tolerant in permitting linguistic forms.
>
> (1956, p. 221)

Relative to a linguistic framework, error can result if we are not scrupulous about respecting the rules of the framework. Since there is no sense in which one framework is true and another false, there is every reason to allow many different frameworks to develop so that we can see their various advantages and disadvantages. Brouwer was right to develop his intuitionist framework for mathematics, wrong to insist that this be developed instead of (rather than alongside) classical mathematics. The only rule Carnap imposes is that we should formulate our frameworks rigorously, explicitly setting out their rules.

Once this is acknowledged, Carnap believes, traditional empiricist scruples about abstract entities – numbers, universals, propositions – are placed in a new light. Are we to adopt a framework which employs the general term '— is a universal', or '— is a number', and contains rules which provide for the settlement of internal questions about universals or numbers? Those who resist such frameworks usually assume that we should only employ them if we believe that reality actually contains such things. But, since all that is at issue is the acceptance of a framework – we are considering an 'external' question – this is the wrong way to look at it. All that is at issue is whether the number framework, or the universal framework, is fruitful and interesting. Once we accept the arithmetic framework, for example, we examine 'internal' questions with determinate answers: we can be wrong about the results of calculations or the validity of proofs. The rules of the framework provide the standards employed in establishing which answers to internal questions are right, and which wrong.

Carnap often attributes metaphysical illusion to a confusion of two styles of speech: the formal and material modes. A philosopher may raise an ontological question about mathematics thus:

Are there numbers?

This is in the material mode of speech: it appears to be concerned with the nature of reality. Given the character of external questions, it is more perspicuously formulated in the metalinguistic formal mode:

Should we adopt a linguistic framework which contains numerals?

'Metaphysical' questions always result from putting an innocuous formal mode question about choice of linguistic framework into the material mode. The material mode formulation deceives us into thinking we are concerned with a question of fact; the formal mode formulation frees us of this illusion.

This sort of picture has been of fundamental importance for the development of analytical philosophy. Quine would have heard a related position defended by one of his teachers at Harvard, the pragmatist C. I. Lewis. And it serves as the core of the logical empiricist philosophy of science which provoked many of the developments in the philosophy of science since the Second World War – for example the work of Kuhn and Feyerabend. Before turning to Quine's response, let us summarize the epistemological implications of this position. When we attempt to reconstruct any body of knowledge, we can expect to find two things:

(1) A framework of analytic principles, whose adoption reflects a practical decision based upon pragmatic considerations. Shared frameworks reflect adoption of conventions to the effect that these principles should be used.
(2) A body of internal knowledge, which is justified by reference to the rules and principles that make up the framework.

When we study a developing body of knowledge, we find changes of two kinds. First, there are internal revisions, adjustments called for by the rules of the framework in response to new experience. Second, there may be external revisions, changes in the framework grounded in a pragmatic concern for a body of opinions which is as simple and fruitful as possible. Carnap offers an account of conceptual change which makes a distinction between rule-governed changes and changes in the rules. This distinction has considerable epistemological importance.

2.4 HOLISM

In *The Logical Syntax of Language* Carnap qualifies his position further. His underlying view of how scientific theories are tested is familiar. He admits, of course, that no finite set of observations can conclusively establish a scientific hypothesis. However, protocol sentences can be deduced from such hypotheses and used in testing them. The more successful predictions that are made with the aid of a theory, the better confirmed it is; and it counts against a theory that its predictions are disappointed.

However, for two reasons, hypotheses are not automatically abandoned when predictions derived from them are disappointed. First, we can retain the hypothesis and reject the 'refuting' observation – we would never abandon a well confirmed theory on the basis of just one surprising observation, but would rather put the surprising result down to observational error. Secondly, protocol sentences are never deduced from single hypotheses: predictions rest also upon other hypotheses which serve as background knowledge. 'Thus *the test applies, at bottom, not to a single hypothesis but to the whole system of physics as a system of hypotheses* (Duhem, Poincaré)' (Carnap, 1937, p. 318). Consequently, when we revise our theories in the light of observational surprise, the rules of the system may leave us with a choice between different revisions which would all restore consistency. In deciding which of these permitted revisions to make, we rely upon the systematic considerations of simplicity and fruitfulness which Carnap claims are also involved in settling external questions. The sharp epistemological contrast between internal and external questions begins to blur.

Hence, if we place our litmus paper into a flask of liquid and it fails to turn red, we are not *logically* constrained to give up our assumption that the flask contains acid. We can restore consistency to our corpus of beliefs in several ways: we might wonder whether the piece of litmus paper we used was faulty, containing imperfections; we might speculate about whether we were misled in thinking it was litmus paper at all; we might reconsider the theory that underlies the belief that the litmus test is a reliable indicator of acidity; and there are many other possibilities.

Immediately after making this point, Carnap qualifies his position still further. Once a framework has been adopted, we might assume that we are to take it as relatively fixed, investigating internal questions subject to the rational standards that it provides. Not so:

> No rule of the physical language is definitive; all rules are laid down with the reservation that they may be altered as soon as it seems expedient to do so. This applies not only to (the rules which formulate basic physical principles) but also to the L-rules (those which correspond to analytic truths) including those of mathematics. In this respect, there are only differences in degree; certain rules are more difficult to renounce than others.
>
> (1937, p. 318)

Thus, Carnap thinks that we must be ready to respond to surprising observations by adjusting framework principles for the sake of a simpler and more coherent position.

Should we conclude that there is no epistemological difference between internal and external questions? No: although pragmatic systematic factors such as simplicity may be involved in answering each kind of question, it is only internal questions that can be settled by appeal to criteria or standards. Indeed, a new observation can conflict with a physical hypothesis (or system of hypotheses), while it cannot conflict with an analytic proposition (1937, pp. 318–19). However, it is also possible that 'under the inducement of new protocol sentences, we alter the language to such an extent that [a given analytic sentence] is no longer analytic' (1937, p. 319). At least, this is Carnap's claim. One of the central themes in Quine's epistemology, by contrast, is that once these qualifications are made, Carnap's philosophical framework – and with it the distinction between analytic and synthetic statements – loses its explanatory force. We must now turn to his arguments for this view.

2.5 'TWO DOGMAS OF EMPIRICISM': THE THIRD AND FOURTH MILESTONES

'Moderate or relative holism' is, according to Quine, the third milestone of empiricism (TT, p. 71):

> We come to recognize that in a scientific theory even a whole sentence is ordinarily too short a text to serve as an independent vehicle of empirical meaning. It will not have its separate bundle of observable or testable consequences. A reasonably inclusive body of scientific theory, taken as a whole, will indeed have such consequences.
>
> (TT, p. 70)

When one of our observational predictions, drawn from a body of theory, proves false, 'the theory is false, but on the face of it there is no saying which of the component sentences of the theory is to blame' (ibid.). Although he passes the third milestone, Carnap stops before reaching the fourth, which is 'methodological monism', the repudiation of the analytic/synthetic distinction (TT, pp. 71–2). Why does Quine think that this additional step is warranted?

If Carnap's theory is correct, then we should be able to identify the linguistic frameworks employed by different inquirers, and in order to do this we must establish which of their confident assertions express analytic truths and which express empirical propositions that are well confirmed relative to their framework. 'Two dogmas' (FLPV) questions whether this distinction can be drawn. Talk of analytic truths reflecting rules or definitions may conceal the difficulty. When we construct an artificial language, then we can list statements under headings such as 'rules' or 'definitions'. But, as Quine sees it, this fails to engage with the difficulty. If we undertake to describe the linguistic framework of a body of practising scientists, how are we to decide which of their utterances articulate rules or definitions and which are synthetic claims? How can we identify from speakers' behaviour which statements articulate analytic principles constitutive of their linguistic frameworks?

Quine's position appears to be that if holism is true, we cannot solve this problem. Towards the end of his paper, he discusses 'reductionism', the 'second dogma' after the analytic/synthetic distinction itself. If the radical reductionist doctrine defended by the early positivists had been true, then any statement would be equivalent to another probably highly complex one cast in purely observational terms. Even when that doctrine is abandoned, the sort of position that we have been considering allows us to derive purely observational consequences from any empirical claim. This seems to provide us with a criterion of analyticity: if a statement is analytic, then no observational consequences can be derived from it. An analytic statement represents 'a limiting kind of statement which is vacuously confirmed, *ipso facto*, come what may' (FLPV, p. 41).

Now, the source of Quine's repudiation of the analytic/synthetic distinction is his rejection of this reductionist picture: 'our statements about the external world face the tribunal of sense experience not individually but only as a corporate body' (FLPV, p. 41). Quine supposes that once we adopt a holistic epistemological outlook, our only hope for clarifying the analytic/synthetic distinction is lost. But 'Two dogmas' does little to show how his position differs from Carnap's considered view – indeed, from reading it, one would not gather that Carnap shared Quine's insights about the holistic character of the relations between evidence and theory.

The simplest answer is that Quine believes that we have a neater and more fruitful picture of how our knowledge grows if we abandon the analytic/synthetic distinction and its related dichotomy of kinds of questions. Once the water is muddied, as it has been by Carnap's more sophisticated treatment in the later pages of *The Logical Syntax of Language*, the explanatory use of the distinction between two sorts of knowledge vanishes. Experience can prompt changes in our body of beliefs: systematic considerations of simplicity and fruitfulness have a role in deciding how to make these adjustments. There simply seems no basis for discerning two different mechanisms. The puzzle is less why Quine made this move than why Carnap didn't.

Consider an example. Alongside analytic truths, the Carnapian picture allows for empirical beliefs, deeply embedded in common sense or scientific theory, which are so well confirmed that we are almost completely certain of them. Perhaps one of these is that physical objects fall when dropped. We might say that this forms part of our concept of a physical object, although it is not one of the analytic principles constituting our linguistic framework. We use it in deriving predictions from other empirical hypotheses, but it is so deeply embedded in our body of opinions that we can think of no observations that would readily refute it. Perhaps we can imagine that it could become questionable, but we do not now think of it as such. We find it impossible to doubt it. Moreover, if another speaker did reject this claim, that would be good evidence of failure to understand one of the words used to express it. Since we are so certain of this fact, we shall rely upon it in identifying things as dropped physical objects, and in explaining words like 'drop' to children or foreigners. Yet it is not analytic – were it to become questionable, we should treat this as an internal question; and there would be no point in the development at which an external question was transformed into an internal question.

Now imagine someone else for whom this statement *is* analytic. He too eventually abandons it, but in this case there is a stage in the development of his views where this statement is transformed from an analytic one to a synthetic one. Just what discernible difference is there in the behaviour of these two agents? For Quine, there is none. Carnap appears to invoke a difference that makes no difference. His theory introduces uncalled-for complexities in the mechanisms whereby our knowledge grows. In each case, surprising experiences together with attention to the pragmatic virtues of our body of opinions cause what was once certain to be debatable. There is nothing for the distinction of two different mechanisms to explain.

In the final section of 'Two dogmas', Quine offers an impressionistic picture of 'empiricism without the dogmas'. He claims that 'total science is like a field of force whose boundary conditions are experience', and continues:

> A conflict with experience at the periphery occasions readjustments in the interior of the field. Truth values have to be redistributed over some of our statements. Reevaluation of some statements entails reevaluation of others, because of their logical interconnections – the logical laws being in turn simply certain further statements of the system, certain further elements of the field. Having reevaluated one statement we must reevaluate some others, which may be statements logically connected with the first or may be the statements of the logical connections themselves. But the total field is so underdetermined by its boundary conditions, experience, that there is much latitude of choice as to what statements to reevaluate in the light of any singular contrary experience.
>
> (FLPV, pp. 42–3)

It is a corollary of this that:

> Any statement can be held true come what may, if we make drastic enough adjustments elsewhere in the system. Even a statement very close to the periphery can be held true in the face of recalcitrant experience by pleading hallucination or by amending certain statements of the kind called logical laws. Conversely, by the same token, no statement is immune to revision. Revision even of the logical law of the excluded middle has been proposed as a means of simplifying quantum mechanics; and what difference is there in principle between such a shift and the shift whereby Kepler superseded Ptolemy, or Einstein Newton, or Darwin Aristotle?
>
> (FLPV, p. 43)

Apart from the final clause, this passage would have been acceptable to Carnap. He may even be able to accept the final clause too, for radical shifts in scientific perspective – as well as changes in logic – probably involve framework changes rather than internal changes relative to a shared framework. Carnap's more complex picture adds nothing to Quine's account.

2.6 EMPIRICISM WITHOUT THE DOGMAS: MODERATE HOLISM

As Quine has admitted, the metaphors he used to express his position at the end of 'Two dogmas' have misled many readers. In the remaining two sections of this chapter, we shall consider the epistemological bearings of Quine's holism and his repudiation of the analytic/synthetic distinction. Readers often assume that Quine claims that we have extraordinary freedom in how we develop our opinions. For example:

(1) As I sit here using my typewriter, I have the option of denying that there is any typewriter in front of me.
(2) When a predicted experience fails to occur – the train does not arrive when I expect it to – I have the option of restoring order to my beliefs by abandoning a fundamental logical law or simple arithmetic assumption.

It seems clear that claims 1 and 2 are false. They do not describe choices that are open to me at all. Does Quine dispute this obvious truth?

He does not. What is at issue is how the truth is to be explained. We could claim that it is *psychologically* impossible for me to deny what my senses tell me, when this coheres with the rest of my beliefs. This falls short of the claim that the meaning of the sentence 'There is a typewriter in front of me' compels me 'logically' or 'semantically' to accept it, and it could be accepted by Quine. In the normal case, denying an observation introduces an arbitrary complexity into our body of beliefs. We seek to keep our system of beliefs as simple as possible, but also to keep its evolution as simple and smooth as possible – changes are to be kept to a minimum (RR, p. 137). So, as rational inquirers, we avoid such arbitrary changes. Still, there are circumstances in which it would be rational (and psychologically possible) to doubt the evidence of our senses. If what I see conflicts with many deeply held beliefs, especially if I am in a position where perceptual error is common, then denying the observational evidence may be the least disruptive recourse, ensuring the least modification in my corpus of beliefs and the simplest and most useful overall corpus. The perceptual judgement which is undeniable now could subsequently come to be challenged – quite reasonably – without any change in its meaning. No semantic rule determines how we should respond in any particular case, for we are always sensitive to the systematic integrity of our beliefs as a whole. Quine's position is secure if he holds that, whenever we talk of what can be doubted or about what must be believed, we are concerned with psychological – rather than logical – possibility, and if he holds that the systematic structure of our corpus of beliefs influences what it is possible for us to doubt at any time.

Let us now turn to logic and mathematics. How can Quine believe that we could ever find it psychologically or rationally possible to abandon such claims? Plainly, if I resolved to abandon the principle that:

If P&Q then P

or, if I gave up the belief that

$$2+6=8$$

and retained consistency by announcing that 6 is, in fact, the successor of 7 in the number series, not 5, or by claiming that only one of the conjuncts has to be true for a conjunction to be true, we should feel that I am simply arbitrarily changing the meanings of the expressions involved. This would not support Quine's doctrine in any interesting sense. Indeed, we cannot conceive of any grounds for giving up those beliefs which would not seem arbitrary in this way. So, is Quine wrong in his claim about the revisability of mathematics and logic?

For the present, I merely wish to argue that it is not yet obvious that he is. I shall do this in two stages. The first point to be made is that the facts just adduced could be explained in several different ways. One possibility is that such statements express linguistic rules, or framework principles, so that they have a different sort of epistemological status from claims that can be revised in response to evidence. A second possibility is that, in some other fashion, statements of logic and mathematics have an epistemological status different from that of statements of physics or common sense: perhaps our knowledge of them reflects an intuitive awareness of various abstract necessary structures. A third possibility is that these beliefs are so deeply embedded in our structure of beliefs – so many other beliefs depend upon them – that it is currently inconceivable that the search for an economical route to a simple and useful body of knowledge could ever challenge them. If this third explanation were correct, then there would be no case for positing two distinct sorts of knowledge: a unified theory which accounts for the bearing of pragmatic and sensory considerations upon our beliefs would account for the apparently special characteristics of these beliefs without giving them a radically different status from other beliefs. We explain the psychological impossibility of doubt without attributing it to semantic rules.

Secondly, we can allow that through a process of lengthy evolution in our opinions, guided by concern for system and concern for evidence, it could gradually come about that we could conceive how one of these statements might be false: it would gradually lose its special status. Consider a geometric example. Two hundred years ago, the claim that parallel straight lines perpendicular to a given line would never meet would have seemed analytic. It was inconceivable that this could ever be doubted; to doubt it would show that one's grasp of the concept of a straight line was imperfect. The product of a hundred years of varied developments in geometry and in physics was that it became a genuine question whether it was, in fact, true. What was 'analytic' before 1800 was rejected after 1900. There is a clear sense in which the meaning of 'straight line' changed during that period, but this did not involve arbitrary shifts of meaning. The change reflected a series of small developments, all of which were guided by considerations of evidence and theoretical economy. The 'analytic' status of the statement at the earlier time is reflected in the extent of the changes in physics that were required to shift our allegiance to it; but it is not reflected in any detailed semantic mechanisms involved in the shift.

In the light of this, we can produce a cautious expression of the Quinean view. There are many statements of logic and mathematics of which we feel certain, quite reasonably, that their truth value will never come into question. This is not because our knowledge of them has a special source which *guarantees* this assurance: some statements which once had this status have lost it as inquiry has progressed. The source of our certainty is the systematic role that such statements have within the body of our beliefs: it is their remoteness from experience rather than their total independence of experiential test. We can explain how this makes it psychologically impossible for us to doubt them. And we can explain the fact that we tend to respond to evidence in similar ways by pointing out that our psychological dispositions – the product of training and natural endowment – have many points of similarity. We have shared standards of simplicity and similarity, shared dispositions to generalize from observed regularities and to find observational reports indubitable. Distinguishing deeply entrenched or highly certain beliefs from conventionally adopted rules or analytic truths does not add to our capacity to explain our ability to use and understand the English language, or our ability to reach a consensus on scientific questions.

In concluding this section, let us return to Quine's insistence that he is only a 'moderate' holist. In 'Five milestones of empiricism' he asks how inclusive the system of sentences which now constitutes the vehicle of meaning should be. He repudiates the suggestion that it is the whole of science, claiming:

> Should it be the whole of science or the whole of *a* science, a branch of science? This should be seen as a matter or degree, and of diminishing returns. All sciences interlock to some extent; they share a common logic and generally some common part of mathematics, even when nothing else. It is an uninteresting legalism, however, to think of our scientific system of the world as involved *en bloc* in every prediction. More modest chunks suffice, and so may be ascribed their independent empirical meaning, nearly enough, since some vagueness in meaning must be allowed for in any event.
>
> (TT, p. 71)

Moreover, insisting that all here is a matter of degree, Quine stresses that observation sentences *do* have a separable empirical meaning: although they *can* be 'recanted in the light of the rest of one's theory', 'this is an extreme case and happily not characteristic'. These points are further developed in 'On empirically equivalent systems of the world', where Quine insists that however correct the claim may be 'in a legalistic way', it is unreasonable to 'extend a Duhemian holism to the whole of science, taking all science as the unit that is responsible to observation'.

> Science is neither discontinuous nor monolithic. It is variously jointed, and loose in the joints in varying degrees. In the face of a recalcitrant observation we are free to choose which statements to revise and what to

> hold fast, and these alternatives will disrupt various stretches of theory in various ways, varying in severity.
>
> (EESW, pp. 313–14)

These claims concern what is psychologically possible for us: this is the only kind of possibility that Quine will countenance here. Notions like logical or semantic compulsion have no explanatory role.

2.7 UNDERSTANDING WITHOUT ANALYTICITY

According to the interpretation that I have offered, Quine's attack on the analytic/synthetic distinction is primarily directed at a model of how beliefs are revised in the course of inquiry. He rejects the suggestion that two distinct mechanisms are involved in these changes: revision of belief in synthetic propositions against the background of a definite linguistic framework; and revisions in analytic framework principles guided by pragmatic considerations. The phrase he uses to describe his position, 'methodological monism' indicates his belief that that all revisions of beliefs conform to a single pattern.

It is a natural complaint that 'methodological monism' leaves us without an account of understanding at all. The analytic/synthetic distinction explained our ability to communicate: it rests upon a shared mastery of the analytic truths of a common linguistic framework. Without this distinction, no explanation of our shared understandings of words is possible at all. Another common objection is that we all agree on which statements count as analytic, which as synthetic. How can Quine deny a distinction as obvious as that between 'All bachelors are unmarried' and 'Thatcher is British Prime Minister in 1986'? (See Grice and Strawson, 1956). The former is 'plainly' *a priori* knowable, necessarily true, and true by virtue of meaning; the latter is equally plainly empirical, contingent and synthetic. These complaints, it seems to me, are unwarranted. I shall suggest what a Quinean could say about shared understanding, and we shall conclude that the 'intuitive' notion of analyticity is untouched by his arguments. What is at stake is whether a notion of analyticity can make the sort of contribution to the *explanation* of meaning, rationality and knowledge that Carnap desires. Quine's conclusion is that talk of linguistic *rules* offers only an illusion of understanding in these areas.

The early positivists held that understanding a word such as 'lemon' or 'proton', 'horse' or 'table' required knowledge of a set of necessary and sufficient conditions for being an item of the appropriate kind. I know which characteristics all tables share and exploit this knowledge when I use the word. My understanding embodies standards which determine whether the term applies to the objects which I encounter. Even Carnap's more sophisticated position grounds understanding in grasp of postulates giving complex necessary conditions for belonging to the extension of the term. Of course, the picture is an idealization: terms of a natural language are vague and amibiguous, so we might be unclear about which rules govern our use of a word. But in principle, we could reform or regiment our language, removing this vagueness, constructing a language which operates according to strict standards.

Among the conditions for the application of a term that we all use, some are constitutive of the *meanings* of the terms in question; they are analytic, resulting from stipulations, or grounded in pragmatically governed conventional decision. Others embody well confirmed empirical generalizations. These synthetic beliefs enter into our 'conceptions' of the kinds of things in question, but are not constitutive of the meanings of the corresponding words. My conception of, say, a proton can change both as my knowledge of physics grows, and as the best current theories are revised and developed. And this happens without the *meaning* of the word 'proton' changing. Of course, Carnap also allows for a second kind of change: meanings, and analytic truths, change as one factor in scientific progress.

There are various grounds for dissatisfaction with this picture. Some – the pervasive vagueness and indeterminacies in ordinary language – have already been alluded to. Wittgenstein has famously remarked that we cannot find any clear necessary or sufficient conditions for the property of being a game: it seems impossible to find any body of clear *rules* which govern our use of this notion, but we have no inclination to think of it as simply ambiguous or to think that it could retain its utility for us if it was brought under a strict set of necessary or sufficient conditions. And this does not mean that we fail to agree in our usage, or that we are prey to indecision about whether some activity is a game (Wittgenstein, 1953, sections 69ff).

Putnam has pointed out features of our use of terms for 'natural kinds' – kinds of plants, animals, minerals etc. – which appear to raise further difficulties for this initially plausible picture (Putnam, 1975, ch. 8). In such cases, we seem to be guided by a sense of what a *normal* member of the kind in question is like, rather than by knowledge of invariable characteristics. We would describe a cheetah as a four-legged animal, very fast, a member of the cat family, with distinctive markings. But we are not disturbed at encountering albino cheetahs, or by those which have lost a leg, and are hence slow. Although we think of lemons as yellow, sour-tasting fruit with a distinctive shape, we grant that skilful plant breeding could provide us with lemons of a different taste, colour or shape. Most of the characteristics that are central to our sense of what a lemon is could be absent without our being forced to conclude that what we are confronted with is not a lemon. And it is far from clear that we have to change the meaning of the word 'lemon' in order to accommodate such deviant fruit.

As we have seen, Quine rejects the view that language use can be explained in terms of the application of rules or standards expressing necessary or sufficient conditions. We do not have rules or standards which determine how a term is to be applied in any conceivable circumstance. How a concept is to be applied to a novel case reflects not only the entrenched beliefs we have about things that fall under the concept, but also considerations of overall coherence and simplicity in the relevant parts of our general body of theory. How our precedents will be interpreted in the new case is not something that they declare unequivocally for themselves. Nor is our sense of simplicity and coherence formulated in a body of rules which can be applied to determine what we should say in the new situation. The holistic character of scientific practice undermines the plausible traditional picture, by requiring that overall coherence or simplicity can, at any time, have a role in how we revise our beliefs in response to perceptual surprise.

A satisfying development of some of these Quinean themes is found in Putnam's paper 'The analytic and the synthetic' (in Putnam 1975). In part, he is criticizing Quine. He thinks that there are analytic sentences like

All vixens are foxes.

What is distinctive about this is that there is just *one* criterion that we make use of for something being a vixen – that it is a female fox. Since there is only one such criterion, it seems evident that no run of experience could lead us to reject the claim. However, even if Quine is wrong about this, Putnam's sympathies in this paper are, in general, Quinean: there aren't any *interesting* analytic statements, and the notion cannot be used for the sorts of purposes that Carnap intended. Most words are employed in accordance with multiple criteria. Theoretical terms from the sciences are 'law-cluster' terms: they derive their meanings from the cluster of laws in which they occur in our latest theories. No one of these laws is analytic: we expect that many of them may have to be refined or substantially revised as knowledge progresses. It is part of our understanding of such terms that any of the laws may turn out to be mistaken, or may turn out only to be a special determination of some other more general law. Considerations of overall simplicity have a role in deciding which are to give when the theory has to be revised. We can imagine that the results of a sequence of changes elsewhere in the theory would be that our sense of which laws in the cluster are more vulnerable would change. Those that 'felt' more analytic would cease to do so, without anything like a conventionally adopted change of meaning being involved.

Understanding requires that we can be confident that others will apply terms to novel cases as we do. Part of the explanation of this is that we all know that we all know that (say) normal lemons are yellow when ripe. This is 'analytic' in a loose sense: no one who denied it would be accepted as understanding the word 'lemon'; we all tend to rely upon it in identifying lemons; it is a truth that we would convey in teaching the word 'lemon'. But, as I have mentioned above, this falls short of the philosophical notion of analyticity which Quine is concerned to combat. A certainty which was 'synthetic', in the philosophical sense, could serve the same role. And it does not require the claim that distinct mechanisms are involved in the growth of knowledge. Another part of the explanation is that we know we have shared senses of simplicity and coherence. Without this shared capacity for judging how to respond to new cases, shared concepts and understanding would not be possible at all. A psychological explanation can be provided for all this. We do not require explanations that talk of conventionally adopted linguistic frameworks. The analytic/synthetic distinction is rejected as part of an inadequate explanatory framework.

The 'loose' sense of analyticity mentioned above may well suffice to account for the intuitive appeal that the concept has. If that is all 'analytic' means, it is a useful everyday concept, but it lacks the philosophical importance which many have wanted for it. The statement is analytic because everyone expects everyone to accept it, and because it is taught as people learn their language. Its analyticity does not contribute to an explanation of its truth, or its obviousness; and its analyticity has little contribution to make to explaining how we have *a priori* knowledge or to explaining scientific rationality. This loose notion is not Quine's target.

Quine's attack on the explanatory value of notions like 'rule', 'analytic' and 'convention' works in other ways too. In 'True by convention', (WP), there is a general argument against attempts to explain logical principles as fixed by conventions. The argument is simple. Since there are indefinitely many logically true statements, we cannot appeal to a separate convention to fix the truth of each: the truth of each of the following reflects the same convention:

> If all men are mortal and John is a man then John is mortal
>
> If all swans are white and this is a swan, then this is white
>
> If all even numbers are divisible without remainder by 2, and 48 is an even number, then 48 is divisible without remainder by 2 – etc.

Our general convention might take the form

> All statements of the form 'If all F are G and a is F, then a is G' are true.

But then we need logic to apply this general convention to establish that particular statements are logical truths. and indeed, we need to use a logical principle of exactly this form in order to apply the principle itself. Conventional rules presuppose logic: they cannot explain its validity.

In spite of their many differences, Quine and the later Wittgenstein are united in combating the tendency of philosophers to view the notion of a rule as part of a powerful explanatory account of understanding and rationality. Language is not, throughout, bound by precise rules; talk of rules has limited explanatory value unless we can explain how the rules themselves are applied or interpreted; talk of being compelled, logically, to use words or draw inferences in particular ways is not explanatory – at root it rests upon psychological or natural necessity. Both were responding to Carnap and the other Vienna positivists; both were struck by holistic features of understanding and inquiry. But we must now turn to aspects of Quine's philosophy which have less echo in the *Philosophical Investigations*.

3

Naturalism, Realism and Pragmatism

3.1 QUINE, CARNAP AND PHILOSOPHY

We should not lose sight of the merits of Carnap's philosophical outlook. The contrast between internal and external questions was a powerful philosophical tool, and it is easy to understand Carnap's resistance to its elimination. First, it provided a plausible diagnosis of the errors of traditional philosophers, and a means of overcoming them. When philosophers debate over whether there are physical objects or universals, they employ the 'material mode' to talk about what is more perspicuously expressed in the 'formal mode' as issues about linguistic expressions: what is really at issue is whether to adopt a certain linguistic framework. Thus:

Are there universals?

is better expressed

> Should we adopt a linguistic framework which employs '— is a universal' as one of its fundamental general terms?

Talk of universals is covertly talk of language. Metaphysics grows out of the error of viewing issues which, when correctly formulated in the metalinguistic 'formal mode', can be seen not to be substantive, as substantive issues formulated in the 'material mode'. Since adoption of frameworks turns on pragmatic convenience rather than correspondence to reality, philosophers delude themselves when they believe they are involved in a substantive debate. It was a corollary of this that Carnap could talk of various sorts of abstract entities in his writings on modal logic and semantics without having to worry about the scruples about such things normally experienced by empiricists.

Secondly, retention of the distinction between internal and external questions provided a distinctive role for a scientific philosophy. Philosophy – in the guise of logical syntax – can describe and study the properties of linguistic frameworks. It can step back, survey the different frameworks, discuss their merits, and provide an account of the normative principles of rationality which the different frameworks impose on those who adopt them. Philosophy as analysis or logical syntax can retain some of the traditional aspirations of philosophy.

A third merit surfaces when we consider relations between pragmatism and objectivity. Our taking a realist attitude towards a subject matter, our seeing it as objective, involves believing that the correct answers to questions arising about it are not up to us. Whether a statement is true is not affected by the processes of inquiry that go toward finding out whether it is true. If we ignore the complexities introduced when Carnap came under the influence of Duhem, we can illustrate the force of this observation by reference to his views. When I attempt to answer an internal question, from within the perspective of a particular framework, it is not up to me what answer I should give. The rules of the framework determine some answer as the correct one, in the light of experience. On the other hand, when the question 'Are there physical objects?' is raised as an *external* question, this form of objectivity is missing. The correct answer will reflect the tastes, interests and standards of simplicity of the the person who asks it. Choice of framework reflects subjective interests and purposes, not correspondence to an objective independent reality.

This illustrates a further advantage of retaining the distinction between internal and external questions. It enables us to disentangle the subjective and objective elements in the growth of knowledge. The objectivity of science can be acknowledged, and explained in terms of the character of internal questions. Once the situation is muddied by the recognition that pragmatic considerations have a role in answering even internal questions, then it is difficult to sustain the claim that the theoretical parts of science are genuinely objective. An 'anti-realism' about the objects of theoretical science was widely adopted by later logical empiricist philosophers of science.

If, with Quine, we abandon this distinction, a number of problems arise. How are the subjective and objective elements in our knowledge to be disentangled? Are all questions analogous to internal ones, or are they analogous to external ones? If neither analogy is appropriate, and apparently subjective pragmatic criteria are invoked when we revise our opinions, can room be found for saying that we investigate an objective reality? And just what theoretical apparatus should the philosopher use in investigating our activities as inquirers? What tasks are left for philosophy? What sort of subject is it?

3.2 QUINE AND PRAGMATISM

In 'Two dogmas', Quine notes two effects of abandoning the analytic/synthetic distinction. One, 'a blurring of the supposed boundary between speculative metaphysics and natural science', will be discussed in the following section. The other is 'a shift toward pragmatism' (FLPV, p. 20). The closing sections of both 'Two dogmas' and 'On what there is' are full of endorsements of pragmatism: Carnap's pragmatic considerations become relevant to all questions once the contrast between external and internal is abandoned. Curiously, these references to pragmatism vanish from Quine's subsequent work. One question we must consider is whether this represents a substantive shift in his views.

We have noticed tensions between the suggestion that pragmatic considerations have an important role in the ways in which knowledge develops, and the idea that knowledge claims are objective. We feared that a corollary of Quine's position was that we could not disentangle subjective from objective factors in the growth of knowledge: all questions have the status of Carnap's external questions. Scientific realism, the doctrine that science is objective, goes by the board. Many passages in *From a Logical Point of View* support such a reading. In 'Identity, ostension and hypostasis' Quine refers (like Carnap) to Duhem and asserts that it is meaningless 'to inquire into the absolute correctness of a conceptual scheme as a mirror of reality' (FLPV, p. 79).

> Our standard for appraising basic changes of conceptual scheme must be, not a realistic standard of correspondence to reality, but a pragmatic standard. Concepts are language, and the purpose of concepts and of language is efficacy in communication and prediction. Such is the ultimate duty of language, science and philosophy, and it is in relation to that duty that a conceptual scheme has finally to be appraised.
>
> (FLPV, p. 79)

Moreover, in 'On what there is', after admitting that choice of ontology like choice of scientific theory rests upon pragmatic considerations of overall simplicity and coherence, Quine appears to advocate a tolerant pragmatist pluralism or relativism. Noting that simplicity is 'not a clear and unambiguous idea' and can present a 'double standard', he contrasts two conceptual schemes for coping with experience. One, a phenomenalistic scheme, talks only of sense experiences and their properties; the other, a physicalist scheme, deals with ordinary physical objects.

> Which should prevail? Each has its advantages; each has its special simplicity in its own way. Each, I suggest, deserves to be developed. Each may be said, indeed, to be the more fundamental, though in different senses: the one is epistemologically, the other physically, fundamental.
>
> (FLPV, p. 17)

From the point of view of this phenomenalistic scheme (FLPV, p. 18), and from Quine's own empiricist outlook (p. 44), physical objects are imported to make coherent sense of our experience as 'irreducible posits comparable, epistemologically, to the gods of Homer'.

> For my part I do, qua lay physicist, believe in physical objects and not in the gods of Homer; and I consider it a scientific error to do otherwise. But in point of epistemological footing the physical objects and the gods differ only in degree and not in kind. Both sorts of entities enter our conceptions only as cultural posits. The myth of physical objects is epistemologically superior to most in that it has proved more efficacious than other myths as a device for working a manageable structure into the flux of experience.
>
> (FLPV, p. 44)

It is easy to take away from this a picture of all inquiry as a more or less useful kind of myth making. In accord with Carnap's principle of tolerance, we can expect Quine to advocate developing a variety of different myths, each with its own merits. There is no sense in which one or other of the myths is objectively true: and as philosophers we can appreciate the variety of conceptual schemes through which we approach our experience without seeing any one of them as fundamental.

Just this sort of view is developed by a thinker who has been close to Quine, Nelson Goodman. In a pluralistic spirit, he developed a number of contrasting schemes in his early book *The Structure of Appearance*; and more recently in *Ways of Worldmaking* he has defended explicitly an anti-realist pluralism or relativism. He contrasts many different 'versions' of the world that we construct – those of science, of common sense, of literature, music and the other arts – and deplores the view that some one of these is closer to reality or more perspicuous as a representation of it than the others. There is not one true account of reality, but as many versions of it as we construct and find to be fruitful.

3.3 PRAGMATISM AND REALISM

In a recent review of *Ways of Worldmaking*, Quine rejects this tolerant pluralism. He increasingly describes himself as a realist, and turns to the physical sciences for a description of reality. Although the term frequently occurs in *From a Logical Point of View*, 'pragmatism' is hardly mentioned subsequently, and does not appear in the index of *Word and Object*. Apparently, the tensions between pragmatism and objectivity are resolved differently in later work.

However, even in *From a Logical Point of View*, we can find grounds for unease about this relativist, anti-realistic reading of Quine's writings. A small clue is the stress he places upon his *believing* in physical objects but not in Homer's gods. This suggests that treating something as a myth need not disparage its reality. More telling is the continuation of the passage from 'Identity, ostension and hypostasis' that was quoted above. Having stressed that our standard for appraising theories is a pragmatic one, rather than one based upon correspondence to the truth, Quine first claims that efficient prediction and communication provides the 'duty of language, science and philosophy' by reference to which proposals must be evaluated. He continues:

> Elegance, conceptual economy also enters as an objective. But this virtue, engaging though it is, is secondary... Elegance can make the difference between a psychologically manageable conceptual scheme and one that is too unwieldy for our poor minds to cope with effectively. Where this happens, elegance is simply a means to the end of a pragmatically acceptable conceptual scheme. But elegance also enters as an end in itself – and quite properly so long as it remains secondary in another respect; namely so long as it is appealed to only in choices where the pragmatic

> standard prescribes no contrary decision. Where elegance doesn't matter, we may and shall, as poets, pursue elegance for elegance's sake.
>
> (FLPV, p. 79)

It is striking that he *contrasts* the pursuit of an elegant theory for its own sake with the choice of a body of beliefs on pragmatic grounds. The 'pragmatic standard' embodies, not a reference to whatever particular interests and purposes might lead someone to construct a world, but an appeal to the pursuit of efficient predictive control over experience which serves as the 'duty' of science. Here Quine's empiricism intervenes to assign a meaning to the 'pragmatic' which puts into question the claim that the presence of pragmatic considerations in scientific growth is in tension with a realist construal of science. Pragmatism requires us to ensure that our beliefs are answerable to experience.

A slightly earlier passage is more instructive still. Quine there suggests that the question of realism, of how far our knowledge is objective, may be spurious:

> Certainly we are in a predicament if we try to answer the question; for to answer the question we must talk about the world as well as about language, and to talk about the world we must already impose upon the world some conceptual scheme peculiar to our own special language.
>
> (FLPV, p. 78)

We initially feared that Quine's pragmatism involved turning every question into an external one. Perhaps it is less misleading to say that he turns every question into an internal one. The philosopher takes for granted a view of the world when he considers questions about knowledge, meaning or ontology.

The anti-realist reading of Quine's early writings results from ignoring the continuities between philosophy and the rest of our knowledge which are required by the holism that Quine urges in 'Two dogmas of empiricism' and elsewhere. Let us return to the quotation from 'Identity, ostension and hypostasis'. How does Quine *know* that the 'duty' of science, and other forms of knowledge, is to guide us to efficient predictive control over our experience? He cannot consistently display this as *a priori* knowledge or as analytic truth. How can philosophers support such claims?

Quine often borrows a metaphor from Neurath. The scientist or philosopher does not resemble a shipwright who places a ship in drydock and rebuilds it from the keel up, ensuring that each plank is secured in its place as he goes. Rather, he is in the position of a sailor on a leaky ship at sea. Repairs can be effected in a piecemeal fashion, the remaining timbers keeping the ship afloat while one is removed and replaced. Our knowledge grows through changes and adjustments made from within our growing corpus. The beliefs not currently under challenge provide the inferential links that are exploited in testing more questionable parts of the structure. Which are the beliefs that keep us afloat when we raise philosophical questions about realism and the possibility of knowledge? My suspicion is that, at the time of writing the papers contained in *From a Logical Point of View*, Quine had not fully thought out his response to this question. By the publication of *Word and Object*, in 1960, his more robust realism and avoidance of talk of pragmatism reflects a greater clarity about just this issue. The rhetoric and metaphor of the epistemological sections of the earlier papers is replaced by a more developed theory.

3.4 REALISM AND NATURALISM

We now encounter the fifth and final milestone of empiricism. This is naturalism: 'the abandonment of the goal of a first philosophy' (TT, p. 72). It reflects a despair of providing reductive accounts of our concepts, induced by taking holism seriously, and an 'unregenerate realism'. The philosopher's epistemological interests are not abandoned, they are pursued within empirical psychology. The scientific epistemologist tries to explain how our knowledge is possible:

> (a)nd he comes out with an account that has a good deal to do with the learning of language and with the neurology of perception. He talks of how men posit bodies and hypothetical particles, but he does not mean to suggest that the things posited do not exist. Evolution and natural selection will doubtless figure in this account, and he will feel free to apply physics if he sees a way.
>
> (TT, p. 72)

The further natural step on from methodological monism is the refusal to see any radical differences between the methods and resources used in philosophy and those used in the sciences. The naturalistic philosopher works within a world view which, he is sure, is flawed in unknown ways. As 'the busy sailor adrift on Neurath's boat', he seeks to locate and remedy these defects from within.

Hence, the philosopher works within a scientific account of the world, exploiting discoveries from physics and, perhaps, psychology, in considering philosophical questions. Our scientific theories and common-sense beliefs about reality serve as the fabric of the boat which keeps it afloat when it is threatened by philosophical perplexities. Epistemology investigates how we can construct our sophisticated theories about the physical world on the basis of the sparse evidence available to us. Information about the physiology of the senses and the evolutionary advantages of our inferential practices have a role in these explanations. Our questions are scientific questions about the growth of science. Epistemology is considered 'an enterprise within natural science' (NNK, p. 68). In the first chapter of *Word and Object*, Quine proposes to 'ponder our talk of physical phenomena as a physical phenomenon, and our scientific imaginings as activities within the world that we imagine' (WO, p. 5). As Quine's work progresses, it loses the programmatic character of *From a Logical Point of View*. Increasingly, it is composed of sketches of, and speculations about, our psychological and physiological relations to our surroundings. Armchair learning theory becomes the vehicle of philosophical analysis. Philosophical problems differ from scientific ones only in their greater generality. Philosophy loses its special character.

The remainder of this volume is concerned with some of the details of Quine's execution of his philosophical project. I want now to raise some issues concerning Quine's naturalistic approach to philosophy, and thus introduce topics that will concern us in later chapters. First, someone could agree with Quine that philosophy should fall into place as part of science while rejecting Quine's own 'scientific' view of reality as excessively impoverished. Quine is a physicalist. It is physics which describes the nature of reality, and sciences other than physics are treated with some suspicion. Quine's psychology is heavily behaviouristic and physiological, having little room for the patterns of explanation used in common-sense discussions of the mind and action. Quine's physicalism is the principal source of the distinctive flavour of his philosophical position. Part II contains a fuller discussion of these views. Part II as a whole explores Quine's philosophical methods and his highly austere conception of reality. This discussion is developed in Part III, where we examine the implications of this austere vision for our understanding of mind and meaning. This will involve a consideration of one of Quine's most influential doctrines, the indeterminacy of translation.

A second issue concerns whether a naturalized epistemology is possible at all. Many philosophers hold that sceptical arguments are the source of our epistemological problems, and insist that naturalized epistemology cannot address them. When sceptical problems are raised, and doubt is cast upon our ability to know *anything* about reality, we cannot, on pain of circularity, make use of scientific information in our response. Since the credentials of science are being challenged by the sceptical argument, it is question begging to assume the truth of scientific results in framing a reply. Quine changes the subject: what he offers is not continuous with traditional epistemology. His psychology of knowledge is irrelevant to philosophical problems. Chapter 11, in Part IV, discusses this topic in detail.

A third issue returns us to the tension between realist and anti-realist themes in Quine's work. What does science tell us about scientific activity? In 'The nature of natural knowledge', we learn that it tells us that 'our only source of information about the external world is through the impact of light rays and molecules upon our sensory surfaces' (p. 68); and that its utility 'from a practical point of view, lies in fulfilled expectation: true prediction'. These claims are equally true of 'sophisticated science' and its 'primitive progenitor' (pp. 68–9); they apply to advanced mathematical physics, common-sense opinions, and the information processing of animals. In the same spirit, the first paragraph of 'Things and their place in theories' runs:

> Our talk of external things, our very notion of things, is just a conceptual apparatus that helps us to foresee and control the triggering of our sensory receptors in the light of previous triggering of our sensory receptors. The triggering, first and last, is all we have to go on.
>
> (TT, pp. 1–2)

Quine denies that these remarks have any sceptical content. This passage is itself about external things – people and nerve endings – and: 'There is nothing we can be more certain of than external things – some of them, anyway – other people, sticks and stones. But there remains the fact – a fact of science itself – that science is a conceptual bridge linking sensory stimulation to sensory stimulation' (TT, p. 2).

A paradox threatens here, and we shall return to it in chapter 11. If science teaches us that science is nothing but a 'conceptual bridge', valued because we are enabled to anticipate the future course of experience, doesn't science itself undermine its claim to give us a true account of physical reality? If different theories, offering alternative accounts of the underlying nature of matter, were equally effective in enabling us to avoid perceptual surprise, what sense attaches to the claim that one is true and the other false? And this threatens to rebound against the scientific theories upon which Quine's theory is based. The 'pragmatist' claims from *From a Logical Point of View* seem not to have been left behind.

Quine's naturalism has been discussed in a very sketchy fashion here. It will concern us repeatedly in the ensuing chapters. However, before we can examine the issues it raises, we must explore some of the fundamental doctrines which shape his philosophical system. Hence, we turn, in Part II, to a discussion of his physicalism and to some of his views about the logical character of a language adequate to describe the physical world.

Part II

Logic and Reality

4

Physicalism and Objectivity

4.1 SCIENCE AND PHILOSOPHY

Holding that science serves as a paradigm for all knowledge, the logical empiricists were ambitious to bring scientific standards of precision and objectivity to philosophy: philosophy could provide knowledge only by employing the scientific method. Furthermore, epistemology – the theory of knowledge – became the philosophy of science: the primary epistemological problems concerned the scientific pursuit of truth. Finally, since many of the claims and assertions that we normally make fail to measure up to the strict standards of science, some philosophical response to them was required. One possibility was to repudiate them: we erroneously claim knowledge of such things. Alternatively, they could be reinterpreted: it was a mistake to think of them as claims to knowledge at all. Thus some philosophers argued that our ordinary practice of making moral judgements reflects an erroneous belief that there are objective values; while others insisted that these 'judgements' should be understood as expressing emotions or attitudes rather than beliefs about reality.

This 'scientific' outlook is present in Carnap's insistence that 'once philosophy is purified of all scientific elements, only the logic of science remains' (1937, p. 279). However, this scientism may sit rather uneasily with his pragmatism and the contrast of internal and external questions. Consider, first, the methodology of philosophy and the question: what framework do we employ when we study the properties of frameworks and draw the distinction between internal and external questions? It would be nice to find that we could know those things in some absolute non-framework-relative way, but, of course, that is impossible. Hence philosophical results have no non-relative validity, and it is important to ask what pragmatic considerations warrant the choice of philosophical frameworks – the framework of 'general syntax' in *The Logical Syntax of Language*, the framework of semantics in Carnap's later work.

The tension runs deeper than this. From the external perspective, relying upon pragmatic considerations to choose a linguistic framework, why should we expect science to win out over non-scientific alternatives? Once we deny that frameworks are to be preferred because they provide better accounts of reality, why should the honorific title 'knowledge' attach to the scientific ones but not to any others? Our practical needs may be best served by the sort of predictive control over our surroundings that the sciences provide, but we need to show further that other pragmatic requirements are not equally important.

In the light of these considerations, we can see the appeal of Goodman's more thoroughgoing pragmatism which deplores the scientism of the positivist movement (see Goodman, 1978). Why should a special status be attached to empirical science? Shouldn't we prefer a pluralist approach which finds complementary merits in the 'versions' constructed by scientists, painters and poets and others, but denies that any is fundamental? Perhaps we should see this scientism as a prior commitment of Carnap's. The rapid scientific progress of the early twentieth century convinced many philosophers that science alone provided genuine knowledge. In that case, it is the desire to make sense of the sciences that motivates choice of framework for analysis of linguistic frameworks; and a more pluralistic outlook was never seriously considered. But that does not relieve us of the need to understand what is so good about science.

Quine is resistant to Goodman's pragmatic pluralism: his commitment to science and to empiricism is as strong as Carnap's:

> One feels that this sequence of worlds or versions founders in absurdity. I take Goodman's defense of it to be that there is no reasonable intermediate point at which to end it. I would end it after the first step: physical theory. I grant the possibility of alternative physical theories, insusceptible to adjudication; but I see the rest of his sequence of worlds or world versions only as a rather tenuous metaphor.
>
> (TT, pp. 97–8)

Like the positivists, Quine insists that scientific knowledge is the only genuine (non-metaphorical) knowledge. Moreover, he seems to go beyond insisting that non-scientific 'versions' are mere 'tenuous metaphor'; sciences other than physics apparently enjoy a similar status. The physical facts, he insists, are all the facts. But the retreat from Carnap's external perspective to Neurath's boat does not offer any obvious basis for adopting this austere conception of the structure of reality. We shall not understand the character of Quine's thought until we see the force of his physicalism.

We have already noticed the impact of this commitment. The fundamental epistemological problem, for Quine, rests upon a 'scientific' view of the aims of scientific endeavour and the methods that scientists employ. In the quotation from 'Things and their place in theories', we were told that all there was to science was the correct anticipation of stimulations of nerve endings on our sensory surfaces: a theory is adequate if it succesfully mediates patterns of stimulations at different times. At first glance, this is very implausible. We are likely to protest that we want our theories to enable us to *understand* or make sense of our surroundings; we want true beliefs about the underlying structure of matter; and so on. Quine appears to have missed out much that seems essential to scientific activity.

These alternative accounts of the aims of science are cast in psychological terms: they use notions like belief and understanding. The oddity of Quine's description may reflect a refusal to make use of this sort of psychological vocabulary: it is the sort of account of science we should expect to be offered by someone who resolved only to make use of a radically impoverished vocabulary in describing human and social phenomena. It looks like a physiological or behavioural account of what science is. If we feel that it misses out much that is important, we shall also suspect that Quine's conception of the facts is too austere, his canon of acceptable versions is too restrictive.

In this chapter and those that follow it, we look at the sources of Quine's austere conception of reality. First, we directly examine his physicalism. Then, we turn to some themes from his logic: particularly his insistence that a very limited logical framework will suffice to handle all discourse concerned with describing the structure of reality.

4.2 QUINE'S PHYSICALISM: SOME QUESTIONS

If we are to come to terms with Quine's physicalism, we must find answers to a number of questions. One of these concerns just what is involved in thinking of a fact as *physical*: until we know what physical facts are, we shall not know what to make of the insistence that they exhaust the facts. A second question, obviously, concerns the sorts of reasons that Quine offers for thinking his doctrine is true. Both of these issues will be discussed later in the chapter. First, I want to prepare for this by discussing some other issues concerning the doctrine and its implications for Quine's theory of knowledge.

Let us contrast two ways in which Neurath's boat metaphor could be developed. According to the first (version A), we start with a vast, somewhat disorganized structure comprising all of our common-sense beliefs and prejudices, together with scientific beliefs drawn from all the different disciplines. As a result of scientific inquiries, this corpus of opinions grows and evolves: new opinions are added, old ones are jettisoned, others are reformulated or revised in other ways. This is the most natural reading of the doctrine. Our remarks about Quine's physicalism, however, might suggest an alternative interpretation (version B). Since only physics describes the facts, all that the boat metaphor is supposed to represent is the development of physical theory. Common-sense assurances, theories from chemistry, biology, economics, historical descriptions, would then have no place in the boat. If this second version is required by Quine's physicalism, it is hard to see why it is preferable to the first.

Of course, the two versions need not compete. One could hold that the austere world view of version B is what we end up with when we begin from the position described in version A. The force of Quine's physicalism could then be that continued use of the scientific method and philosophical analysis will eventually transform the rich, familiar boat of version A into a refined, honed down racing model composed just of physical theory. There is support for this. He endorses Smart's remark that 'the physicist's language gives us a *truer* picture of the world than does the language of ordinary common sense' (TT, p. 92). So perhaps he proposes that, eventually, serious fact-stating discourse will only be permitted if formulated in the vocabulary of physical theory.

What I want to take from this discussion are two questions which bring us to the heart of what is involved in defending physicalism. The first concerns what we might call the institutional implications of the doctrine. Should the physicalist shut down all but Physics departments in universities; or are some non-physical sciences still respectable? If, as we surely must, we allow that chemists and biologists contribute to the growth of genuine scientific knowledge, then we have to explain how this can be so. If, as Quine would, we question the scientific credentials of some disciplines and some common sense, then we must explain how the line is to be drawn: how are scientific sheep to be sorted from discredited goats?

The second related question concerns the idioms we use in our everyday lives. Is it suggested that we must abandon all those which are not respectable from a physicalist standpoint? This would require a radical reconstruction of ordinary consciousness. And the suggestion that a philosophical defence of physicalism *could* have such far-reaching consequences seems absurd. So, the two questions force us to consider what it is like to be a physicalist: what is to happen to those forms of discourse (scientific and everyday) which do not employ the vocabulary of physical theory?

4.3 EXPRESSION AND DESCRIPTION

In *Word and Object*, Quine informs us that 'if we are limning the true and ultimate structure of reality' we should use an austere conceptual framework which does not refer to states like beliefs and desires (the propositional attitudes) but only 'the physical constitution and behavior of organisms' (WO, p. 221). But he qualifies this: 'Not that I would foreswear daily use of such intentional idioms, or maintain that they are practically dispensable' (ibid.). He does not assert that 'the idioms thus renounced are supposed to be unneeded in the market place or the laboratory'. Rather, he suggests that many of our 'assertions' should not be seen as attempts to describe the facts, to 'limn' the structure of reality. Once we appreciate that such discourse is 'non-cognitive' in this sense, it is untouched by any philosophical doctrines about what facts there are. The aim is not to ban all but one of Goodman's versions, but to claim that only the physical one is properly descriptive of reality.

Two kinds of stories can be told to support tolerating idioms which are not, in this sense, descriptive. First, we may ascribe to them an expressive function. Not all the things we say can be treated as equally *objective*. For example, when I describe something as having a pleasant taste, this does not reflect an objective trait of the external object; rather it expresses how I respond to it. Some philosophers hold that moral judgements express the attitudes of the judgers, and do not ascribe real properties to external objects or events. There may be idioms which, at first glance, look like attempts to describe the objective character of reality, but which really reflect the tastes, attitudes or interests of the person who makes the judgement.

We can easily find many philosophical views which account for a certain sort of judgement by giving it what I shall call an 'expressive function': it expresses an attitude or interest of the judger and does not simply describe the external world. A famous example would be Hume's theory of causation. Hume denies that causation involves a necessary connection between external objects or events: the aspects of our idiom which suggest that we think it does simply express the fact that our thoughts leap very easily from thought of the cause to thought of the effect. We 'project' or 'spread' a subjective attitude onto reality by speaking *as if* it reflected an objective feature of the world. In a number of recent publications, Simon Blackburn has advocated employing such projectivist theories to explain a variety of facets of our linguistic behaviour. He calls the strategy 'quasi-realist' for it undertakes to show that many utterances which look like ordinary assertions about reality need not be taken at face value (Blackburn, 1984).

Let me offer a Quinean illustration of this strategy: it concerns judgements of necessity. We make statements such as

Necessarily, all vixens are foxes

Necessarily, 2+2=4

A natural interpretation of this is that there is a fundamental classification of facts into those that are necessary, and those, like the fact that it is now raining, which are contingent. If that were so, we should need to use an expression like 'necessarily' in order to describe the true structure of reality. Quine famously denies that this is required (see chapter 7). However, it is evident that he does not wish to prevent us using this adverb in the laboratory, study or market place.

In a recent paper, Edward Craig discusses a view of necessity which he calls 'minimal non-cognitivism' (Craig, 1985). Someone who accepts that necessarily all vixens are foxes does not disagree about the *facts* with someone who, admitting that all vixens are foxes, is reluctant to acknowledge that this is *necessary*. The latter holds back from 'the policy of treating the unimaginable as necessarily false': what the former does when he deems this statement necessary 'is not recognitional; it is more like the projection on to the world of a fact about himself' (pp. 93–4). What this policy would involve may not be wholly clear. It cannot be all that remote from Quinean suggestions that use of the adverb signals the decision to hold the statement true whatever experience should come along, that it signals that the statement's role in our corpus of opinions means that we cannot conceive of what could show it false, or that the statement is grounded in the deeper reaches of our body of theory. However this thought is developed, it entails that the idiom may indeed be practically indispensible while not being required if our sole concern is with the perspicuous description of the facts.

This projectivist move is not the only way of continuing to employ a form of discourse while sceptical that it reflects the structure of reality. We can treat it simply as a useful technique, something that helps us to carry out our practical activities, although it is not part of descriptive science. Its value is instrumental. Some philosophers have regarded only the common-sense world as properly real, and valued physical theories as useful instruments valuable for the predictions they yield about familiar things. By contrast, Quine is ready to regard the world revealed by physics as real and to attach instrumental value to those useful features of our familiar scheme which are not vindicated by physics. Just as engineers prefer to employ a simple although refuted physical theory which is accurate enough for building bridges and machines, so we are happy to explain behaviour using our familiar 'folk psychology' of beliefs and desires, even if we are aware that this does not yield a scientifically perspicuous account of the mind.

Such an attitude towards our everyday psychological concepts is not uncommon. It is defended by D. C. Dennett, S. Stich, and possibly by Davidson. A very sophisticated version is found in the writings of Wilfrid Sellars (1963, ch. 1). Sellars contrasts two images of mind and the world: the scientific image which is physicalist – we are just matter in motion; and the manifest image – the framework of persons, beliefs and intentions which has no ready home in the scientific image. The manifest image is the one in which we first become aware of ourselves as persons, and begin to reason about our beliefs and projects. Sellars would agree with Quine that the scientific image is ontologically prior – it captures the ultimate structure of reality. The manifest image does not purport to describe reality, but reflects the framework of normative standards that are employed in controlling our actions and investigations. But in one respect he appears to go further than Quine: where the latter stresses that this framework may be very *useful*, Sellars wants to insist that without it we cannot become conscious of ourselves as persons, agents, reasoners or inquirers. The activities which yield the ontologically fundamental scientific image crucially depend upon the manifest image.

So a physicalist such as Quine is not committed to discarding vast stretches of ordinary talk. Of course, to make use of one of these strategies, we need some way of deciding which speech acts have descriptive intent, and which are expressive or instrumental. And that raises once again the question of how Quine establishes that physics has this fundamental role.

4.4 TRUTH AND METHOD

It is tempting to account for the virtues of physics, or of whatever sciences are included in the canonical list, by claiming that they alone yield truths. It is only in these sciences that propositions are accepted because they are *true*: expressive discourse lacks this kind of link with truth.

This is not Quine's strategy. In order to carry it out, we should need some sort of substantive characterization of what it is for a claim to be true and then demonstrate that scientific results fit this characterization. We should risk circularity if we took our account of truth from the sciences, so the strategy will only work if there is a philosophical discipline, independent of and more fundamental than science, whose task is to provide such a substantive characterization of what it is for a claim to be true. It is a consequence of Quine's naturalism that there can be no such discipline.

Indeed, Quine's remarks about truth indicate that he thinks this strategy deeply misconceived. In *The Web of Belief*, he insists that 'Truth is a property of sentences; it is a trait shared equally by all that would be rightly affirmed' (p. 13). This suggests that we are to explain truth in terms of the property of being rightly affirmed, rather than – as the proposal under discussion would require – vice versa. The suggestion is confirmed by *Word and Object* and *Philosophy of Logic*, where Quine insists that 'true' is simply a predicate of 'disquotation': 'To say that the statement "Brutus killed Caesar" is true, or that "The atomic weight of sodium is 23" is true, is in effect simply to say that Brutus killed Caesar or that the atomic weight of sodium is 23' (WO, p. 24). In that case, the property of truth cannot be used to mark fundamental philosophical distinctions: it simply follows our practice concerning what is assertible or 'rightly affirmed'. It cannot be exploited to justify it. Indeed, someone who denies the objectivity of (say) values could happily admit that 'Cruelty is wrong' is *true*: since to say *that* is just to say that cruelty is wrong, it is just as expressive or subjective as the latter claim – for further discussion, see section 12.2.

Quine does consider a proposal which he attributes to Peirce, which is to 'define truth outright in terms of scientific method, as the ideal theory which is approached as a limit when the (supposed) canons of scientific method are used unceasingly on continuing experience' (WO, p. 23). However, he despairs of such methodological definitions of truth on several grounds: he is sceptical of the assumption of a 'final organon of scientific method'; and he sees little reason to think that there would be a unique such 'ideal theory'. Moreover, it is worth stressing that Peirce is only able to defend such a view (insofar as the attribution is correct) by rejecting naturalism, and studying this ideal method within a purified first philosophy.

If not via an account of truth, or through some idealized model of scientific method, how are we to decide which disciplines are truly scientific or truly descriptive? Granted Quine's constant insistence that we start inquiry in the middle of things, equipped with a body of beliefs and prejudices, concerned to rebuild our boat at sea, perhaps we rely upon a list of those disciplines which, we would all agree, are sciences: physics, chemistry, biology and so on. Then we identify the scientific method by observing the methods those disciplines employ. Since there is much consensus about which disciplines are scientific, this seems a sensible Quinean starting point.

However, it is natural to object that this consensus is limited. Although no one doubts that physics and chemistry are sciences, the status of psycho-analysis, psychology and history is controversial. Moreover, since, as we saw, Quine operates with a restricted list of respectable scientific disciplines, he must have some basis for discriminating among those subjects which are popularly described as sciences. Fortunately, this is not a devastating objection. The debates turn upon identifying and evaluating the respects in which the more controversial disciplines differ from what is uncontroversially scientific. Hence, we can begin from our untutored sense of what is scientific, refining our list as we compare the controversial cases with the straightforward ones.

4.5 PHYSICALISM

Quine, then, defends physicalism, a modern version of the traditional materialist creed that all that there is is matter in motion. The doctrine is attractive in its rejection of the claim that there are minds or spirits which are not located in space, and its insistence that mental phenomena are somehow grounded in occurrences in the brain. In this section I wish to become clear about just what this doctrine involves, and about the arguments that Quine offers in its defence. Subsequently, we shall explore its wider philosophical implications. For the present, I aim to cut a broad swathe through these issues, leaving several difficult issues of interpretation and evaluation to emerge when we return to Quine's physicalism in Parts III and IV.

A natural way of formulating physicalism is as a reductionist doctrine. Consider a chemical law:

All C are D.

In the course of reducing chemistry to physics, we might look for a predicate 'P' cast in the language of physics which characterizes exactly the same events as the chemical predicate 'C', and another, 'Q', which corresponds in the same way to 'D'. We should then show that it is a truth of physics that

All P are Q.

This offers a physical explanation of the chemical law. Since 'P' and 'Q' are likely to be more complex than the chemical predicates that correspond to them, we can appreciate the value of staying with the chemical vocabulary. But, in principle, the laws of chemistry could be explained, or formulated, in physical terms.

A physicalist would then hold that any significant factual discourse could in this way be reduced to physics. Searching for such reductions would be an important focus for research; and finding them would offer empirical support for the physicalist claim that all the facts are physical ones. Short of reducing all of science in this way, a physicalist can point to such supposed triumphs as the reduction of natural selection to Mendelian genetics, and the reduction of genetics to molecular biology.

Like Davidson and many other modern physicalists, Quine denies reductionism. It is doubtful whether even biology or chemistry is reducible to physics, but in the following passage, Quine is specifically concerned with the implications of physicalism for our concept of mind.

> It is not a reductionist doctrine of the sort sometimes imagined. It is not a utopian dream of our being able to specify all mental events in physiological or microbiological terms. It is not a claim that such correlations even exist, in general, to be discovered; the groupings of events in mentalistic terms need not stand in any systematic relation to biological groupings. What it does say about the life of the mind is that there is no mental difference without a physical difference. Most of us nowadays are so ready to agree to this principle that we fail to sense its magnitude. It is a way of saying that the fundamental objects are the physical objects. It accords physics its rightful place as the basic natural science without venturing any dubious hopes of reduction of other disciplines.
>
> (FM, p. 163)

Physics is, in some sense, the basic natural science: it describes the fundamental particles which make up the world together with the laws that govern their behaviour. What we have to understand is how Quine proposes to make precise sense of this.

In his paper 'The material mind' Davidson invites us to imagine that we have constructed *l'homme machine*, 'in the shape of a man and out of the very stuff of a man'. We are reasonably sure we have built him right because we have replicated all that we can learn about the physical structure of human brains and bodies, and because 'He' ('Art') behaves like a man in all observable ways (1980, pp. 245ff). Unless told of Art's origin, no one could distinguish him from a 'real' man on the basis of his physical make-up, behaviour, utterances, expressions and so forth. Even if, as Davidson argues, we can expect to find no systematic theoretical links between psychological and physical properties, we can find plausible the claim that mental phenomena depend upon the physical: two individuals cannot differ mentally unless they differ physically. Once the physical properties of Art are fixed, there is no further question whether he really has mental states: the physical facts fix or determine all the others.

We can see why this captures a sense in which physics is the fundamental natural science. It suggests the thesis that Fodor has christened the 'generality of physics': 'roughly, the view that all events which fall under the laws of any science are physical events and hence fall under the laws of physics' (1975, p. 10). However, it forces us to face two questions. First, of course, why should we take this doctrine to be true? And second, why should it be taken to support the view that the physical facts are all the facts, that claims from psychology or biology are 'metaphor'? We shall begin by considering Quine's arguments for his 'determinationist' doctrine.

Sometimes he insists that the first objects we become aware of as we grow up are familiar physical objects such as human bodies, tables and chairs. The rest of our conceptual equipment is developed as a means to make sense of, and systematize, these primary objects: unless a body of belief helps us to make sense of changes to these physical things, we have no reason to think it true. But there is a deeper and more important argument than this which emerges in 'Facts of the matter' and elsewhere.

This rests upon the claim that a major aim of physics is 'to find a minimum catalogue of states – elementary states, let us call them – such that there is no change without a change in respect of them'.

> If the physicist suspected there was any event that did not consist in a redistribution of the elementary states allowed for by his physical theory, he would seek a way of supplementing his theory. Full coverage in this sense is the very business of physics, and only of physics.
>
> (TT, p. 98)

While the determinationist claim may not be true about physics as we have it now, we should not be satisfied that we have an ideally adequate physical theory unless it made the determinationist claim true. Were it not that the term is anathema to Quine, we could say that it is analytic of 'physics' that the determinationist claim is true: if physics is possible, then physicalism is true.

A fanciful example will illustrate this point, as well as indicating the sort of philosophical use to which Quine's physicalism can be put: it will also alert us to a problem in the use of this doctrine. Imagine a dispute arising within a chemistry laboratory about how current theory should be revised in order to accommodate some anomaly. The dispute is fierce, and the disputants stress the elegance of their respective theories and their usefulness, each claiming that his own theory is probably true. Suppose that reflection upon the structure of these theories and the conditions of their application should show that – according to our current best physical theories – it makes no *physical* difference which of these theories is correctly adopted.

Consider two responses to this discovery. First, we can conclude that it is not a factual matter which of the two chemical theories is correctly asserted, although a multitude of pragmatic considerations, reflecting the purposes for which we pursue chemical investigations, can lead us to prefer one to the other, or to dispute about which to adopt. The principle of physicalism enables us to identify the question as a pragmatic, as opposed to a factual, one.

In that case, physics provides a standpoint from which something analogous to Carnap's distinction of internal and external questions can be drawn. It enables us to see how concerns other than a disinterested pursuit of the fundamental laws of the universe influence the development of nonbasic science. We might even expect the disputants tolerantly to agree that there might be some value in pursuing each of the strategies so that their respective pragmatic merits can be assessed. As we shall see below, this kind of move – the use of physics as a standard for distinguishing objective from subjective or expressive – recurs in Quine's philosophy. Where earlier empiricists might claim that two theories are equivalent if they make the same empirical predictions, Quine will insist that they are equivalent when it makes no physical difference which is true.

But another response is available to our disputants. If they are sufficiently convinced that their dispute is a factual one, they may – in principle – claim that all that is revealed is the poverty of our current best physics. Finding the physical differences that underlie this chemical difference, they may urge, should become a prime focus of physical research, even if it involves radical revision of physical theory. Since what makes a theory physical, on Quine's account, is largely the fact that it has this fundamental role, there are, so far, very few constraints upon what a physical theory can look like. Hence, this move seems to be available.

Since we cannot rule out the possibility that our conception of the physical world will alter radically as science develops, we might suppose that we can say nothing very helpful about what makes a property a physical one. Suppose that someone defended a Cartesian theory of mind, claiming that there were ultimate fundamental mental substances and events which interact in various ways with a 'physical' realm by which they were not determined: these events are thoughts and sensations which are revealed in the private experience of each person.

There is a danger that Quinean physicalism could then be trivialized by the claim that since these occurrences are fundamental, all that the Cartesian does is to posit a new, unusual kind of physical occurrence: the Cartesian does not challenge physicalism, but only our narrow conception of the physical.

How are we to resist this trivialization of the doctrine without imposing an arbitrary conception of what counts as a physical property? We might identify the physical by using an argument alluded to earlier. At an early stage, our ontology was of ordinary physical objects – human bodies, rocks, items of furniture and the like. These are our first paradigms of the physical. Our body of knowledge then grows as we seek explanations of the behaviour of these bodies; and our conception of the physical develops as we discover what kinds of laws and entities we have to appeal to in order to do so. And, of course, we then seek further explanations of the behaviour of the physical objects discovered at this first stage. Then, a property is physical if it has a fundamental role in the explanatory practice which grows out of our initial concern to master the behaviour of spatio-temporal physical things. This leaves it open what the physical world is actually like while keeping that world anchored through those spatially extended objects which were our first paradigms of the physical. Hence, the Cartesian picture is excluded insofar as it grows out of the insistence that the most primitive items of our experience are not 'physical objects' but thoughts and sensations of which only we are directly aware.

4.6 REDUCTION AND REALITY

How defensible are the claims Quine makes for physics? We might question whether vindicating the determinationist thesis really is a fundamental aim of physics. For the most part, physicists are not motivated by thoughts of a 'long run' when such a complete physics might be obtained. They are content to solve particular physical problems that have arisen within the tradition, or to expose errors in currently accepted theories. Quine could hardly deny this, and would presumably only claim that his was *one* of the controlling aims of the subject; we might wonder whether even that was true (for further discussion, see Healey 1978). There is also scope for debate about whether an 'ultimate' physics that vindicates the determinationist thesis is achievable at all. However, for purposes of this discussion, I am prepared to grant Quine his conception of physics: it is a plausible way of explaining the sense in which physics is the basic or foundational natural science.

In this section, I shall raise some issues concerning the philosophical consequences that Quine draws from this position. Granted his rejection of reductionism, how does the claim that physics occupies this determinationist role support the claim that the physical facts are all the facts there are? We have not yet discussed why reductionism has seemed implausible to many philosophers, so we now turn to that.

We shall begin with a simple illustration: a straightforward law from economics. Other things being equal, increasing the price of something will lead to a fall in demand. We can appeal to this law to explain a particular fall in demand; we can use it to make 'counterfactual' claims like

> If the price had not been raised last month, demand would not now have fallen.

The law relates events of increasing prices to patterns of events of purchasing goods. For the sake of argument, we shall accept that all of these occurrences have rather complex physical descriptions, and that none of these events fails to accord with the laws of physics. What is the force of denying that this law could be reduced to physics?

The law collects together a disparate set of occurrences which are all instances of raising prices: they are recognized as similar in some significant respect; and, indeed, the fact that the classification enables us to formulate a law of economics with wide application shows why the classification is significant. When we take into account the variety of economic and currency arrangements, the variety of ways in which prices can be raised in any of these, the physical variations between people, the variety of different transactions that can count as expressing demand for an item, it is clear that the events that are brought together under this law will differ physically in untold ways. We would expect the law to continue to hold in economic systems which, at present, we can hardly imagine (see Fodor 1975).

In that case, if we imagine a physical predicate that collects together all those events which we describe as raising prices, it will be highly disjunctive, of the form:

( ) is P1 or P2 or P3 or P4 or P5 or . . .

A physical 'law' which corresponded to the economic one would be very complex indeed. One ground for denying that the law could be reduced would simply be that we are incapable of understanding statements with that degree of complexity. But there are deeper grounds for concern than that.

First, one thing that the economic law conveyed was that these events formed a 'kind'; they were significantly alike. Without this, the law had no explanatory force. This is wholly lost in an immensely disjunctive physical law: physics can offer us no explanation at all of why *these* occurrences should be grouped together in a single law. We can justify this only by returning to our economic vocabulary and explaining that they are all instances of raising prices. Hence, the highly complex physical 'law' lacks the systematizing or explanatory advantages of the economic one, although it gestures towards the different physical mechanisms which ground the economic interactions.

Secondly, since our knowledge of possible economic arrangements is obviously limited, the disjunctive characterization of raising prices invoked above would inevitably be incomplete – we should have to leave it open so that new disjuncts could be added. Our grasp of the economic vocabulary enables us to recognize events as cases of raising prices which are very different from those we have so far encountered: it is a feature of the events forming a kind that we can identify new cases which differ from familiar ones. So a concept of raising prices developed for the economics of developed societies can often be applied unproblematically in studying barter economies. But a mere grasp of the complex physical descriptions of price raisings gives us no clue about which other physical descriptions should be added to the disjunction. Once again, economic theory finds a significant pattern which cannot be captured in physical terms.

By rejecting reductionism, Quine wishes to acknowledge all this without having to abandon his physicalism. As will emerge in later chapters, Quine's views about translation may lead both him and Davidson to find even deeper difficulties for reductionism about the mental. My present concern is with the philosophical significance of these points: I shall raise the question to which we shall return in later chapters.

Suppose that somebody accepted Quine's determinationist thesis, but attempted to deny that the physical facts are the only ultimate ones. In order to understand the ultimate structure of reality, they might argue, we need to know about more than the ultimate events there are, and the physical laws governing their behaviour. We also need to know how they are to be classified, the fundamental kinds into which they fall. In that case, there are structural features of reality which we shall not know until we have developed economic theory; there are classifications which reveal structure but which cannot be identified by physicists. Hence, Quine's physicalism does not entail that it is physics alone that describes ultimate structure. Physics describes the trees: the broader geographical properties of the wood are no less structural features of reality.

There seem to be two Quinean responses to this argument. One is that physicalism amounts to no more than the determinationist thesis, so that there is nothing in the view just described which a physicalist cannot acknowledge. This would defuse physicalism in a rather disappointing fashion. The alternative, and more likely, response is that the kinds discerned by economists do not represent part of 'ultimate structure', but reflect classifications determined by our practical interests and concerns. They are justified in an expressive or instrumentalist fashion. In a more complex way, it would parallel the classification of things as yellow. We employ this term because it groups things in a way that is easy to identify perceptually. Physical theory may teach that this is a superficial or subjective classification: it collects together things which exhibit very different dispositions to reflect light rays, e.g. from the red and green parts of the spectrum, or predominantly from the yellow part of the spectrum (Averill 1985). In that case, physics promises a kind of objectivity which is lacking in those disciplines which employ classifications that are relative to human interests, practical concerns, or epistemic limitations.

Much now depends upon the defensibility of these claims about objectivity. Our problem is that chemistry, biology and the rest seem to be autonomous: they are not reducible to physics, and the perspicuous generalizations they investigate do not correspond to physical laws in any straightforward manner. It is easy to see that, for many reasons, we should be more interested in these high-level generalizations than in the fundamental ones described by physical theories. The question we are carrying forward for later discussion concerns how far recognition of this can be reconciled with the claim that the 'versions' provided by these disciplines are 'metaphor'– more or less fruitful ways of thinking about a world whose real character is given by physics.

By way of summary, let us distinguish three physicalist theses. The first is the doctrine of the generality of physics. This is suggested by Quine's 'determinationist' doctrine, but it is far from obvious that it has the ontological implications which Quine often has in mind. Secondly, there is the claim that the physical facts are all the facts. Quine hints that this is a mere reformulation of the first thesis, but it is difficult to see why that is so. Finally, there is the claim that the only kind of explanation which is properly scientific is physical explanation, explanations from other sciences being of value only because they allude to (known or unknown) physical explanations. This thesis seems stronger still: we shall see below that it is operative in Quine's applications of his physicalism.

5

Logic: Canonical Notation and Extensionality

5.1 LOGIC: CALCULUS AND CATEGORIAL FRAMEWORK

The primary concern of logic is with validity, with classifying arguments into those that are good and those that are not. An argument is valid if the premisses cannot be true when the conclusion is false – the conclusion follows from the premisses. This aim is usually pursued by seeking a short list of general patterns of argument, each with the property that no argument fits it that has true premisses but a false conclusion. Hence, any argument obtained through consistently substituting sentences for 'P' and 'Q' in the schema below is valid:

P or Q

It is not the case that P

So Q

Quine usually says that logicians are concerned with a certain range of statements, the 'logical truths'. This does not conflict with the observation that the subject's principal concern is with the validity of arguments. Corresponding to the validity of the schema just given, there is a form of implication statement all of whose instances are logical truths:

If (P or Q and it is not the case that P) then Q.

This suggests that the chief goal of logic is to create a calculus or algorithm for deduction, something that will serve to 'dissolve verbal perplexities or facilitate deduction' (WO, p. 221). Just as arithmetic provides an instrument which improves our control over numbers, so logic helps us to reason efficiently. The contribution of logical calculi to the development of computing machinery illustrates this.

However, logic promises more than an efficient instrument for deduction. It can prompt us to ask why valid arguments are valid, and, by displaying the structures of sentences involved in arguments, can help us to understand why the conclusion must be true when the premisses are. This was alluded to in sections 1.3 and 2.2: remarks there suggest that the validity of certain simple arguments can be explained by reference to the truth functional character of expressions they contain. Moreover, it is plausible that understanding a sentence puts us in a position to evaluate arguments in which it occurs. In that case, the abstract logical structures discerned through logical analysis may help us to see what is involved in understanding the expressions of a natural language. Studying logical calculi can contribute to the construction of a theory of meaning for the sentences used to formulate arguments. For example, Russell's theory of definite descriptions may reveal the underlying semantic structure of sentences containing them.

Since Kant, some philosophers have looked for a different sort of insight from logic. A study of the logical forms of statements used in scientific or descriptive discourse reveals to us some of the broadest structural features of reality. Kant claimed, for example, that the presence of subject–predicate statements and conditional statements in our language shows that we must think of the world as composed of substances standing in causal relations. An account of these pervasive abstract features of reality is a theory of categories. In similar vein, Frege drew a fundamental contrast between objects and concepts from the logical or grammatical distinction between name and predicate; and Peirce found philosophical insight in the observation that an adequate language would contain 'unsaturated expressions' (predicates) of different valencies – monadic predicates such as '— is red', dyadic ones such as '— loves —' and triadic ones such as '— gives — to —'. The underlying thought is that if we know what sorts of logical structures must be used to describe reality, we know something about the abstract structure of reality. In similar fashion, the broadest features of a conception of reality are determined by a logical or linguistic framework in the writings of Carnap, as we have seen. (See Hookway 1985, ch. 3 for a much lengthier discussion of these topics.)

Particularly in *Word and Object*, Quine adopts a similar project. The logician seeks to construct a notation which, using as few resources as possible, would be adequate for expressing the contents of all scientific theories:

> Each reduction that we make in the variety of constituent constructions needed in building the sentences of science is a simplification in the structure of the inclusive conceptual scheme of science . . . The same motives that impel scientists to seek ever simpler and clearer theories adequate to the subject matter of their special sciences are motives for the simplification and clarification of the broader framework shared by all the sciences. Here the objective is called philosophical, because of the breadth of the framework concerned; but the motivation is the same. The quest of a simplest clearest overall pattern of canonical notation is not to be distinguished from a quest of ultimate categories, a limning of the most general traits of reality.
>
> (WO, p. 161)

We gain philosophical insight into the broadest features of reality by inquiring into the kinds of logical complexity that will be found in a language adequate for all scientific theory: we seek a 'canonical notation for science', a notation that reflects the simplest kind of grammatical structure that will serve all *scientific* purposes.

The goal of seeking a system of categories can conflict with that of 'facilitating deduction'. If there are forms of inferential behaviour which are 'practically indispensable', but which are not required for displaying the structures of scientific theories, then we cannot ignore them in a general theory of inference although they would have no place in a canonical notation for science. Quine speaks of a bifurcation in the development of logical systems. Different systems of canonical notation are required for different purposes (WO, p. 221). In this chapter, our primary interest is with the second source of what I have called Quine's austere vision: the restricted character of the canonical notation which is supposed to be adequate for scientific purposes.

Before looking at what a canonical notation or system of formal logic involves, we should consider a further question about the role of logic in the Quinean canon of sciences. How do we distinguish *logical* implications – such as those mentioned above – from claims drawn from the special sciences: what distinguishes truths of logic from those of physics and the other special sciences?

Like other sciences, according to Quine, logic studies a body of truths, but these are truths of a particularly general and obvious kind which are deeply embedded in the vast structure of our knowledge.

When, in 'Five milestones of empiricism' and elsewhere, Quine contrasts his own moderate holism with the more extreme doctrine that is sometimes ascribed to him, he qualifies his insistence that the 'unit of significance' is generally some 'modest chunk' of science by saying: 'All sciences interlock to some extent; they share a common logic and generally some common part of mathematics, even when nothing else' (TT, p. 71). Logic studies the implications which serve as the bonds holding the ship together: the truths it studies turn up in the study of *all* subject matters.

If we consider a simple example of a logical truth, we shall see the force of Quine's position:

> If the liquid in the flask is either acid or alkaline but is not acid, then it is alkaline.

We have seen that Quine believes that, in principle, in the interests of overall simplicity in our conceptual scheme, we might decide that this sentence was not after all true, even if we cannot now imagine any circumstances that could drive us to this. The fact that analogous truths arise in connection with any subject matter indicates that it is very unlikely that we would ever be driven to this: it is rational to keep revisions in our body of knowledge to a minimum, and abandoning such a claim would have consequences that we can hardly begin to envisage. Hence, in *Methods of Logic*, we read:

> Our system of statements has such a thick cushion of indeterminacy, in relation to experience, that vast domains of law can easily be held immune to revision on principle. We can always turn to other quarters of the system when revisions are called for by unexpected experiences. Mathematics and logic, central as they are to our conceptual scheme, tend to be accorded such immunity, in view of our conservative preference for revisions which disturb the system least; and herein, perhaps, lies the 'necessity' which the laws of mathematics and logic are felt to enjoy.
>
> (ML, p. xiii)

In consequence of this, Quine concedes that logical truths are 'true simply by virtue of our conceptual scheme':

> For, it is certainly by virtue of that scheme that those laws are central to it; and it is by virtue of being thus central that the laws are preserved

from revision at the expense of statements less strategically situated.
(ML, p. xiv)

Let us return to our example of a logical truth. The statement is true whatever general terms we substitute for 'liquid in the flask', 'acid' and 'alkaline', so long as we make the substitutions uniformly throughout the sentence. Indeed, we may uniformly substitute any sentences we like for 'the liquid in the flask is acid' and 'the liquid in the flask is alkaline', and the result will be a true sentence. The sentence is true simply in virtue of its grammatical form – any sentence with the same form will also be true. Only 'logical words' like 'if', 'or', 'and' and 'not' occur 'essentially': we can make substitutions for any nonlogical words without risking that the resulting sentence will be false. (I shall ignore the massive but interesting question of just how to identify 'logical words' or features of 'grammatical form', but see WP, p. 110, and PoL *passim* for Quine's discussions of these issues.)

As Quine notes in *Philosophy of Logic*, this dependence of logical truth upon grammatical form rather than any specific 'lexicon' of terms or predicates explains several of its features. It is applicable to all sciences because it relies upon no special lexicon, but just the general logical vocabulary that is used universally. Its results are obvious – 'everyone will unhesitatingly assent to them if asked' – because they are acquired with the grammatical habits upon which all of our linguistic behaviour depends. And, finally, we find it useful to express them as general metalinguistic principles or schemata. Thus, we might articulate the logical law that

Any statement of the form 'If ((P or Q) and not P) then Q' is true.

Formal logic seeks a body of such schemata that capture all the logical truths (PoL, pp. 101–2, and *passim*). Instances of any of these schemata may turn up in any area of discourse.

So Quine's holism does not prevent him from seeing how logic differs from other sciences: it is more secure than other disciplines, it has a kind of obviousness which they can lack, and it has no special subject matter. A question that remains open concerns the claim that logical principles are *necessary* truths: while we may be able to conceive of possible states of affairs which contravene the laws of physics or psychology, the laws of logic appear to be operative in all possible states of affairs. Quine appears to want to trace our sense of this necessity to an awareness that logical principles are so deeply embedded in our framework of beliefs that it is unlikely that any evidence could force us to undertake the enormous revisions that would be required if we were to abandon one of them. We saw above, in the quotation from *Methods of Logic*, that our use of the adverb 'necessarily' here may signal our decision to hold these principles immune from falsification in the light of new evidence.

5.2 THE CANONICAL NOTATION FOR SCIENCE

We shall now examine some of the idioms permitted by the canonical notation that Quine favours. We have encountered some of them already. The simplest 'atomic' sentences might contain predicate expressions and singular terms having the forms:

Fa, Gb, Rab etc.

Lower-case letters here represent singular terms, and upper case letters stand for predicates or general terms with different numbers of places, different valencies. Thus '— is red' is a one-place predicate; '— admires —' is a two-place predicate; '— gives — to —' has three places; and so on. One special 'logical' two-place predicate has already been mentioned, and will be familiar from elementary arithmetic. This is the identity or sameness relation, and is expressed '='. The claim that Cicero is the same as Tully (alternatively, that Cicero is Tully, or Cicero is identical to Tully) is of the form:

c=t.

Next, there are some simple means for constructing complex sentences out of simple ones. These are the truth functional connectives, such as 'and', 'or' and 'if — then —'. With their aid, we form complex sentences like

It is not the case that Carnap wrote *Word and Object*

Carnap wrote *Word and Object* or Carnap wrote *The Logical Syntax of Language*

If Carnap wrote *Word and Object*, then Carnap is identical to Quine

Carnap wrote *The Logical Syntax of Language* and Quine wrote *Word and Object*

It should be obvious how these relate to more idiomatic, less clumsy English sentences. Their forms are expressed in the canonical notation

$$\sim Wc$$

$$Wc \vee Lc$$

$$Wc \rightarrow c=q$$

$$Lc \;\&\; Wq$$

It is easy to see how – using brackets to avoid ambiguities – we can construct sentences with complex forms like

$$\sim Wc \rightarrow (Wq \rightarrow \sim c=q))$$

If Carnap didn't write *Word and Object*, then, if Quine wrote *Word and Object*, Carnap is not the same person as Quine

And so on. (Note that there is controversy over the claim that ordinary English conditionals are truth functional. I shall mention some conditionals that are not truth functional in the following chapter. I lack the space to discuss these controversies.)

Let me now discuss a standard way of explaining the meanings of expressions in such a formal language. The explanation proceeds relative to a domain or universe of discourse – the class of objects that forms the subject matter of the discourse in question. We interpret each of the names by indicating which member of the universe of discourse it names. For each one-place predicate, we identify its 'extension'– the class of members of the universe of which it is true. Then, for a sentence of the form

$$Fa$$

we can explain its truth conditions by saying that it is true if, and only if, the object assigned to 'a' belongs to the extension of 'F'. The extension of a two-place predicate is a class of pairs of objects from the universe of discourse. Thus, to the predicate '— admires —' is assigned the class of pairs of objects such that the first admires the second. Then, a sentence of the form

Rab

is true when the pair of objects made up of the object assigned to 'a' and the object assigned to 'b' belongs to the extension of the relational expression 'R'. A sentence of the form

a=b

is true if, and only if, the same object is assigned to 'a' and to 'b'.

This may seem fairly trivial, and does not look a part of a valuable explanatory theory of the workings of language. For the present, its interest lies in providing a systematic description of how the truth conditions of complex sentences depend upon certain semantic properties of their parts. For example, what is involved in saying that the connectives discussed above are 'truth functional' is that the truth value of a sentence formed by their use is determined by the truth values of the sentences from which they are formed. A sentence of the form

~A

is true when 'A' is false, false when 'A' is true: that is all there is to the semantic functioning of '~'. A sentence of the form

A & B

is true when 'A' and 'B' are both true; otherwise it is false. And so on for the other connectives.

I shall introduce just enough of this semantic apparatus to enable the reader to understand simple formal representations used in subsequent discussions, and to enable me to explain what Quine has to say about quantification. So far, we lack the means to represent sentences of the forms:

Something is F

There is an F

Everything is F

If we had names for all the objects in the universe of discourse, we might be able to understand the first two of these as very long disjunctions, and the third as a very long conjunction:

Fa v Fb v Fc v Fd v . . .

Fa & Fb & Fc & Fd & . . .

But this is not very satisfactory. First, there is no reason to suppose that every object will have a name. Second, if, as may be the case, the universe of discourse contains infinitely many objects, then we should have to use infinitely long formulae to express these claims. Third, as Ramsey pointed out when Wittgenstein defended a similar view in *Tractatus Logico-Philosophicus*, a very long (even infinite) conjunction does not fully capture the meaning of 'Everything is F'. For the conjunction does not guarantee that there is a conjunct corresponding to *every* object. We should require a rider to the effect that everything has been taken into account, and that requires a sentence of just the sort we have been trying to analyse.

Hence, the canonical notation will contain additional idioms to express 'existential quantification' – 'there is' or 'some' – and to express 'universal quantification – 'all' or 'every'. A clue to how this is done may be be provided by the clumsy English forms:

Something is such that *it* is F

Everything is such that *it* is F

We introduce pronouns or variables, and by putting them in the place of names in atomic sentences we provide 'open' sentences which cannot be used to say anything until we have determined what the pronouns are to stand for.

Fx: it is F

Rax: a stands in relation R to it

We then introduce quantifiers' 'something is such that' or 'everything is such that': (Ex) and (x) respectively.

(Ex) Fx: something is (such that it is) F

(x) Rax: everything is such that a stands in the relation R to it

For present purposes, we can restrict our attention to simple sentences containing just one quantifier. For an open sentence like 'Fx', we can consider all the different interpretations that result from assigning to the pronoun or variable the different objects in the universe of discourse: the open sentence may turn out to be true on some of these assignments, false on others. Each assignment attaches a different 'value' to the pronoun or variable. Then, we can say that the existential quantification of this open sentence is true if the open sentence is true on at least one of these assignments; its universal quantification is true if it is true on all of them.

As I said above, it would be a mistake to attach too much philosophical importance to these semantic explanations. Their value lies in providing a description of the truth conditions of different sentences which can be used to explain which arguments are valid. For example, the argument

Fa, so (Ex)Fx

is valid. This can be seen because the premiss will only be true if the name stands for an object from the universe of discourse which belongs to the extension of 'F'. When we consider the interpretations of the open sentence 'Fx' that result from assigning all possible different values to the variable, there will be at least one according to which the open sentence is true. This is because the object for which 'a' stands is in the universe of discourse, and is thus one of the values of the variable; and it is in the extension of 'F'. In a similar fashion, we can exploit the descriptions we have given to explain the validity of much more complex arguments than this one.

Another value of the systematization is that it enables us to state Quine's criterion of ontological commitment more rigorously. A theory is committed to the existence of entities of a certain kind if, and only if, 'some of them must be counted among the values of the variables in order that the statements affirmed in the theory be true' (FLPV, p. 103). Notice that the formulation retains the 'must' which, we saw earlier, has raised the suspicion that it is incompatible with Quine's views of modality.

Such notations enable us to formulate simple rules which classify arguments into valid and invalid. I shall not describe any such systems of rules here; they can be found in any logic textbook. In two respects, the notation we have described here is more complex than Quine would wish: a simpler language will suffice for scientific purposes. First, as we saw in chapter 1, Quine thinks that we can get by without singular terms or names and that our logic is simplified if we do so: we replace them by special predicates and employ Russell's theory of descriptions. Secondly, if we wish to, we can economize on connectives and quantifiers. For example, if we eliminate '&' from the notation, its expressive capacities are not diminished. A claim of the form P & Q is equivalent to one of the form ~(~P v ~Q): 'The weather is neither not hot nor not sunny' is simply a more long-winded way of saying 'The weather is hot and sunny'. And, for example, we can eliminate the existential quantifier and express 'There is a horse in the field' using the more long-winded 'It is not the case that everything in the field is not a horse'. While the search for the simplest system of canonical notation may call for such economies, I shall conform to customary practice; we note that they are possible, but, in the interests of readable formulae on the page, stick to the richer system of notation.

5.3 EXTENSIONALITY

As is evident from the previous section, the validity of arguments turns upon the structural features of sentences. Atomic sentences are formed from names and predicates; other sentences are built up with the aid of truth functional connectives, quantifiers and variables. Formal validity never depends upon particular choice of names or predicates, but upon the grammatical structures in which they appear. Moreover, the validity of arguments was explained by an account of how the truth values of sentences depended upon the semantic properties of their parts. The semantic significance of the structural features alluded to is crucial because it consists in the ways in which they establish such dependencies.

The sketch for a semantic account of the Quinean canonical notation for science was very simple. All we took account of was the extensions of predicates and relations: once these are fixed, the truth value of every sentence cast in the language is fixed. 'Taking the canonical notation thus austerely,' Quine writes, 'we have just these basic constructions: predication, universal quantification, and the truth functions' (WO, p. 228). The truth values of atomic sentences depended upon no more than this; quantification was explained in terms that took account of no other semantic properties; and when complex sentences are constructed from simpler ones with the aid of connectives, we need to know only the truth values of the parts to establish the truth value of the complex. Thus, no semantic properties of predicates or names other than their extensions is relevant to establishing the validity of arguments cast in Quine's canonical notation.

It follows from this that the Quinean language of science has the following properties:

(1) Whenever a complete sentence occurs as part of a complex one, the truth value of the whole is unchanged when we replace this sentence by another with the same truth value.
(2) Whenever a predicate or relational expression occurs in a sentence, we can replace it by another with the same extension and the truth value of the whole will not be affected.

We might consider a third condition too:

(3) Whenever a name occurs in a sentence, we can replace it by another with the same denotation and the truth value of the whole will not be affected.

However, if we follow Quine in replacing names by special predicates like 'pegasizes', this is already accounted for by condition 2. The denotation of the name is replaced by the single-membered extension of the corresponding predicate. Thus, the members of the pairs of sentences below have the same truth values.

1a Cicero was an orator
1b Tully was an orator

2a Cicero was a creature with a heart
2b Cicero was a creature with a kidney

A sentence with these properties is called 'extensional', and an extensional logic is one that deals only with inferences involving extensional sentences. Hence, Quine's canonical notation for science is extensional: this is the second element of the austerity of his conception of reality. If an extensional language is adequate for formulating scientific theories, this reveals a general and philosophically important point about the nature of reality.

How much of a restriction is this? Many of the most pervasive idioms of ordinary discourse (especially talk about the mind) are non-extensional (are intensional). Hence, by favouring an extensional canonical notation, Quine excludes much familiar ordinary talk from it. Just as Quine's physicalism may be used as a critical tool for purging certain forms of discourse from serious science, so his favouring an extensional language provides another critical technique. Once it is shown that a region of discourse is not extensional, then, according to Quine, we have reason to doubt its claims to describe the structure of reality. In the following chapter, we take up these issues. First, we shall examine the variety of intensional claims that we normally make; secondly, we shall begin to ask how this thesis of 'extensionality' is to be defended; and we raise the crucial question of whether an extensional language is adequate even for physics.

5.4 FORMAL LOGIC, CANONICAL NOTATION AND ORDINARY ENGLISH

As we have already seen, logicians construct artificial systems of 'canonical notation' in which they represent statements and arguments, and which they use to provide a systematic account of which argument forms are valid. What is Quine's view of the relation between these representations and the familiar sentences we use to present arguments and state theories? One possible answer is that the formal representations reveal the logical or semantical structures which are present in familiar English sentences: this enables us to apply the logical notation to the evaluation of arguments cast in ordinary English. Alternatively, Quine might be constructing an artificial language structure which he proposes that we should adopt in place of English for serious scientific work. In fact, neither of these answers captures Quine's position. We must look more closely at his claims for his canonical notation.

While we could attempt to formulate all of the logical truths by attending closely to the grammatical structure of English or some other natural language, 'simplification of theory' counsels us to keep our list of logical words or grammatical constructions to a minimum by employing 'sweeping artificialities of notation'. Hence, it is clear enough that Quine is not attempting to describe the logical structure of our everyday sentences. Since, as we have seen, the logician joins in the scientific attempt to improve our overall body of theory of the world, it is easy to conclude that he is a reformer. In that case, Quine would belong with those philosophers who propose that we replace our imperfect natural language by an artificial, constructed framework which lacks its failings. However, it counts against this that Quine insists that our formal notations must be explained by relating them to locutions from familiar English: English is not being repudiated.

We interpret the logician's formalisms by translating them into the stilted forms often known as 'logician's English'. This is a clumsy fragment of the language which, as we have seen, uses awkward forms like 'it is not the case that' in place of our more common idioms of negation. In addition it uses special predicates in place of names and, perhaps, even economizes on connectives and quantifiers as Quine's formal notation does. If Quine proposed that we actually adopted his canonical notation, then we should speak in this artificial, stilted portion of English. But he does not propose that:

> It is the part of strategy to keep theory simple where we can, and then, when we want to apply the theory to particular sentences of ordinary language, to transform those sentences into a 'canonical form' adapted to the theory.
>
> (WO, p. 158)

> By developing our logical theory strictly for sentences in a convenient canonical form we achieve the best division of labour: on the one hand there is theoretical deduction and on the other hand there is the work of paraphrasing ordinary language into the theory.
>
> (WO, p. 159)

So, we continue to speak in ordinary English. When we wish to apply our logical notations to the evaluation of arguments or the clarification of hypotheses, we first paraphrase them into this stilted, clumsy form. Quine's claim is that any serious scientific assertion can receive such a paraphrase. He does not think we can construct any straightforward rules to take us from English to these canonical forms. Nor does he think that the paraphrase provides a synonym of the original. It is enough that we can agree on which paraphrases are appropriate, or that the speaker is prepared to accept a sentence in the canonical form as an adequate replacement for his assertion.

The picture that emerges, then, is as follows. Logicians study validity, for the most part, by constructing artificial notations. These lend themselves to rigorous mathematical treatment, and help us in the activity of conceptual simplification: we can reduce basic laws and fundamental constructions to a minimum. Of course we have to explain the meanings of these notations, and this is done by showing how to interpret them in stilted 'logician's English': we associate them with rather long-winded, but structurally unambiguous and perspicuous sentences of a slightly butchered form of English. The link with ordinary English is informal. Usually, we will all agree which stilted expression captures the relevant content of a more idiomatic utterance. If there is uncertainty or controversy, we will normally allow the speaker's choice of an interpretation to fix 'what he meant'. And if uncertainties often arise, we may take this to reveal unclarity or incoherence in ordinary discourse. There may then be a case for making small revisions in ordinary scientific discourse in the direction of the regimented or stilted forms. The stress throughout is upon the value of logic for clarification and disambiguation, and for providing a framework in which our scientific claims *can* be expressed: there is no suggestion that the forms discerned by the logician are somehow latent beneath the surface of our familiar idioms, or that we should use the logican's notation as a more satisfactory replacement for ordinary English.

6

Intensionality

6.1 INTENSIONALITY: EXAMPLES

Quine claims that serious scientific theory can be expressed in an extensional language. Our first task is to see just how pervasive intensionality is in ordinary language: if we are properly to enjoy the renunciation that Quine urges upon us, it will be good to know what we have to give up. This section simply provides some examples of intensionality.

A natural language such as English involves lots of expressions that are used to construct complex sentences out of simpler ones, but which are not truth functional: the truth value of the whole *does* vary according to the simple sentence involved, even when the simpler sentences have the same truth values.

It ought to be the case that there is no suffering

results from prefixing 'It ought to be the case that . . .' to the sentence 'There is no suffering.' If the complete sentence is true, and 'There is no suffering' is false, then we should expect that we would obtain another true sentence if we replaced 'There is no suffering' with any other false sentence. Hence it would be true that

It ought to be the case that everyone is in pain.

Since this is plainly false, 'It ought to be the case that . . .' is not truth functional. So, such sentences could not be accommodated within Quine's notation.

Other examples are easily found. 'It is 1973' and 'It is 2073' are both false. 'It was the case that it is 1973' is true; it does not follow that it was the case that it is 2073. So familiar tense operators like 'It was the case that . . .', and 'It will be the case that. . .' are non-truth functional and would seem to have no place in Quine's austere notation.

'It rained all summer in England in 1985' and '2+2=4' are both true. But whereas it is necessarily true that 2+2=4, the claim about the weather is not necessarily true. Thus, the Quinean notation seems to have no place for statements of necessity. Nor, it seems, can it allow belief ascriptions. Given that John believes that 2+2=4, it does not follow that he believes that England has just had a bad summer. And so on: it seems easy to show that a natural language is full of idioms that would have no place in Quine's canonical notation for science.

One more example – a familiar kind of subjunctive conditional claim:

> *If* I had left five minutes earlier *then* I would not have missed the bus.

Or, in a more perspicuous 'logician's form':

> *If it had been the case that* I left five minutes earlier than I did, *then it would have been the case that* I did not miss the bus.

These conditionals are not truth functional. If I replace the antecedent with the equally false supposition that I left five minutes later than I did, the truth value is not unchanged. So once again, a very familiar kind of locution is missing from Quinean science. Moreover, unlike some of the other examples we have mentioned, such subjunctive or 'counterfactual' conditionals appear to be important for science.

Now for some examples of non-extensional occurrences of predicates. Suppose, as an example, that 'is red' and 'is the same colour as a London bus' have the same extensions. If our language is fully extensional there could not be two sentences which differed only in that one contained 'red' where the other contained 'is the same colour as a London bus', and which had different truth values, one being true and the other false. But it is easy to imagine such cases. If John does not know London, he may believe that his book is red while believing that his book is not the same colour as a London bus. Once again, we see that sentences built up using 'believes' are intensional. Parallel examples could be constructed for 'ought' and 'necessarily' and with tense operators.

Finally, to names – although, strictly, these have been eliminated from our canonical notation. A linguistic context for names or singular terms is *referentially transparent* if replacing a name within it by another name for the same object cannot affect the truth value of the whole sentence. Granted that 'Cicero' and 'Tully' refer to the same person, then, if a language contains only transparent contexts for singular terms, there could not be sentences with different truth values which differ only in that one contains 'Tully' where the other contains 'Cicero'. Insofar as Quine ever does admit names or singular terms to his notation, he insists that any contexts for names are transparent rather than *opaque*. But English evidently contains opaque contexts for singular terms. Consider the context

John wonders whether Cicero is —.

If the gap is filled by 'Tully', we obtain a sentence which could well be true if John is at an early stage in the study of Roman history. Filling it with 'Cicero' could not produce a true sentence.

Our way of accounting for the semantic properties of expressions cannot explain the validity of arguments containing intensional contexts as it can those involving only extensional language. A more complex and sophisticated semantic framework would be required if an intensional logic was to be developed. There is a large body of work by logicians concerned with developing tense logic, the logic of subjunctive idioms, doxastic logic (concerned with belief), deontic logics (concerned with 'ought' and obligations) and modal logics (concerned with necessity and possibility), which finds no place in the logical framework that Quine develops as a canonical notation for science. Quine is highly sceptical of these activities. Some of his grounds for scepticism will emerge as the discussion develops. He also holds that, if our concern is to develop a canonical notation for science, we have no need to attend to intensional logic. We now turn to some of his reasons for thinking this.

6.2 TIME AND TENSE

Quine can use a number of strategies for 'explaining' intensionality: our use of such idioms reflects an erroneous conception of reality; it reflects expressive or projective features of discourse; such idioms have an instrumental value. The absence of intensionality from the canonical notation shows only that it is not required for physics. In this section, we consider just one variety of intensionality – tensed language.

There are several reasons for doing this. One is that tense does not seem to be merely subjective; it is hard to see how serious science can ignore time. Thus, it is a good subject for a first case study to illustrate Quine's attitudes towards intensionality. The advantages of such a case study are more than just illustrative. Quine's extensionalism is not just a consequence of his physicalism: he does not simply notice that extensional language will do for physics and so decide he needs nothing more. Indeed, at first sight, one might suppose that physics requires a language with tense indicators and subjunctive conditionals. Rather, he has independent reasons for doubting whether he can make sense of intensionality: he is sceptical of whether the richer semantic framework it calls for can be worked out. By considering tense, we shall begin to see what some of these difficulties are supposed to be – although, it should be noted, he thinks that the difficulties are far more pressing in connection with other forms of intensionality. Finally, when we understand how extensional logic is supposed to account for time without running into these difficulties, we will uncover another fundamental Quinean doctrine – about the nature of objects.

Tense logic introduces the additional operators 'It was the case that . . .' (*P*) and 'It will be the case that . . .' (*F*). When these are combined with the other elements of a canonical notation, we can form schemata such as

P(Rab)

It was the case that Brutus killed Caesar

(Ex)*F*(Txa)

Someone will travel to London

~*F*(Ex)(Gx v Hx)

It is not the case that there will be something that is either G or H

This seems a fairly straightforward development of our standard logic: we have no difficulty in understanding what these sentences mean.

As well as introducing non-truth functionality and other forms of intensionality, tense introduces another complexity into standard logic. So far, we have assumed that any sentence is determinately true or false: once tense is introduced, then a sentence will be true at some times, false at others.

The Olympic Games were in Los Angeles

is now true, but in 1981 it was false. On the other hand, the false sentence

The Olympic Games will be in Los Angeles

was then true. If we adopt a tensed language, we can only ask what truth value a sentence has, relative to a context (a time). Similar context-relativity is introduced by expressions like 'here', 'now' (which is likely to be used in a tense logic), 'you', 'that', as well as many others. Quine's canonical notation appears to lack sentences whose truth values are relative to context: it contains no 'indexical' expressions.

So how does his logic handle time? Rather than relativizing truth value to time, Quine adds an extra argument place to predicate expressions. Thus, '— is red' is seen as an abbreviation of '— is red at —' where the second place is to be filled by a reference to a time. Since it is now June 1987, the past tense sentence

Brutus killed Caesar

can be paraphrased in a stilted, regimented form:

There is a time before June 1987 at which Brutus kills Caesar

or

(Et)(Before (t, June 1987) & Kills (Brutus, Caesar, t)).

The verb 'kills' has then to be understood as *untensed*. By introducing explicit reference to dates and times, by mentioning relations between them, and by quantifying over them, tense operators are eliminated. There is no longer the appearance of a non-truth functional operator; the language is extensional, because the extension of a term like 'red' becomes a set of pairs of objects and times; and the truth value of a sentence no longer varies from time to time.

What is there to recommend this manoeuvre? One advantage is that science can make use only of *eternal sentences* whose truth values do not change from time to time – in contrast to tensed sentences and those involving indexicals. This means that readers of scientific journals and research reports do not have to discover the context in which sentences were written in order to understand them or evaluate them. In *Philosophy of Logic*, Quine celebrates such ploys because they provide a reduction to 'standard logic, the neat and efficient logic of truth functions and quantifiers that we understand so well. When we paraphrase a theory into standard form we are, in effect, programming our standard logical computer to deal with the logical problems of the theory' (PoL, p. 77).

Another advantage is simplicity of logic. We avoid adding further fundamental constructions to our canonical notation, and so we are able to make do with a more economical logical apparatus. Moreover, we are spared the complexities that would be involved in reformulating logical laws to allow for the fact that sentences are not straightforwardly just true or false, but true or false only relative to a time. But Quine admits that these benefits are a minor consideration (PoL, p. 31).

He occasionally claims that modern physics calls for a system of notation that treats time and space in a similar fashion, and thus plays down tense. Sometimes he misleadingly claims that the Theory of Relativity requires us to treat time as simply one more space-like dimension (WO, p. 172; but see Newton-Smith 1980, pp. 186–7). But it does seem true that if judgements of simultancity are relative to an arbitrarily adopted frame of reference, a system of notation whose temporal indications rest upon a sharp distinction between past and future (as the tensed system does) will be unsatisfactory (see Mellor 1981, pp. 67–8). However, the most important considerations lie elsewhere, in Quine's views about the nature of *objects*.

6.3 OBJECTS AND EVENTS

Our familiar conceptual scheme distinguishes substances from events or processes. Substances are things like persons, rocks, tables, ships and so on, which continue to exist through a period of time, and have different properties at different times. An event, like my getting up this morning, or the outbreak of the Second World War, does not continue to exist over a period with different properties at different times. We gain some grip of the distinction when we notice that events are things that can happen to substances: undergoing the event of getting up this morning is one of my properties. We can think of something like the Second World War, or the giving of a lecture as a sequence or sum of events. Clarifying this distinction is not easy; but since it is a fairly familiar or obvious one, we can use it without getting stuck on these difficulties.

I have already mentioned that substances can be involved in events – the events can be things that happen to them. Indeed, we can associate with any substance a set or sequence of events that makes up its *history*: my history simply contains all of the events in which I have figured. In fact, we can contrast two sorts of 'history' here. First, there is one that contains occurrences such as getting up, giving a lecture, eating meals and so on – this is how we would naturally think of someone's history. Secondly, there is what we can call something's *physical* history: this would be the set or sequence of physical events which occurs within its 'body' during its lifetime. In the case of a person, this would involve every physical event that has occurred within his or her brain, muscles, skin, bones etc. Histories are things of the same kind as the Second World War, or a lecture, at least in this one respect, that they are sequences of, or sums of, events.

Intuitively, persons (or any substances) and their histories are not the same things. I could have had a different history without being a different person. My giving a lecture is part of my history but it is not a part of me. Furthermore, while we can distinguish times at which I exist from those at which I do not (before my birth or after my death), we do not make similar claims about (say) my lecture. We can talk about when it occurred, and say that it has finished, but we should not express this by saying that it no longer exists. This distinction emerges importantly in the ways in which tense interacts with quantifiers. Thus, we shall feel cheated if someone tries to support his claim that there *is* someone who met Henry VIII by mentioning Thomas Cromwell: the present tense idiom 'there is' suggests that he is making a claim about someone who exists now. On the other hand, there is no parallel difficulty in supporting the claim that there is a battle in which cavalry was decisive by pointing to one that occurred over a century ago. We should not attach too much importance to these linguistic facts, but they do help to point to some differences in our ways of thinking about substances and their histories.

Quine holds that serious scientific discourse will not refer to substances: reference to people, animals or inanimate objects can be replaced by reference to the sequences of events that make up their histories. Hence, conceptual simplification is to be achieved by eliminating substances from our conceptual scheme, and talking only of events and sequences or sums of events. Indeed, in keeping with Quine's physicalism, his position seems to be that reference to me (or to my typewriter or the table on which I write) can be replaced by reference to our physical histories (the sums of physical events that occur within our boundaries). In consequence of this revision in our conceptual scheme, it follows that the movements of my mouth as I lecture are parts of me (and parts of the lecture), rather than things that happen to me or parts of my history.

Of course, it may still be 'practically indispensable' to retain this distinction between substances and events, processes or histories. The claim is only that we can abandon it when our concern is with 'limning the most general features of reality'. Before asking why Quine should favour this revision in our conceptual framework, we must develop the story one stage further. Our universe of discourse is to contain sequences of, or sums of, events: these will be our 'objects' from now on. Which collections of events are to count as genuine objects? Plainly, my physical history is to count as one. But what about the history of my thumb, or the history of me between the ages of 16 and 17, or the history made up of every event occurring within the body of whoever happened to be Prime Minister of Great Britain between 1800 and 1900? We seem to need some principle for deciding which collections of events are to count as 'objects'. What should it be?

Quine doubts that such a principle can be found. If this does not lead him to despair, it does provoke what some might think a desperate remedy. He is prepared to look on *any* collection of physical events as an 'object', as a member of his universe of discourse. Thus, alongside familiar ones, there will be the 'object' which contains not only the events involved in my typewriter key just being pressed, but also those involved in the first wave striking Dover beach on 4 May 1639, and those involved in printing the first page of the first copy of *Word and Object*. The events need not 'belong together' in any natural or intuitive fashion. Why does Quine adopt this curious revisionary account of what objects there are?

The view is neatly summarized in 'Things and their place in theories':

> More objects are wanted, certainly, than just bodies and [kinds of stuff]. We need all sorts of parts or portions of [stuff]. For lack of a natural stopping place, the natural course at this point is to admit as an object the material content of any portion of space–time, however irregular and discontinuous and heterogeneous. This is the generalization of the primitive and ill-defined category of bodies to what I call physical objects.
>
> [Kinds of stuff] fall into place now as physical objects. Milk, or wood, or sugar, is the discontinuous four-dimensional physical object comprising all the world's milk, or wood, or sugar, ever.
>
> (TT, p. 10)

He appears to hold that both modern physics and modern logic call for the replacement of objects by their histories. I have already expressed some hesitancy about the thought that the Theory of Relativity suggests abandoning any conception, such as that of a continuing object, which rests upon sharply distinguishing space and time. In the light of our discussions from the end of chapter 5, it should be clear that Quine is partly motivated by the desire to frame his understanding of objects in ways that accord with fundamental physics: basic physics, it could be argued, does not need to talk of persons, tables, thumbs and the like, so we should regard those things as built up out of the kinds of reactions which physics *does* describe. In *Theories and Things*, Quine suggests that one natural support for the view comes from molecular theory: 'if even a solid is diffuse, why stop there?' (TT, p. 13).

The logical foundations for the doctrine are of more immediate concern. Sometimes, one gets the impression that Quine holds that, unless we adopt his theory of objects, we shall be committed to a tensed theory of quantification, so that what can be talked about depends upon what exists at any given time. Replacing traditional object talk by talk of histories enables us to avoid this difficulty.

> Think how awkward it is, without some such view, to make sense of applying a predicate to something that no longer exists; or to make sense of quantifying over objects that never co-existed at any one time, and assembling such objects into sets.
>
> (PoL, p. 77)

However, there are straightforward technical means of avoiding those difficulties without such a radical revision in our conceptual scheme.

The best approach to Quine's motivation is through a famous puzzle, first discussed by Thomas Hobbes. At one time (t1), there was a ship, the ship of Theseus. As time went by, this required repair: occasionally, a plank would be replaced by a new one. Eventually, afer a long period, it transpired that every plank in the original ship had been replaced. Thus (at t2), there is a ship which has no material in common with the original, but which has resulted from the piecemeal replacement of bits of it. The puzzle is: does the original ship of Theseus still exist at t2, or has it gradually been replaced by another ship? A deeper version of the puzzle supposes that all of the original planks were stored and used, at t2, to build a ship exactly like the original. We then ask which, if either, of the ships existing at t2 is the original ship of Theseus.

At first sight, this puzzle seems to point to vagueness or incoherence in our concept of an object or our concept of identity: we feel at a loss to say whether the ships are the same or not. In that case, there would be incoherence in concepts that are absolutely fundamental to our conceptual scheme. If those concepts are not clear, then we may doubt the capacity of our framework for coping adequately with the demands of science. They are concepts with, it seems, an essential role in our canonical notation, but which cannot play that role with the sort of precision that is required for scientific purposes.

At the same time, we feel that the puzzle is basically trivial: it does not raise a fundamental question of fact. I think that Quine would claim that it is one virtue of his concept of objects that he can answer the puzzle without admitting the incoherence of fundamental concepts. He claims that the vagueness concerns the concept of a ship rather than the concept of an object.

Do we have the same object before and after repair? According to Quine's position, this comes down to the question: are there any objects which contain all those physical events within the boundary of the ship of Theseus at t1 and also those events occurring within the boundary of the repaired ship at t2? The question is easily answered: there are numerous objects that contain all of these events, as well as objects that contain some but not all of them. There are also numerous objects containing all events within the original ship and those within the rebuilt ship – and indeed some containing all events within both of the ship's existing at t2. The question has a perfectly clear sense, and a perfectly clear answer. We may continue to ask whether any of those objects are (the physical histories of) ships. That may prove hard to answer, for the concept of a ship is vague: we have never bothered to lay down how it should be applied to cases like this. But problems with the concept of a ship do not trouble the deeper reaches of our conceptual scheme, and they are easily resolved by a new stipulation if they become pressing. Hence, Quine's theory replaces a concept of an object which is threatened by paradox by one which is clear and coherent, which can handle the paradox straightforwardly.

The benefits of this broad conception of an object are clarity and precision. The bizarre objects which are thus introduced stay tidily out of the way for all serious purposes. When we formulate laws or generalizations, we always specify which sorts of objects they are to apply to. Even when speaking most generally, we may claim that all physical bodies have some property. We often restrict attention to those collections of events which count as *bodies*: an object that is 'roughly continuous spatially and rather chunky and that contrasts abruptly with most of its surroundings and is individuated over time by continuity of displacement, distortion and discoloration' (TT, p. 13). This is very vague, particularly because molecular theory teaches us that the boundaries of such things are ill-defined (ibid.): so much the better, Quine would say, for his generalized conception of a physical object in general. It acknowledges that concepts such as body and substance are not as fundamental to our conception of reality as some have thought.

6.4 PHYSICS AND EXTENSIONALITY

There are a number of intensional idioms which appear to have an essential role in basic science, most of which involve the subjunctive conditional. First, scientists look for scientific laws, and they contrast these with generalizations that are true 'by accident'. The distinction can be introduced through some examples:

(1) All samples of ice melt when heated above 0°C, in normal circumstances.
(2) All the cars in the car park are red.

(1) may not be general or abstract enough to count as a scientific 'law', but it is 'lawlike': when we accept it, we acknowledge that heating ice (causally) *explains* its melting; and, relatedly, the generalization sustains counterfactual or subjunctive conditionals. It is not making a claim

simply about those samples of ice that have been heated, but rather speaks of all ice, whether heated or not. Thus, given (1), we would conclude:

(3) If this piece of ice had been heated above 0°C, then it would have melted.

Normally, we should expect that if a statement such as (2) is true, it is accidentally so: the cars are not red *because* they are in the car park; and we should not use it to justify (4):

(4) If I had placed my car in the car park this morning, it would have been red.

Science is interested in generalizations that yield subjunctive conditionals, and is not interested in the accidental ones.

Within Quine's system of canonical notation, this difference between (1) and (2) seems not to appear; (1) is naturally represented:

$$(x)(\text{Ice}(x) \rightarrow (\text{Heated}(x) \rightarrow \text{Melts}(x))).$$

This involves the non-subjunctive 'material conditional': the generalization is true so long as no sample of ice which is heated fails to melt. It carries no suggestion that the heating causes the melting: it would turn out true, for example, if no ice had ever been heated, or if the ice that had been heated was about to melt anyway. The only relevant difference between (1) and (2) that is represented is that (2) concerns a specific time, whereas (1) seems to make a claim about all times. But, in principle, there is no obstacle to there being an accidentally true generalization which is not temporally limited in this way. A trivial example would be:

(5) Every dodo taken to America dies immediately on landing.

This is true simply because no dodo has been (or will be) taken to America.

The source of intensionality that Quine most often discusses involves dispositional properties – for example, the properties of being soluble, or intelligent, or fragile. Can we handle predicates which express them in extensional language? Quine accepts that Carnap had shown the impossibility of this in the 1930s:

> To say of a particular lump of stuff that it is soluble in water is, as Carnap has stressed, to say more about it than just that whenever it is in water it dissolves. For perhaps this particular lump will never be in water. By default, then, even if the lump is quartz, it would be true that whenever the lump is in water it dissolves; but we cannot on that ground call it soluble in water. For a lump to be soluble we must be able to say of it that if it *were* in water it *would* dissolve; we need an 'if–then' conditional governed by necessity, and by a necessity that goes beyond mere generality over time. To say that the lump dissolves at each time that it *is* in water is too weak.
>
> (WP, p. 71)

The problem is that any material conditional with a false antecedent is true. Thus, if we know that a certain iron bar has never been, and never will be, placed in water, we can know that it is soluble, since

> (t)(If the iron bar is placed in water at t, then it dissolves soon after t).

Thus, if science is to refer to dispositional properties – and it is hard to deny that it must do this – it must make use of intensional idioms.

Another kind of scientific statement that appears to be intensional concerns probability:

> The probability that the reaction will occur is n.

If we replace 'The reaction will occur' by another sentence with the same truth value, there is no guarantee that the resulting sentence will have the same truth value as the one we started with: all true statements do not have the same probability. Since there is evidence that fundamental physical theories attribute probabilistic dispositions to things in order to explain their behaviour, Quine's extensionalism looks implausible.

Quine has little to say about probabilities. He claims that such statements are used to make tentative assertions, based upon limited evidence. All that is *asserted* when I say that it will probably rain tomorrow is that it will rain tomorrow. By using 'probably' I cover myself, admitting that I am making, at best, an informed guess or speculation. The penalties for making a false assertion so qualified are considerably less than those for making one unqualified. The auditor is made aware of the risk he takes when he relies upon my testimony. This does not account for the role of statistical hypotheses in finished scientific theories: the probability of patients with a certain disease surviving is n. According to Quine, such judgements are correctly formulated as numerical hypotheses about the proportion of those who incur the disease that survive. In that case, there is no challenge to extensionality: intensional probability judgements have no role in a canonical notation for representing finished scientific theories.

That leaves the problems about laws, dispositions and subjunctive conditionals. Quine's response to these is firmly within the empiricist tradition. Like Hume, he does not accept that laws and subjunctive conditionals express necessities which are present in nature; the material conditional is the only one which his notation allows; and the apparent intensionality of laws and dispositions is to be explained away rather than accommodated. Part of the difference between sentences 1 and 2 (see p. 104) as we have noticed, is that (2) involves specific temporal reference. The rest of the difference reflects the greater embeddedness of (1) in our conceptual scheme. A counterexample to (1) would embarrass us more than a counterexample to (2): we could not abandon (1) without substantial revision of other beliefs. Faced with a sample of ice that appears not to melt, we should prefer to hold on to (1) and explain the counterexample away: the thermometer was faulty, or the ice impure . . . The subjunctive expresses our determination to hold on to the law unless forced to abandon it: we have no such determination with respect to (2). If we heard that a dodo had been taken to America, we should be ready to abandon 5 immediately.

The story Quine tells about dispositions is more complicated (see WO, pp. 222–5; RR, pp. 4ff, 10–15; WP, pp. 71–4; OR, pp. 130–1) This is because appeal to dispositions like solubility can help to *explain* dissolvings. If all that it means to say something is soluble is that it dissolves when placed in water, such explanations would be empty. Chemical theory has described the 'subvisible structure' which leads to dissolving. We can, if we wish, simply identify the disposition with this underlying chemical or physical mechanism. When I claim that a dry cube of sugar is soluble, I claim that it is similarly structured to objects that have dissolved: *theory* leads us to expect such things to dissolve when placed in water. This can be expressed in extensional terms. If 'M' is read 'are alike in molecular structure', then 'x is soluble' can be glossed:

(Ey)(Mxy and y dissolves).

Use of subjunctive conditionals generally alludes to the fact that the generalization or conditional in question is licensed by theories which explain the underlying structures of the objects involved.

It is no objection that we can talk of solubility while ignorant of the molecular structures accounting for it; nor that we can talk of intelligence while no one is aware of how to explain the capacity to solve problems quickly. The merit of subjunctive talk is that it enables us to gesture towards explanatory mechanisms that we little understand:

> Early and late, solubility has been meant to be some causal agency or mechanism or arrangement in the lump, however little understood. From the start of a scientific attitude anyway, the term has been a sort of promissory note which one might hope eventually to redeem in terms of an explicit account of the working mechanism . . . [The] promissory character of the unredeemed solubility idea was never an obstacle to glib use of the term. For this much one is assured of early and late: whenever a soluble thing is in water it does dissolve. We intend in advance that solubility consist precisely in those explanatory traits of structure and composition, however ill-pictured or unpictured at the time, that do make things dissolve when in water.
>
> (WP, p. 72)

While dispositional terms have an essential heuristic or regulative role in formulating ideas and problems as science progresses; and while they provide an excellent shorthand in alluding to great stretches of theory, and a useful means for covering up our relative ignorance – there is no reason to think they need have a role in formulating the true finished theory of reality. Subjunctive conditionals have no place in 'an austere canonical notation for science': in principle, we can always turn to the underlying mechanisms and dismiss such indirect – albeit useful – means for referring to them.

We have here an elegant illustration of the strategies Quine employs to vindicate his extensional canonical notation. There are philosophers who dispute this position. They hold that subjunctive conditionals and other intensional idioms are indispensable for science. Sometimes, this involves pointing out how such notions are used in describing the results of experiments (Suppes 1985, p. 187). This would not bother Quine, who would agree that his canonical notation omits locutions which are indispensable in the laboratory but which have no role in stating finished scientific theories. More troublesome is the suggestion that even physical theory is intensional: this could be grounded in doubts about Quine's accounts of law and probability. Since I am currently more concerned with understanding Quine's austere view of the world than with evaluating all of the details, and because space is limited, I cannot enter into these debates here. In fact, these Quinean doctrines are not particularly original. They place him squarely in the empiricist tradition, and resemble Hume's attempt, in his analysis of causation, to explain away our sense that a necessary connection holds between cause and effect. An extensional language is adequate for all *descriptive* purposes. Subjunctive conditionals, and talk of what is probable, have a role in communication. But this is through expressing, or indicating, our attitudes towards the propositions we assert, or through alluding to other bodies of theory. Consequently, we lose little by omitting them from our austere canonical notation for science.

7

Necessity: Logic and Metaphysics

7.1 NECESSITY AND EXTENSIONALITY

Most philosophers feel very confident in using the words 'possibly' and 'necessarily'. Explaining them clearly is another matter. One way to introduce them is through examples. It is possible for a vixen to be well fed or hungry, but it is not possible for a vixen to be male or a rabbit; it is not possible that the sum of 3 and 4 should be 9; it is not possible that a statement and its negation should both be true, while it is possible for both to be believed (at least, by different people); and so on. These examples are cast in terms of 'possibly', but the light they throw on 'necessary' becomes clear when it is noted that to claim that some truth is necessary is to claim that its negation is not possible. Thus: it is necessary that 3+4=7, that a statement and its negation are not both true, or that vixens are female foxes.

Such examples are usually accompanied by vague, unhelpful explanations. These are required because of an apparent ambiguity in 'possibly'. Sometimes, it has an epistemic meaning: when I say that it is possible that it snowed before Christmas in 1977, I may mean simply that I do not know that it did not. Philosophical interest in the concept rests upon the belief that not all possibility is of this sort. In some 'broad logical' sense of possibility, there is a fundamental distinction between two kinds of truths: those (like mathematical ones) which hold in all possible states of the world; and those (like ordinary contingent claims about material objects) which, even if we know them to obtain, we also know might not have obtained. I might not have worn a blue sweater today, had I made a different decision; the roses might now have been in flower, had the weather been different; but under no such supposition could a vixen have been other than a fox. If the distinction can be made good, its philosophical importance is evident. The problem is that it is very hard to advance beyond informal elucidations of the distinction to a full explanation of it. Notoriously, Quine is sceptical that this can be done.

A natural starting point is that many of the statements we judge to be necessary are established by proof or calculation rather than by observation and experiment. The truths of logic and mathematics provide paradigms of necessity. This is not surprising. When we arrive at an opinion by observation and experiment, we respond to features of our actual situation, so it is problematic how we can thus arrive at truths about all possible situations. Proof and calculation, on the other hand, lack this sensitivity to the actual environment: if a proof is convincing here and now, it would be convincing if our physical surroundings were different. Moreover, since these subjects depend upon little in the way of specific lexicon, forming a framework which is used in connection with all subject matters, we readily accept that they provide a general frame of reference that can contain all possibilities.

It looks as if we should introduce the expression 'necessarily' into our canonical notation, employing the rule:

If it is a truth of logic or mathematics that p, then necessarily p.

We should then have introduced a non-truth functional operator into our language: extensionality would have been sacrificed. But it is hard to see that we have lapsed into incoherence.

In fact, Quine is perfectly happy with this much necessity, but denies that it compromises his extensionalism (see WP, pp. 158ff). Compare

(1) Necessarily, if the dog is a bulldog or a boxer, and it is not a bulldog, then it is a boxer.
(2) 'If the dog is a bulldog or a boxer, and is not a bulldog, then it is a boxer' is a necessarily true statement.

Statement 2 is extensional. It is of simple subject–predicate form, containing a singular term referring to a statement, and a predicate 'is a necessarily true statement' which ascribes a property to it. Quotation marks transform expressions into singular terms that refer to linguistic items (words, phrases or sentences). The sentence 'If the dog . . .' is not *used* to talk about animals in (2). Rather, it is *mentioned* : when we utter

(2), we are talking about that sentence. Its occurrence in (2) is like that of 'The cat is on the mat' in

'The cat is on the mat' contains six words.

It is no sacrifice of extensionality that substituting another sentence for 'The cat is on the mat' can lead to a change in truth value. All that is required is that no such change result if we introduce another singular term referring to that sentence. Thus

John's favourite sentence contains six words.

This sentence (2) retains extensionality by talking about language. Does this show us how to regiment all of our modal discourse within an extensional language? Can we accommodate necessity (and possibility) within Quine's canonical notation through some such linguistic theory?

If we could do so, then, in line with Quine's views about such notations, there is no obstacle to our continuing to use the intensional idioms, so long as we are prepared to agree upon extensional paraphrases when we need to resolve unclarities or ambiguities. Let me illustrate this. There seems to be no grammatical obstacle to iterating modal expressions like 'possibly' and 'necessarily'. We can talk of what is possibly necessary or necessarily possible and produce complex claims such as

Necessarily, possibly, necessarily, it is possible that 3+4=7.

It is unclear what these sentences mean, however. We have little idea how to go about establishing whether they are true or false, and this can be a source of apparently deep philosophical problems about possibility and necessity. On the view now under consideration, we begin by seeking an extensional metalinguistic paraphrase of the sentence in question. It will involve a complex system of nested quotation marks:

''''3+4=7' is possible' is necessary' is possible' is necessary.

We then simply hunt through the theorems of logic or mathematics in order to see whether the sentence is there: since 'possible' and 'necessary' belong to the vocabulary of neither logic nor mathematics, we shall not find it. The problems dissolve. If we were happy with the Carnapian notion of analyticity, then this approach would have further applications.

Necessarily, vixens are foxes

would receive an extensional metalinguistic paraphrase:

'Vixens are foxes' is analytic.

Quine objects to a *logic* of necessity and possibility on two grounds. First, if all modal talk can receive such a paraphrase, then it calls only for an expansion in our lexicon: it does not deal with specific operators or modes of construction, so does not demand a distinctive logic. Second, if, like most of the work actually done in the field, it deals with forms of modal discourse that cannot receive such a paraphrase (or can receive one only by using the notion of analyticity) then it runs into intractable logical and philosophical problems. Our concern in the remainder of this chapter is with these problems.

As Quine points out, there are limits to what can be achieved by this strategy of metalinguistic paraphrase – even if we help ourselves to the notion of analyticity. There are features of our ordinary talk of necessity which cannot be accommodated by this kind of paraphrase We can take them seriously only if we augment the canonical system of notation to incorporate 'necessarily' and 'possibly' as statement operators, analogous to negation. They involve the use of quantifiers in tandem with modal operators: only a full-blooded modal logic allows 'the possibility of quantifying into modal positions, for we know we cannot quantify into quotation' (WO, p. 197).

The best way to understand this is through considering a parallel proposal. Could we replace the negation operator with the metalinguistic predicate '— is false'? How far would doing so reduce our expressive capacities? Problems arise when we compare the two claims:

There is someone who is not bald

It is not the case that there is someone who is bald

They plainly do not mean the same: the first is true and the second false. Whereas we could paraphrase the second as:

'There is someone who is bald' is false

no such paraphrase is available for the first. This is because the existential quantifier 'There is someone who —' occurs outside the 'scope' of the negation operator and binds a variable within it. We should require some such paraphrase as

Ex 'x is bald' is false.

Once an expression occurs within quotation marks, Quine insists, it refers to a linguistic expression and loses its normal reference. In the example above, the second occurrence of 'x' refers to the twenty-fourth letter of the alphabet; it does not function as a variable. Hence, the existential quantifier fails to engage with the 'variable' in the quoted sentence. The moral, according to Quine, is: if variables occurring within the scope of operators can be bound by quantifiers that do not occur within their scope, then the operator cannot be paraphrased as a metalinguistic predicate. The proposed metalinguistic construal of negation fails.

As a corollary of this, Quine claims, we require a genuine modal logic, which treats 'possibly' and 'necessarily' as operators, if, and only if, we need to make sense of sentences in which quantifiers bind variables occurring within the scope of modal expressions. Unless we need a quantified modal logic, we have no need for a modal logic at all. (In 'Intensions revisited' (TT, ch. 13) Quine suggests that even quantified modal logic can be handled with a special metalinguistic predicate – but this development does not seriously affect the points I wish to discuss here.)

It is easy to find sentences of ordinary language which look as if they can only be regimented within a quantified modal logic. The claim that there is someone who could meet the train from the station, like the judgement that there is a number that is necessarily greater than seven, seem to have this form. Over thirty or forty years, Quine has campaigned against the intelligibility of quantified modal logic. The most evident effect of these writings has been the development of sophisticated systems of quantified modal logics designed to resist Quine's challenges. We begin our examination of this debate, in the following section, by describing the most influential of Quine's arguments.

7.2 *DE DICTO* AND *DE RE*

Quine has discussed the sins of quantified modal logic on several occasions, most notably: 'Reference and modality' (in FLPV), 'Three grades of modal involvement' in (WP), and 'Intensions revisited' and 'Worlds aways' (both in TT), as well as in *Word and Object* (pp. 195ff). Throughout, he stresses that, once we allow quantifiers to bind variables within the scope of modal operators, we are committed to making sense of *de re* modalities. Therefore, our first task is to explain the *de re*/*de dicto* distinction.

As we have seen, one kind of necessity claim is concerned with the modal status of complete propositions: for example, necessarily all bachelors are unmarried or necessarily 3+9=12. In contrast to this, some philosophers talk of necessity in connection with the ways in which properties attach to things. Some object – a person for example – has some of its properties by necessity, others accidentally: a necessity claim 'specifies the modal status of an object's exemplification of an attribute' (Loux (ed.) 1979, p. 31). For example, the number two is necessarily even, but only contingently the number of books on my desk; Quine is necessarily a person, but only contingently a logician. We can envisage possible worlds in which Quine (that individual) chose not to be a logician; we can envisage none in which he was not a person. The first kind of claim concerns necessity *de dicto*; the second kind concerns necessity *de re*. The statement

> The number of books on my desk is necessarily even

is ambiguous. There is a *de dicto* reading according to which it means

> It is a necessary truth that: there is a even number of books on my desk.

So understood, it is false. It also has a *de re* reading according to which it means that the number of books on my desk (viz. two) has the property of being necessarily even: if *de re* necessities are intelligible at all, this is true.

The distinction can be drawn for tensed statements too. A *de dicto* tensed statement attaches a tense operator to a complete statement: it was the case that Italy was a monarchy. A *de re* claim attaches a tensed property to an object: my typewriter used to work better than it now does. As we have seen above, Quine would systematize tensed discourse by regarding properties as applying to individuals at times, rather than by introducing tense operators. This is most naturally thought of as a *de re* conception.

Quine's view is that *de dicto* modality is bad enough. But, even if we understand how to make sense of that, perhaps in terms of analyticity, *de re* necessity is beyond redemption. There is to be no provision for *de re* modality within his austere canonical notation: his view of reality requires no distinction between different modes of exemplification of properties.

It is easy to see the link between quantified modal logic and *de re* modality. When we make a statement of the form

Ex (necessarily Fx)

we claim that some object has the property of being necessarily F. No complete proposition follows the modal operator: it is hard to see how the necessity, in this case, could be explained in terms of the analyticity of some proposition.

7.3 TENSE AND MODALITY

Since Quine finds problems in modal discourse where there are none in discourse about time, it is useful to compare the two cases. Many philosophers are struck by a parallel between them. Tensed discourse illustrates how property ascriptions are relative to time: an object can have a given property at one time and not at others. Our use of modal distinctions illustrates that properties apply to objects only relative to a possible situation: an object can have a given property in some situations, and not in others. The term 'possible world' is used to refer to these possible situations. So the proposal is that a predicate such as 'is red' expresses a triadic relation. The simplest colour judgements are of the form

The book is red at time t in possible world w.

Just as an object is *always* F if it is F at all times, so it is *necessarily* F if it is F at all times in all possible worlds. Most recent work in modal logic develops this analogy.

Reference to possible worlds has been criticized from a number of perspectives. Many philosophers find possible worlds too alien, and too abstract, for their taste. They point out, for example, that events occurring at remote times can affect us causally, while other possible worlds are cut off from this one. A philosopher with a taste for desert landscapes is unlikely to be happy with an ontology of possible worlds. While Quine would almost certainly sympathize with such complaints, they are not central to his critique of *de re* modality. Rather, he focuses on problems of cross-world identity.

Consider a *de re* tensed claim:

> There is someone who is now a politician and who was once an actor.

In order to establish whether this is true, we have to understand how one and the same object (in this case, a person) can exist at different times. The individual that is a politician now, and the individual that was an actor in the past, are the same. Bearing in mind Quine's conception of a person, we can see what this requires. First: is there a Quinean object (a set of events) which includes both events constitutive of political activity now and events constitutive of being an actor in the past? Of course, there are very many such objects. Secondly, are there any such objects with the property that all of the events within them form a single human life? There are rather fewer of these, but one is enough to make the statement true. A person existing at a lot of different times consists in a Quinean object having the kind of structured unity that makes up the life of a single human being.

Our ordinary talk of things reflects the role of the predicate 'body' in our conceptual scheme. The matter of the world is sufficiently clustered and patterned that thinking of things as bodies which slowly change and evolve is crucial to our conceptual grasp upon reality. We discussed this in the previous chapter. The important point here is that concepts like *body* and *person* are required to make sense of our ordinary tensed talk: it is only because of the prevalence of bodies that we are interested in whether we encounter 'the same thing again'. It is the availability of this predicate, picking out a favoured class of things, which confers stable sense on talk of cross-temporal identity.

How should we extend this picture to account for modal discourse? In 'Worlds away', Quine suggests that we would need a yet more liberal conception of a physical object. Physical objects would be:

> simply the sums of physical objects of the various worlds, combining denizens of different worlds indiscriminately. One of these values would consist of Napoleon together with his counterparts in other worlds . . .; another would consist of Napoleon together with sundry dissimilar denizens of other worlds.
>
> (TT, p. 126)

In David Lewis's usage, the counterpart of Napoleon in some other world is the object in that world which is most like Napoleon (Lewis 1981, chs 3–4). Our ordinary modal claims would be about those among these 'objects' which count as persons or bodies: these will be made up of bodies from each world which stand in some intimate relation to each other.

Quine holds that we can make sense of quantified modal discourse, on the model of quantified tensed discourse, only if the concepts of object and body can be developed in this fashion. He thinks that this is impossible, insisting, in 'Worlds away', that the problem with *de re* modality lies with the predicates 'body' or 'person' which are used to identify those Quinean objects which are of special concern to us.

> We could accommodate them if we could somehow extend our principle of individuation or integration of bodies so as to identify bodies not just from moment to moment, as we do so well, but from world to world. However, our cross moment identification of bodies turned on continuity of displacement, distortion and chemical change. These considerations cannot be extended across the worlds, because you can change anything to anything by easy stages through some connecting series of possible worlds.
>
> (TT, pp. 126–7)

At least one commentator has found this a weak argument:

> For it is equally true of the temporal case that you can change, if not anything to anything as time passes, at least certain things to startlingly different things, and the philosophical difficulties that arise in virtue of this phenomenon appear to be precisely parallel to those which arise in the modal case.
>
> (Forbes 1985, p. 53)

Forbes finds at best a challenge to the modal logician to explain the basis on which objects can be identified across worlds.

But Forbes does not quote the sentence which follows the passage from 'Worlds away': 'The devastating difference is that the series of momentary cross-sections of our real world is uniquely imposed on us, for better or for worse, whereas all manner of paths of continuous gradation from one possible world to another are free for the thinking up.' The point is that the different 'momentary cross-sections of our real world' arrive *ordered*. Consequently, when we identify bodies by reference to slowly evolving parcels of matter, we have no choice as to which order to take the different momentary cross sections in. Possible worlds do not have a unique ordering imposed upon them, and this prevents our constructing a coherent modal concept of body.

An example may illustrate this, based upon what is often referred to as Chisholm's paradox (Chisholm 1967). Consider two possible worlds, which differ only slightly: in wn Noah is one ounce heavier that in w1 – the only other differences are those involved in this being the case. Since this is a very slight difference, we can expect that Noah in w1 and Noah in wn would both belong to the same Quinean modal body. But, in fact, I have described the case in a question-begging fashion. We can construct a sequence of worlds, starting from w1, ending with wn, which suggests that this is not so.

In w1, Noah and Adam have all the properties they have in the actual world (as described in the Old Testament). For example, Adam lived for 930 years and Noah for 950. In w2, Adam lived for 931, and Noah for 949; and so on through the sequence of worlds until Adam lived for 950 years and Noah for 930. We then continue, and very gradually Noah and Adam exchange all of their properties, until we reach wn. If we follow this sequence of worlds, looking for the gradual evolution which makes up a Quinean body, it seems that the person in wn that we described above as Noah is in fact Adam: he is very similar to the Adam of the immediately preceding world, and very unlike the Noah of that world. Then it seems likely that, simply by ordering the worlds in different ways, we shall find that any body in this world will be part of a very large number of 'modal' bodies: there is no basis for saying whether a body or person in some world is me or is Noah. Since *every possibility* is available to be included in one or other of these orderings, the modal notion of a body lacks the coherence of Quine's temporal notion. For the latter, we take account only of the events that actually occur, and their ordering is given.

The puzzle about Noah and Adam can appear rather silly. Quine would sympathize with this view. His claim is just that *if* you wish to extend his notion of a body in order to make sense of modal discourse, then you have to respond to it. The parallel between times and worlds is not sufficient to force us to admit *de re* modality on the coat-tails of analogous talk of time.

7.4 ESSENTIALISM

The philosophical literature does not lack responses to these puzzles. They have stimulated much work on the semantics of modal logic and the nature of necessity, and few philosophers have agreed with Quine that they demonstrate the incoherence of modal notions or the emptiness of modal logic. I shall suggest in this section that many of these discussions do not respond directly to Quine's worries about modality.

Some of these responses involve arguing that the doctrine of *essentialism* holds the key to making sense of *de re* modalities. An essential property of an object is one which it could not lack without ceasing to exist: there could not be a situation which involved that object but in which it lacked an essential property. A plausible, but ultimately not very interesting, example of such a property is that of self-identity: Noah could not exist while not being the same thing as himself. We might hold too that *being Adam* is an essential property of Adam's: but, once again, that does not get us very far. If we can find substantive essential properties of Adam and Noah, this may help to solve our paradox. For example, if it was an essential property of Adam's that he was not born of human parents, or that he was the first man, this would place restrictions upon which objects in which worlds could be combined with Adam's history in this world to form a modalized Quinean object. Similarly, if it was essential to Noah that he was born of a particular set of parents (or of a particular sperm and ovum), he could not then acquire all of Adam's properties. Our long route from w1 to wn would be blocked because, at some point, both Adam and Noah would lose their respective essential properties (and at some point, each would acquire the essential properties of the other).

Quine agrees that quantified modal logic could be developed coherently if essentialism were true. 'Evidently, this reversion to Aristotelian essentialism is required if quantification into modal contexts is to be insisted on' (FLPV, p. 155; cf. WO, p. 199). 'Essence is needed to identify an object from one possible world to another.' (TT, p. 118). In *Word and Object* he complains that the distinction between essence and accident is 'surely indefensible' (p. 200). For the most part, he sees little need to argue that, if quantified modal logic is committed to essentialism, then it has no place in our austere canonical idiom: the notion of essence has been left behind with Aristotelian science.

In a famous passage, Quine writes:

> Perhaps I can evoke the appropriate sense of bewilderment as follows. Mathematicians may conceivably be said to be necessarily rational and not necessarily two-legged; and cyclists necessarily two-legged and not necessarily rational. But what of an individual who counts among his eccentricities both mathematics and cycling? Is this concrete individual necessarily rational and contingently two-legged or vice versa? Just insofar as we are talking referentially of the object, with no special bias toward a background grouping of mathematicians as against cyclists, or vice versa, there is no semblance of sense in rating some of his attributes as necessary, and others as contingent. Some of his attributes count as important and others as unimportant, yes; some as enduring and others as fleeting; but none as necessary or contingent.
>
> (WO, p. 199)

The passage importantly suggests that the appeal of the notion of essence involves confusing it with other, more interest-relative, distinctions. The problem with it is that no friend of essences would rely upon such examples. If better examples are attended to, they suggest, our bewilderment may abate. Let us consider one adapted from a much fuller discussion in Forbes (1985).

As I write, I can see an ash tree in the garden. Clearly, that tree could have been planted elsewhere: it is not essential to it that it have just that location. It could have grown differently, have been stunted due to lack of light, or pruned: its physical constitution depends upon the nutrients taken up from the soil, and that too could have been different. On the other hand, a different tree could have been planted where this one is. And it could have grown to a similar shape and size as this; and it could have developed the same physical constitution through taking up the same nutrients from the soil. We can easily imagine a situation in which the tree that I now see was elsewhere and of a different size and shape, while a different tree qualitatively like this one took its place in my garden. The ease with which we understand these counterfactual possibilities suggests that our concept of a tree (or of an ash tree) provides us with a basis for telling which tree is which. And it is plausible that our understanding of the case rests upon imagining a tree eleswhere growing from the seed which produced this one, and a tree just like this one which resulted from a different seed. In any conceivable situation in which this very tree exists, it grows from the same seed: the origin of the tree constitutes an essential property.

In like vein, any concept which characterizes a sort or kind of thing must provide us with some basis for distinguishing and re-identifying different things belonging to that sort. If we agree that Caesar, for example, could not exist without being a human being, and we also agree that human beings are individuated by reference to their origin in a sperm and ovum, then we have an essential property of Caesar's. A lot of work is required for this to be more than suggestive. My present concern is simply to break the spell of Quine's bewilderment: if we think about the right sorts of examples, the doctrine of essentialism loses its bizarre character. If this doctrine, 'the essentiality of origin', is correct, it is easy to see how to solve the puzzle about Adam and Noah. Many philosophers would hold that it is a major, unintended, contribution of Quine's to awake us to the pervasive essentialist themes in ordinary thought.

It is one thing to argue that many of our ordinary idioms can only be formalized in a quantified modal logic, or that our ordinary concepts of sorts of things provide the materials for defensible talk of essential properties; it is quite another to claim that such idioms have a role in Quine's austere idiom for expressing the contents of finished scientific theories. If they are not required for describing 'the facts', then the Quinean logician can ignore them. We should expect Quine's resistance to quantified modal logic to focus on the claim that, if there are any essentialist idioms in our ordinary usage, they have no role in a physicalist science.

Hence, in 'Intensions revisited', we read that the notion of essence makes sense 'in context': 'Relative to a particular inquiry, some predicates may play a more basic role than others, or may apply more fixedly; and these may be treated as essential' (TT, pp. 120–1). Essence reflects our interests, and projects these onto the world. Essence belongs with the concept of substance which, as we saw in the previous chapter, is viewed by Quine as dispensable for scientific purposes.

My present concern is with how Quine's scruples about modal logic are linked to his views on the nature of logic and science. His constant pairing of 'essentialism' and the name of Aristotle indicates that he sees essentialism as belonging with a discarded scientific tradition. His empiricist approach to science ensures that he sees the notion of analyticity as the only hope for clarifying necessity – albeit a forlorn one. As he writes in a slightly different context: 'I do not see the markings here of a proper annex to austere scientific language' (TT, p. 128).

If this is correct, then those scholars most active in developing systems of quantified modal logic differ from Quine primarily in their view of the proper goal of regimentation. Their concern has not been with constructing a system of canonical representations with the property that 'all traits of reality worthy of the name can be set down in an idiom of this austere form if in any idiom' (WO, p. 228). Rather, they have sought a system of representations which will enable us to understand all our familiar forms of speech and the inferences we use them to perform: they wish to express the logical forms of all the different sorts of thoughts we can have. The ultimate concern is with the content of thoughts rather than with the broadest features of reality. Insofar as this is not the case, they have taken for granted a far more liberal conception of reality and 'the facts' than Quine. Taken on its own terms, Quine's approach is not defeated by pointing to features of our ordinary practice which it fails to reflect, or by showing that the inferences we perform using idioms that Quine dislikes can be described systematically. For Quine, the crucial question is whether they are needed for describing the facts, and that comes down to whether they are needed for physics.

7.5 CONCLUSION

In Part II of this volume we have tried to clarify two things. The first was Quine's somewhat unusual conception of philosophical analysis, his goals in trying to construct a system of canonical representations for scientific claims. The second was Quine's austere world view. He defends an unrelenting physicalism; and he holds that a language adequate for scientific purposes will be extensional. In Part III, we shall begin to trace some of the most important consequences of this philosophical outlook. It is important to be clear about how much weight is being carried by Quine's exceedingly austere conception of reality, and by his restricted conception of the task of the philosopher. He is not primarily interested in clarifying or describing the idioms we use to relate to each other or to understand ourselves. He is concerned, rather, with understanding, and developing the broad outlines of, a physicalist account of language and science.

We have discovered a variety of idioms that appear to be intensional. In each case, the Quinean response has taken one of two forms. Either analysis reveals that an extensional paraphrase of the area of discourse in question is available; or the idiom in question, while needed in the laboratory and market place, has no role in the formulation of finished physical theories. We now turn to what are, potentially, the most disturbing challenges to the thesis of extensionality. These are descriptions of the beliefs and other mental states of people, and statements describing the semantical properties of expressions from our language. Sentences ascribing beliefs to people, for example, are intensional. It is hard to see how we could take them seriously without augmenting the austere linguistic framework which Quine employs. Unless such discourse can be shown to be extensional – and I shall not discuss various attempts to show that it is – then either Quine's conception of an adequate canonical notation is mistaken or our ordinary talk of the mind is of no value when it comes to 'limning the ultimate structure of reality'. The next three chapters are concerned with Quine's attack on the factual status of much ordinary talk of meaning and mind.

In concluding this section, we should note that Quine's physicalism and extensionalism seem to be independent of the doctrines discussed in Part I. It is not out of the question that someone could accept the views defended in 'Two dogmas' yet deny Quine's version of physicalism – indeed, Goodman probably defends just such a position. (For a similar suggestion, see Hylton 1982.) One could even accept, with Quine, that empiricism has passed the fifth (naturalistic) milestone, yet deny that the scientific resources available to a properly scientific philosophy are as limited as he supposes. For example, we could follow Fodor and take more seriously than Quine the claims of non-basic sciences, psychology or economics, to reveal the nature of reality. In the chapters that follow, we shall be examining some controversial doctrines which develop out of this austere conception of reality.

Part III

Mind and Meaning

8

Indeterminacy of Translation

8.1 THE THESIS

The indeterminacy of translation is Quine's best known and most controversial thesis: few claims have been discussed so often, or refuted so frequently, in recent philosophical journals. Challenges to its truth have been matched by puzzlement over its meaning and importance. It will occupy us for three chapters, this first of them providing an introductory survey of the ground. In sections 8.4 and 8.5 we consider the philosophical implications of the doctrine – first for Quine's conception of mind and meaning, and second for issues of ontological commitment, reference and truth. Before this, we must explain its content and introduce Quine's arguments in its defence (for a much more detailed and careful examination of different versions of the doctrine, see Kirk 1986).

We are to imagine field linguists attempting to construct manuals which will enable them to translate from another language into English. The manuals must provide English equivalents for all of the sentences of the alien language. According to Quine: 'Manuals for translating one language into another can be set up in divergent ways, all compatible with the totality of speech dispositions, yet incompatible with each other' (WO, p. 27). He holds that there is no fact of the matter over which of these manuals is actually correct. The 'facts' rule out some manuals, on the grounds that they are incompatible with 'the totality of speech dispositions'. Many will remain. When we adopt one of these rather than another, we are guided by its utility in facilitating co-operation or conversation rather than by the thought that it alone assigns their 'true' meanings to expressions of the alien language.

> Two translators might develop independent manuals of translation, both of them compatible with all speech behavior, and yet one manual would offer translations that the other translator would reject. My position was that either manual could be useful, but as to which was right and which wrong there was no fact of the matter.
>
> (FM, p. 167)

Quine is not offering a description of the experience of translators. He does not hold that they actually find themselves overwhelmed by an excess of translations between which they can make no objective choice. Concrete examples of translational indeterminacy may be hard to come by. Nor is he suggesting that translation is much harder or easier than commonly supposed. He can allow that we may find one translation manual to be obviously the best and reasonably expect other translators to agree with us. Skilled translators gain access into alien languages very rapidly. Moreover, he is not making the familiar point that differences in nuance and tone mean that no translation will be wholly satisfactory; there are too many adequate translations, not too few. The problem runs deeper than that and concerns how we are to *describe* what occurs in translation. Does the translator 'discover' some objective 'fact of the matter' – about whether an alien word is *synonymous* to some word or phrase of English? Or is his choice determined by subjective, pragmatic, non-factual considerations?

This will remind the reader of themes from chapter 4. Quine's physicalism leads him to distinguish those areas of discourse that are 'fact-stating' from others best understood as involving subjective or projectivist elements. Our question here is: to what extent is meaning or translation talk required if we wish to describe the structure of reality? Must our canonical notation provide room for such idioms? Or do our choices of translation manuals reflect pragmatic, subjective considerations which require us to give a projectivist account of our practice? We naturally assume that it is an objective factual matter whether the meaning of an alien utterance is the same as that of some English sentence. Quine challenges this assumption.

Why does Quine defend this thesis? How does it relate to the semantic themes discussed in earlier chapters? The differences between Quine and Carnap concerned the explanatory value of notions like analyticity and linguistic framework in accounting for rationality, understanding and the growth of knowledge. Quine claimed that these notions lost all explanatory value once the holistic character of empirical testing was admitted. I do not think that Quine believes that abandoning the analytic/synthetic distinction commits us to the indeterminacy of translation. However, if there is such indeterminacy, it can provide further arguments against Carnap's position. If the 'facts' do not fix translation determinately, then there may be no fact over whether an alien utterance is to be translated as the 'analytic' 'vixens are foxes', or as a well confirmed but synthetic claim. Similarly, if there is no fact of the matter which of two translation manuals is correct, and if they attribute different linguistic frameworks to speakers, then it would not be a matter of fact which linguistic framework the alien speakers had. The explanatory value of talk of linguistic frameworks would then evaporate.

In an article published in 1955, Carnap attempted to respond to Quine's challenge that his approach to language was viable only if he could show how we could establish the rules employed by a speaker on the basis of observations of his verbal behaviour. He contrasted 'pure semantics' – the construction of formal systems by laying down precise syntactic and semantic rules – from 'descriptive semantics' (sometimes, confusingly in this context, described as pragmatics) – the use of semantic concepts to describe existing natural languages. In fact, Carnap questions Quine's insistence that 'a semantical concept, in order to be fruitful, must contain a prior pragmatic counterpart' (Carnap 1956, p. 235). Fortunately, he does undertake to show how his semantic notions can be employed in descriptive semantics, claiming that verbal behaviour can justify semantical descriptions of alien languages.

Consider now Quine's first 'unclear' formulation of his thesis, in *Word and Object* (p. 26):

> [Two] men could be just alike in all their dispositions to verbal behavior, and yet the meanings or ideas expressed in their identically triggered and identically sounded utterances could diverge radically, for the two men, in a wide variety of cases.

If this is correct, then Carnap's enterprise cannot succeed. It is unsurprising that the lengthy discussion of the analytic/synthetic distinction of *From a Logical Point of View* is replaced by the discussion of the indeterminacy thesis in *Word and Object*. The concern, on each occasion, is with 'how much of language can be made sense of in terms of its stimulus conditions, and what scope this leaves for empirically unconditioned variation in one's conceptual scheme' (WO, p. 26).

Quine usually discusses the special case of 'radical translation'. The radical translator is attempting to decipher an unknown language with no links to familiar ones. He cannot appeal to dictionaries or existing partial translation manuals; he cannot appeal to a practice of translation into a third language for which translations into English already exist. Nor can he profit from historical studies tracing common origins of English and the language under study. It should be obvious that this is the fundamental case: we study how semantic facts are manifested in behaviour with no risk of relying upon information which already embodies a semantic interpretation of the alien language. By abstracting from institutional frameworks involving both linguist and informant, we are free to focus upon the relations between physical fact and verbal behaviour; and these are Quine's prime concern.

8.2 THE ARGUMENTS

A translation manual is a function which maps expressions of one language onto expressions of another language. So, if T is such a function:

T('Schnee ist weiss') = 'Snow is white'.

Since most languages contain indefinitely many sentences, the function will probably break alien sentences into parts and select a translation on the basis of the parts and their arrangement in the sentence. A translation manual is adequate if the sentences which serve as argument and value (in this case, 'Schnee ist weiss' and 'Snow is white') are semantically equivalent: the traditional view is that they must be synonymous.

Quine's thesis is that between any two languages there are likely to be many translation manuals, all of which are adequate, yet which offer radically different translations of many sentences. For example, different manuals may offer as translations of the German sentence 'Schnee ist weiss' English sentences which a native English speaker would judge non-synomymous – indeed, the native English speaker may even claim that they have different truth values, one being false and the other true.

Plainly much depends upon our understanding of 'semantic equivalence' and the related notion of the adequacy of a translation manual. In 'Use and its place in meaning' Quine discusses this notion: sentences, he claims, 'are equivalent if their use is the same. Or, trying to put the matter less vaguely, we might say that they are equivalent if their utterance would be prompted by the same stimulatory situations' (TT, p. 48). As Quine admits, this is far too vague. So many factors influence linguistic behaviour that no two sentences could have exactly the same use: 'the motives for volunteering a given sentence can vary widely, and often inscrutably' (p. 48). Hence we narrow our focus: we limit our attention to 'cognitive equivalence' and ignore other aspects of meaning – Quine admits that he will say nothing about 'emotional and poetic' aspects of meaning (p. 53). We begin by trying to discover the native signs for assent and dissent. Then, in varying circumstances, we volunteer the native sentence ourselves, inviting the informant to tell us whether it is true or false, and noticing the stimulatory conditions when he does so. In order to describe these stimulatory conditions in unambiguously physical terms, Quine chooses to do so by reference to the impact of external things on the informant's nervous system 'by triggering his sensory receptors': 'the stimulation that he undergoes at any moment is the set of receptors triggered at that moment' (TT, p. 50). Two sentences are cognitively equivalent if assent to (or dissent from) them is prompted by the same stimulations. We give the stimulus meaning of a sentence when we describe those stimuli that will prompt assent to it, together with those that prompt dissent from it.

Quine holds that no physical facts other than those about stimulus meanings are relevant to translation: if a unique correct translation manual is not determined by facts about stimulus meanings, then there is no fact of the matter which manual correctly conveys the cognitive significance of sentences of the alien language: or, perhaps better, many manuals equally accurately capture this cognitive significance, choice among them depending upon practical usefulness. Evidently, this provides a very thin factual basis for translation. If Quine is right that these are the only relevant facts, his doctrine may seem unsurprising. Before looking at the defensibility of these claims about stimulus meaning, however, we should introduce the arguments Quine employs for the indeterminacy of translation. But, first, some terminology.

Occasion sentences are distinguished from *standing* sentences. The former, like

It is snowing

The newspaper has just arrived

are assented to on some occasions, but not on others. Standing sentences lack this context-relativity:

2+2=4

Snow is white

If assented to at all, they are assented to all the time. Quine acknowledges that this is not a hard and fast distinction. His chief concern is with a subset of occasion sentences – *observation* sentences. He defines this notion behaviourally: an occasion sentence is observational to the extent that all speakers assent to it in response to the same stimulations. We might expect all competent English speakers to agree about when it is snowing. The claim that it is Thursday is less observational: background knowledge is required if we are not to make a mistake. Occasion sentences cast in the vocabulary of theoretical physics form the other end of the continuum: when they can be accepted may be controversial even among the tiny minority who understand them.

A standing sentence is *stimulus analytic* when any competent speaker assents to it in any circumstances that arise: it may be a sentence traditionally described as analytic, or it may express a common-sense truism like

There are plants and animals.

Two sentences are *stimulus synonymous* when they are assented to in just the same circumstances.

Our claims about stimulus meanings are fallible, like all empirical knowledge, but observation and induction can teach us:

(a) which sentences are occasion sentences, and which are observation sentences;
(b) under what circumstances the observation sentences are accepted;
(c) which sentences are stimulus analytic and which pairs of sentences are stimulus synonymous.

Quine also suggests that we can identify truth functional connectives. This provides a bridgehead for a translation: ideally we want to translate observation sentences by sentences of our own language with the same stimulus meaning, and (presumably) stimulus analytic sentences by sentences we treat as stimulus analytic.

The first argument recalls the second milestone of empiricism, the shift of attention from terms to sentences. Stimulus meaning is a property of sentences; it does not attach a semantic property to words directly. Quine's first argument concludes that facts about stimulus meaning leave us considerable lattitude in how to segment utterances into words and how to translate individual words. As we shall see, stimulus meanings do not even enforce determinate translations for observation sentences.

We shall approach the argument indirectly. In 'Use and its place in meaning' (TT, ch. 5) Quine suggests that our familiar talk of word-synonymy *can* be grounded in stimulus meanings. Consider the synonyms 'vixen' and 'female fox'. Quine holds that, so long as we ignore direct quotation and the like, the stimulus meaning of a sentence is unaffected when an occurrence of 'vixen' is replaced by 'female fox'.

There is a vixen behind that tree

There is a female fox behind that tree

have the same stimulus meaning. So, we have a test for cognitive synonymy: terms are synonymous when substituting one for the other within a sentence never alters stimulus meaning.

This test will only detect synonyms *within* a language. Since they cannot be placed in the same 'sentence frames', we cannot apply the test to establish that the English word 'vixen' means the same as the French word 'renarde'. Application between languages would require that we had already translated the French expression corresponding to

There is a — behind that tree.

An attempt to vindicate talk of synonymy between languages which took for granted that we had synonyms for such sentence frames would be question begging – indeed, Carnap's proposals fail for just this reason.

Since there are pairs of English sentences which are plainly not synonymous but which are stimulus synonymous, this raises a serious problem for the translator. In chapter 2 of *Word and Object*, Quine considers a native utterance of an alien expression 'gavagai'. Careful observation suggests to us that the stimulus meaning of this is the same as that of the English sentence

There is a rabbit.

However, many other English sentences have the same stimulus meaning:

(1) An undetached part of a rabbit is over there.
(2) Rabbithood is instantiated over there.
(3) A stage in the history of a rabbit is over there.
(4) That spot is one mile to the left of an area of space one mile to the right of a rabbit.

Quine claims that by making compensating adjustments in our translations of the 'sentence frames' in which it occurs, we could construe some native expression as true of rabbits, of stages in the histories of rabbits, and so on. Different translation manuals thus lead to very different translations of the native utterances while compatible with all of the facts about stimulus meanings. Since translation involves assigning meanings to words and stimulus meanings attach to sentences, there is a leeway that allows for translational indeterminacy.

Since we do have tests for synonymy within a language, we can see how the different candidate translations are not synonymous. Quine's test could be applied to show how sentences 1–4 are built out of non-synonymous words. Although the argument does not provide competing translations of 'gavagai' which differ in truth value, it does provide ones which differ in their ontological commitments: (1) involves quantification over rabbit parts, (2) over the universal rabbithood, (3) over stages in the histories of rabbits, and (4) over areas of space. This argument will be examined in more detail in the next chapter; the relations between the indeterminacy thesis and Quine's account of ontological commitment will be mentioned in section 8.5 below.

In section 2 of 'Meaning and synonymy in natural languages' (1955) Carnap considers the 'pragmatical' or 'descriptive' concepts of denotation and extension. He claims that only ordinary inductive uncertainties can prevent our being confident that Karl (his informant) applies 'Hund' to dogs. Quine's first argument challenges Carnap's conclusion: from the fact that Karl only predicates 'Hund' of his experience when dogs are present, it does not follow that 'Hund' applies to dogs. Our inability to settle whether he is talking of dogs or undetached dog parts is not just inductive uncertainty. The indeterminacy remains when *all* the facts are in.

The second, deeper argument relates to milestone three: moderate holism. For the most part, facts about stimulus meanings do not reflect semantic properties of individual sentences. If I assent to a sentence when you do not, it does not follow that it has a different meaning for both of us. If, unlike me, you know that other animals are easily mistaken for rabbits, you may not share my confidence that rabbits are present. If you know about a species of rabbit fly which is unknown to me, the sight of a hovering insect may prompt you to affirm that rabbits are present while I remain agnostic. If you have the mistaken belief that a hare is a species of rabbit, then, once again, our stimulus meanings will diverge. In these cases, the divergence need not reflect a difference in meaning but rather the influence of other beliefs. Hence, we are free to offer different interpretations of sentences, so long as compensating adjustments are made in our translations of other claims. A variety of translation manuals can be reconciled with the facts.

A translation manual provides a kind of description of an overall pattern of dispositions to verbal behaviour. Owing to the holistic character of these dispositions – each reflects the impact of many beliefs – different systematic descriptions are possible which fit all the facts. This means that whichever we use, we will make just the same predictions of the speaker's dispositions to assent or dissent from sentences: they agree with the facts. On the other hand, the translation manuals differ simply in that their translations of the same native sentences are English ones which would fail any test for intra-linguistic synonymy.

It is natural to complain that Quine ignores much of the evidence available to a translator. For example, a community is more likely to have terms for rabbits than for undetached parts of rabbits or stages in their histories. Hence, the first of our putative translations for 'gavagai' looks much more promising than the others. We could easily think of similar considerations which will reduce the number of candidate hypotheses.

Interestingly, Quine agrees that we should prefer the first translation for a similar reason. He admits that linguists use 'supplementary canons' which restrict choice of translation. 'If a question were to arise over equating a short native locution to "rabbit" and a long one to "rabbit part" or vice versa, they would favor the former course, arguing that the more conspicuously segregated wholes are likelier to bear the simpler terms' (WC, p. 74). Such standards are perfectly in order, Quine suggests, 'unless mistaken for a substantive law of speech behavior'. The suggestion seems to be that the canon provides a pragmatic reason for preferring one manual over another without giving any reason for thinking it *true*. It is not a principle of evidence but rather guides us in choosing a useful manual among those that fit the facts.

Parallel remarks occur when Quine discusses what he calls the 'principle of charity'. When we attempt to move beyond the bridgehead described above, we are likely to prefer translations which maximize agreement between the aliens and ourselves: the best translation will be one that minimizes inexplicable error, enabling us to attribute to them desires or goals similar to our own. Quine's view is that such principles should not be understood as reducing the amount of indeterminacy. Rather, they represent our ways of living with the extensive indeterminacy that obtains. They are not principles of evidence: it is not a *truth* that the aliens are more likely in agreement with us than not, although Quine *may* believe that we are constrained to read our Logic into the verbal behaviour of the natives, his views on this matter are not clear (WO, p. 59, and see Davidson's interpretation, 1984, p. 136 (n. 16). Rather, it suits our *purposes* to use a translation scheme which maximizes agreement: it makes it easier for us to learn from their testimony, and helps us to co-operate with them. The justification is pragmatic.

This illustrates how Quine's arguments rely upon a distinction between two distinct sorts of considerations influencing choice of translation manual. Sensitivity to stimulus meanings is sensitivity to (physical) fact: a manual 'fits the facts' so long as it conforms to stimulus meanings. Choice also depends upon 'regulative' standards, which reflect subjective or pragmatic aspects of our concept of meaning. The role of these standards reflects a projectivist account of our ordinary talk of meanings. The judgement that one manual is better than another sometimes reflects the view that it fits the facts better; on other occasions, it expresses the sense that it better serves our practical needs in looking for a translation manual. Quine's thesis is that the first sort of consideration leaves translation indeterminate. The defensibility of his position will depend upon the acceptability of his way of drawing this distinction.

8.3 EPISTEMOLOGICAL UNDERDETERMINATION, ONTOLOGICAL INDETERMINACY

At risk of labouring a point which might already be obvious, I want to clarify Quine's thesis by considering a popular objection to it. Many commentators take his point to be epistemological: more than one manual of translation will always be compatible with our best *evidence* of speakers' verbal behaviour. They then complain that, since Quine does not take the parallel phenomenon that physics is underdetermined by evidence to refute a realist understanding of physics, he has no reason to take these observations to undermine the objectivity of meaning (e.g. Chomsky 1969, Rorty 1972).

Although the misreading is understandable, it is clear that Quine's point is not primarily epistemological: his claim is not that correct translation is underdetermined by available evidence, but rather that it is not determined by the *facts*. In light of his physicalist conception of 'the facts', he holds that correctness of translation manuals (and semantic claims generally) is not fixed by physics. All of his discussions bear this interpretation, but it is clearest in 'Things and their place in theories':

> suppose, to make things vivid, that we are settling . . . for a physics of elementary particles and recognize a dozen or so basic states or relations in which they may stand. Then when I say there is no fact of the matter as regards, say, the two rival manuals of translation, what I mean is that both manuals are compatible with all the same distributions of states and relations over elementary particles. In a word, they are physically equivalent.
>
> (TT, p. 23)

Hence, Quine has several times stressed that, while theory choice in physics is not determined by all possible evidence, his point now is that, once we have made a choice of physical theory, our choice of translation manual is still open. The illusion that his point is epistemological is encouraged by his views about which physical facts are relevant to questions about translation. His stress upon behavioural notions like stimulus meaning does not reflect an interest in what is epistemologically fundamental in attempting to discover the meanings of someone's utterances. Rather, his claim is that the only physical facts which could possibly be relevant to fixing the correctness of translation manuals are facts about stimulus meanings. The point is ontological rather than epistemological. He holds that a unique correct translation manual is not determined by facts about stimulus meaning. And he also holds that if a unique correct translation manual is not determined by facts about stimulus meanings, then neither is it determined by physical facts. Ordinary talk about synonymy and translation is not determined by physical facts, so it is not factual discourse.

If the objection misses the point, it does not follow that Quine's thesis has been proved. It can be disputed in several ways. For example, we could argue that facts about stimulus meaning do determine a unique best translation manual. More promisingly, we could question whether facts about stimulus meanings are the only physical facts relevant to these semantic issues. Perhaps information about the structure of the brain is relevant too: once we look into the neurophysiological process involved in perception or inference, we may be forced to construe a particular utterance as about rabbits rather than rabbit parts.

The restriction to stimulus meanings reflects Quine's sense that he is an heir to the empiricist tradition, defending a moderate empiricism freed from indefensible traditional dogmas. Stimulus meanings relate judgements to undiluted, unconceptualized experience, even if the notion of 'experience' is transformed into physiological terms which have no direct links with conscious awareness. But why should we accept that these are the only relevant physical facts?

Bearing in mind that Quine's interest is in the cognitive significance of expressions in a 'scientific' language, we should turn to Quine's supposed scientific claims about what science is. We have noticed these before. They emerge most clearly in 'Things and their place in theories':

> Our talk of external things, our very notion of things, is just a conceptual apparatus that helps us to foresee and control the triggering of our sensory receptors in the light of previous triggering of our sensory receptors.
>
> (TT, p. 1)

If this is viewed as a claim about the role of science in general, it would follow that scientific language is best understood as an instrument for securing predictive control over our sensory input. The notion of stimulus meaning, it then seems, records the sole relevant features of the impact of reality upon our cognitive activities. If this is what physics teaches us about physics, then we can see some foundation for Quine's conception of the facts of translation.

Another consideration surfaces in 'Facts of the matter', where Quine considers the (tempting) suggestion that facts of neurophysiology, which certainly have a role in *explaining* verbal behaviour, could be invoked to choose between competing manuals. His response: 'Since translators do not supplement their behavioral criteria with neurological criteria, much less with telepathy, what excuse could there be for supposing that one manual conformed to any distribution of elementary physical states better than the other manual?' (FM, p. 167). If translators would not judge brain scan equipment relevant to their exercise, it is implausible that information only obtained through such a scan could be what makes one manual correct and another incorrect. It is unsurprising that some commentators mistakenly ascribe to Quine an epistemological thesis: an appeal to the sorts of things that could possibly be treated as evidence for the correctness of a translation manual is used to establish what sorts of physical facts could possibly determine its correctness.

We must return to the foundations for Quine's behaviourist naturalistic approach to language below. It is important to notice here that his argument for the indeterminacy of translation ultimately appears to rest upon it. If we find the indeterminacy thesis unsatisfactory, we may have to re-examine Quine's physicalism. The scientistic vision that grounds it may eventually prove to be the weak link in Quine's system.

These are topics for subsequent chapters. In the remainder of this one, we shall consider the philosophical consequences of the indeterminacy thesis.

8.4 CONSEQUENCES: MIND AND MEANING

Semantic notions are of two sorts. Those from the theory of reference are properly extensional: Quine has no hesitation in making use of them in logic and philosophy of language. Concepts belonging to the theory of meaning or sense – such as synonymity and analyticity – are intensional. They resist capture in Quine's extensional canonical notation, and he thinks that responsible philosophers should spurn them. In this section, we consider the bearing of the indeterminacy of translation upon some intensional notions. Section 8.5 turns to reference and truth.

Our ordinary concept of mind seems to be irredeemably intensional. We explain actions in terms of propositional attitudes such as belief and desire, and our ordinary practices for describing and explaining mental events presuppose that we can identify the propositional contents of these states. We normally rely upon two sorts of evidence in doing this: we observe the behaviour of the agents, attempting to guess their beliefs and desires from what they do; and we attend to their avowals, treating their utterances as manifesting their beliefs and desires. If Quine's arguments work, the behavioural dispositions we thus uncover do not fix the contents of propositional attitudes like beliefs. Most straightforwardly, if translation is indeterminate, there is no fact concerning which propositional content is expressed by an assertion. Verbal behaviour fixes the propositional contents of beliefs only relative to a translation manual. When we ascribe a belief to somebody, we specify its content by using a sentence: it is the belief that *there are rabbits in the garden*, or that *snow is white*. If that sentence does not express a determinate content, then we have not assigned a definite content to the belief through using it.

If the indeterminacy thesis is correct, then propositional attitudes have no place in the scientific study of mind and language. For, according to that thesis, it will be indeterminate what the content of any particular utterance or psychological state is. As Quine has stressed, the indeterminacy of translation underwrites his rejection of such intensional entities as senses, propositions and attributes. If it is correct, we can attach no sense to the question whether we are confronted with two propositions or one: it is indeterminate whether two utterances have the same content (SWP, p. 238).

Parallel remarks can be made about other semantical or intensional notions like possibility and necessity. There is likely to be no fact of the matter whether a given sentence expresses what we intuitively take to be an analytic or necessary truth or whether it expresses what we take to be contingent. If the indeterminacy thesis is correct, then there is no basis for assigning determinate intensional contents to propositions. And if we cannot do that, we cannot assign determinate necessarily true contents to them.

In consequence, Quine's idea of a science of mind and language is tough-mindedly extensional. It uses behavioural and physiological language and remains close to the behaviourist approach to the mental that Quine learned from J. B. Watson in the 1920s. In a much-quoted passage, Quine remarks that his arguments for translational indeterminacy resemble arguments used by the proto-phenomenologist Brentano. The latter took the irreducibility of intentional notions (i.e. concepts like belief and desire and meaning) to physical ones as refuting naturalistic or physicalistic approaches to mind. Quine differs:

> One may accept the Brentano thesis either as showing the indispensability of intentional idioms and the importance of an autonomous science of intention, or as showing the baselessness of intentional idioms and the emptiness of a science of intention. My attitude, unlike Brentano's, is the second.
>
> (WO, p. 221)

Talk of such 'intentions' or contents requires us to postulate objective translation relations. These promise little explanatory insight, and their postulation receives little justification from the fact that it is required by 'the vernacular of semantics or intention'.

Many readers may feel that this consequence of the indeterminacy thesis – apparently, the overthrow of our everyday conception of mind – shows that something has gone wrong. It may reinforce the feeling that the focus on stimulus meanings was unduly self-denying and was bound to yield a distorted and impoverished picture of meaning and mind.

8.5 CONSEQUENCES: REFERENCE AND TRUTH

The indeterminacy thesis also affects the ways in which we can think about reference, truth and ontological commitment. When the native mutters 'gavagai', what ontological commitments does he incur? What is he talking about? Quine suggests that adequate translation manuals can be constructed according to which he is talking of rabbits, of rabbit parts, of rabbit stages. So there is no objective fact of the matter what his ontological commitments are: different translation manuals will deliver different ontological commitments. The inscrutability of reference is the doctrine that the referents of terms in an alien language and the range of the quantifiers is not determined by physical or behavioural facts. Statements about the ontological commitments of theories will always be relative to translation manuals.

If the reader imagines that this point relates only to our understanding of alien languages through radical translation, then the depth of this claim will be missed. The same claims can be made of the English speaker's understanding of other English speakers – and, indeed, of his understanding of his own idiolect. 'The resort to a remote language,' we are told, ' was not really essential. On deeper reflection, radical translation begins at home.' (OR, p. 46).

In understanding other English speakers, our normal practice involves the 'homophonic rule': if I hear people say 'There is a rabbit' I take them to mean just that, rather than 'There is an undetached rabbit part'.

> The homophonic rule is a handy one on the whole. That it works so well is no accident, since imitation and feedback are what propagate a language. We acquired a great fund of basic words and phrases in this way, imitating our elders and encouraged by our elders amid external circumstances to which the phrases suitably apply. Homophonic

> translation is implicit in this social method of learning. Departure from homophonic translation in this quarter would only hinder communication.
> (OR, p. 46)

As Quine notes, we do sometimes abandon homophonic translation, preferring to read misunderstanding or idiosyncrasy into others' usage in order to avoid concluding that they hold some absurdly false belief. But it is clear that homophonic translation has a role in the domestic case to which nothing corresponds in radical translation.

Quine denies that this special role is to be explained by saying that the homophonic translation uniquely captures the facts about what our fellows mean. If we wished, especially when we move away from sentences in whose use we received explicit training, we could interpret our fellows non-homophonically while respecting all of the truths about stimulus meanings. By systematically reinterpreting words and constructions of English, I *could* take an utterance of 'There is a rabbit' to be about rabbit parts. Other than relative to a translation manual, there is no fact of the matter about what ontological commitments other English speakers incur by their statements. 'In short, we can reproduce the inscrutability of reference at home . . . The problem at home differs none from radical translation ordinarily so called except in the willfulness of this suspension of homophonic translation' (OR, p. 47).

Quine's underlying point may still elude the reader, for this may suggest a picture whereby each individual speaks a kind of private idiolect with determinate meanings and fixed ontological commitments. The problems would concern how these are matched up for purposes of public communication. Reflection should make clear that Quine denies that even what *I* say has any determinate meaning for me: the ontological commitments of my own assertions are inscrutable to me. I can systematically reinterpret my own utterances and conclude that 'rabbit' in my mouth is true of rabbit parts or stages. The conclusion is that there is no fact of the matter about the ontological commitments of any sentence of theory. All we do is provide statements of the ontological commitments of one sentence by interpreting it in another sentence of the same or another language. This can be philosophically interesting, but its importance – and absolute validity – should not be exaggerated. A different adequate manual of translation or interpretation could have led to a different result; and the significance of the terms used in stating what these ontological commitments are is itself subject to the indeterminacy of translation. The conclusion: there is no objective fact of the matter what we are talking about.

If Quine's indeterminacy thesis is correct, then there may be no fact of the matter whether a sentence is true or false, other than relative to a translation manual. We are familiar with the claim that sentences employing, for example, vague terms have no determinate truth value. But the present point does not depend upon phenomena like vagueness which can be viewed as semantic imperfections. It concerns perfectly ordinary sentences, albeit ones from the more theoretical reaches of our conceptual scheme.

I shall illustrate this through what may seem an unconvincing example, suggested by a case discussed by Quine in a different connection. The illustration will be valuable because it will show us how weak the constraints are which stimulus meanings impose about the adequacy of translation manuals. Consider two words which never occur in observation sentences: 'proton' and 'neutron'. Imagine that, in translating the utterances of a physicist, we depart from homophonic translation in just one respect. We translate his utterances of 'proton' by 'neutron' and vice versa. The result will be: most of the things we take to be true of protons, he takes to be true of neutrons; and most of the things we take to be true of neutrons, he takes to be true of protons. According to this 'translation manual', he is massively mistaken.

Since these words do not occur in observation reports, the two manuals will agree about the stimulus meanings of all observation sentences. However, they will differ over what is stimulus analytic. Only one of the manuals will carry 'Neutrons carry no electric charge' into a sentence we take to be stimulus analytic. This may be enough to ensure that the deviant manual is false, although – accompanied by a statement of what the agents believe – it is perfectly adequate for identifying their dispositions to verbal behaviour. We can account for dispositions to verbal behaviour equally well by insisting that speakers all believe to be true something we take to be controversial as by revealing that they believe what we take to be stimulus analytic. Otherwise we could not decide that a community is universally confident of what we know is false – e.g. of the flatness of the earth. Both manuals are effective at identifying the relevant physical facts. Of course, no sensible person would adopt the non-homophonic one. The principle of charity is against it: we should interpret our subject's utterances in order to minimize inexplicable error. But, according to Quine, this principle is not a substantive law of linguistic behaviour. Rather, it is a regulative maxim which guides our practical choice of which translation manual to use. So far as the *facts* are concerned, it may be indeterminate which is correct, and thus indeterminate whether his utterance of 'Neutrons carry no electric charge' is an obviously true claim about neutrons or an obviously false one about protons. There is no objective fact of the matter as to the truth value of his utterance.

If a manual is 'false' when there is another which is better at preserving stimulus analyticity, then the example does not illustrate how the indeterminacy of translation can leave it indeterminate what truth value a statement has. Quine sometimes suggests that he would accept this criterion of adequacy for translations – although, for reasons indicated in the previous paragraph, I am uncertain how well motivated this is. His grounds for unease about such examples is also clear from the discussion in, for example, TT, p. 29. However, even if we do abandon this example, there might be more complex cases of the same general kind. For example, it may be impossible to translate all the sentences taken to be stimulus analytic as stimulus analytic (or even true) ones of our language. Alternative manuals may then be available which resolve this in different ways, so that a given sentence is mapped onto a true sentence acording to one, and onto a false sentence according to another.

Alternatively, manuals may offer different translations for a standing sentence about which the aliens are undecided. We could be certain that the two translations differ in truth value even if we are unsure which is true. This would be enough to establish Quine's point. For present purposes, we need only the weak conclusion that Quine's account of the factual basis for translation does not guarantee that this will not happen. And that seems to be so.

My concern in this chapter has been to present some of the principal elements of Quine's controversial doctrine. It will be evident that it leaves intact very little of our familiar concept of mind, and undermines most of the traditional aspirations of philosophy. We are left with an impoverished, highly naturalistic, vocabulary for describing and explaining human practices, including the search for knowledge. The Humean picture, that many features of our discourse project our subjective or practical concerns onto reality, rather than being designed for the description of reality, extends to our ordinary styles of talk about meaning and mind.

We naturally feel that these arguments constitute a *reductio ad absurdum* of something, although it is hard to see quite what. Do we have a refutation of a certain picture of philosophy, of a philosophical conception of fact, of physicalism, of a distinctive view of what physicalism involves, or of a particular account of which physical facts are relevant to claims about mind and meaning? In the remaining chapters, I want to explore in more detail the issue of how one can dissent from Quine's position, in the hope of focusing more clearly upon the precise nature of the challenge his work presents for contemporary philosophy.

9

Translation and Explanation

9.1 INTRODUCTION

We shall now explore one of Quine's arguments for the indeterminacy of translation in more detail. After introducing the structure of the argument in section 9.2, we shall discuss some objections. This serves two purposes: considering possible Quinean responses to them clarifies the structure of his position; and we also begin to move towards an understanding of how his conclusions can be resisted.

The argument in question was introduced in the previous chapter. It builds on the observation that the stimulus meanings of sentences do not fix the translations of the words that they contain. By making compensating adjustments in our translations of other expressions, we can defend alternative translations – even of observation sentences – which agree with all the facts about stimulus meanings but offer markedly different translations of alien sentences. Even their ontological commitments are not determined. The argument is the one about rabbits, and we now turn to a closer look at it.

9.2 RABBITS

When considering how to translate 'gavagai', once it is established that its stimulus meaning corresponds to that of our 'There is a rabbit', two questions have to be asked. First: is it used to talk of *objects* at all? Secondly, if it is used to talk about objects, which objects is it actually used to talk about?

We must distinguish several kinds of general terms. Count nouns like 'rabbit', 'table', 'proton' divide their reference. We think of them as applying to definite objects and as incorporating principles which fix when one object ends and another begins. We can answer questions about how many rabbits there are in a certain vicinity. The claim that there is a white rabbit nearby is correct only if whiteness fills the boundaries of at least one whole rabbit. We use such expressions to identify *objects*.

A mass term, like 'snow' or 'water', similarly picks out a physical feature of our surroundings, but it does not divide its reference. We can talk of snow or water while making no sense of where one water starts and another finishes. The question 'How many snows are there in the garden' makes no sense. Rather we ask *how much* snow there is.

Terms like 'white' or 'furry' are primarily predicative in function. They are not used to identify or refer to portions of our environment but rather to characterize objects or stuffs that have already been referred to, as when we say

The rabbits are furry

The snow in the garden is white

There are terms (sometimes called 'feature-placing') which are neither count nouns nor mass terms, but which are not simply used to characterize things that have already been identified. We can say

It is cold

for example, with no suggestion that there is any thing of stuff that we are saying is cold. The claim simply signals the presence of coldness. It is not impossible that people could have a term which similarly signalled the presence of rabbits without referring to rabbits or objects – they might say, for example,

It is rabbity.

So, the first question we have to ask, when trying to translate 'gavagai', concerns whether it involves a term of 'divided' reference – rather than a mass term or, simply, a term like 'rabbity'. Is it used to talk about *objects* at all? Once it is settled that it is used to speak of objects, the second question arises: which objects belong to its extension? What basis for settling questions of 'how many' does it embody? Does it refer to rabbits, stages in the histories of rabbits, parts of rabbits?

Quine appears to believe that the facts about stimulus meaning do not give a determinate answer to either of these questions. It will be indeterminate whether a term in an alien language is a term that divides its reference, a mass term, or a term like 'rabbity'. And, once we have decided to treat it as a term that divides its reference, it will be indeterminate how it does so – there will be no fact about *which* objects it refers to.

If all we have to go on is the individual utterance and its stimulus meaning, then this seems plausible. The position is complicated because words or phrases drawn from the utterance also occur in other utterances. Since we seek a systematic translation manual which accounts for an indefinite number of sentences, we shall form what Quine calls 'analytical hypotheses', breaking sentences into words or morphemes and grounding translations of sentences in our translations of their parts. The translation we give of a word will have to account for its behaviour in all of the sentences in which it occurs. This will restrict our freedom in proposing different eccentric translations. Thus, Quine admits that if an expression occurs in contexts like

There are three Fs

That F is the same as the one we saw yesterday

There is only one F present

then we have no choice but to interpret it as a term of divided reference.

Moreover, since the following pairs of sentences have different stimulus meanings, we shall be limited too in our choice of translation for the alien term in question:

1a There are three rabbits
1b There are three undetached parts of rabbits

2a That rabbit is the same as the one that I saw yesterday
2b That stage in the history of a rabbit is part of the same animal as the one I saw yesterday

Once we take into account the systematic structure of sentences – and we observe how the term occurs in connection with statements of identity and quantification – then we have no choice but to translate 'gavagai' as a statement about rabbits.

Quine agrees that we should not treat a term as dividing its reference unless we find it occurring in identity statements and quantificational statements. However, he does not view the observations of the last paragraph as a refutation of his position. The argument assumed that the translation of alien expressions corresponding to 'there are three' and 'is the same as the one that I saw yesterday' was itself determinate. But that would beg the question against him. The translation of 'gavagai' as a claim about the undetached parts of rabbits can only be sustained if the expression previously translated 'there are three' is translated as something like 'there are three animals which are composed of'; 1c is stimulus synonymous to 1a:

1c There are three animals which are composed of undetached rabbit parts.

If what is normally translated 'is the same animal' is translated 'is a part of the same animal', then we obtain 2c, which is stimulus synonymous to 2a:

2c That rabbit stage is a part of the same animal as the rabbit stage we saw yesterday.

This is supposed to illustrate how systematic adjustments in the most 'natural' scheme of translation can yield another which is compatible with all of the facts. Quine supposes that similar ingenuity may even allow us to translate 'gavagai' as involving a feature-placing term.

It is important to remember that Quine is not disputing that we would be crazy to prefer a translation manual which yielded 1c or 2c to one that yielded 1a and 2a. His point is that the choice between them does not rest upon preference for the manual that is actually *true*: the choice is grounded in pragmatic considerations. The more natural manual is much easier to work with. It makes it easier to co-operate with the aliens and learn from them: we are spared the feeling that they conceptualize their experience in a radically alien fashion.

The reader will probably object that this is insufficient to establish Quine's point. Once we take into account *all* of the systematic relations between the sentences of the alien languages, it will be claimed, it soon becomes clear that many of these proposals will not work. For example, if the aliens also say things 'naturally' translated as:

3a There are three books on my desk

the translation manual that gave rise to 1c will provide some absurdity such as 3b or (hardly better) 3c.

3b There are three animals which are composed of books on my desk
3c There are three animals which are composed of undetached parts of books on my desk

If the expression normally translated 'there are three' is used to talk about anything but rabbits (or other animals) the alternative translation we proposed will not do. It is a tall order to provide an alternative translation manual which will account for all of these complexities and interrelations.

I think that this objection is misplaced, and sympathize with Gareth Evans when he suggests that 'It is a quarrelsome man who would bicker with Quine over the indeterminacy of translation – the constraints upon that enterprise being so slight' (1985, p. 26). My response to the objection will appear *ad hoc* – and it is not a response which, so far as I am aware, Quine has used. However, it will be valuable for pointing us towards the underlying philosophical source of Quine's position. Imagine that the alien language contains a sentence containing two parts: Q^R ('^' expresses the concatenation of expressions). The 'natural' translation manual (T1) says:

T1(Q) = 'There are three'

T1(R) = 'Rabbit'

Thus, T1(Q^R) = 'There are three rabbits'.

Our alternative manual (T2) tells us that

T2(R) = 'Undetached rabbit part'.

The objection assumed that

T2(Q) = 'There are three animals composed of

and then objected that this would not work if Q occurred with terms other than R. But T2 could offer a more complex translation of Q. For example:

T2(Q) = (a) There are three animals composed of', when Q occurs 'together with' R
(b) 'There are three' in all other cases

With a few similar adjustments, we shall have a translation manual which calls for translation of 'gavagai' as about undetached rabbit parts and which respects all the facts about stimulus meaning. Adopting this manual does not limit our capacity to predict which sentences will be assented to in which circumstances: the speakers' 'verbal dispositions' are equally captured.

We find this *ad hoc* because, while T1 accounts for the translation of Q through a single clause, T2 needs an additional clause to deal specifically with statements about rabbits and their parts. But, while this does show that T1 is *simpler* than T2 and that it will be easier to use, it does not show that T1 is true and T2 false. Simplicity is a pragmatic consideration which influences our choice of manual without reflecting faithfulness to the facts.

The reader may still feel that we have failed to do justice to his sense that there is something wrong or *ad hoc* about T2. In order to respond to this, we shall examine a criticism of Quine's argument offered by Gareth Evans, in his paper 'Identity and predication' (1985; this rich and challenging paper contains much fascinating material besides the arguments that I shall discuss). I shall argue that his criticisms do not succeed against the position Quine defends. However, reflection upon them will help us to identify some of the more debatable aspects of Quine's position.

9.3 TRANSLATION AND MEANING

As should be clear by now, a translation manual is simply a mapping from expressions to expressions. It tells us that

'Rouge' is the French translation of German 'rot'

'Snow' is the English translation of German 'Schnee'

As the first of these indicates, someone could know such truths about translation without thereby understanding 'rouge': the statement explains the meaning of 'rouge' only to someone who already understands the German word 'rot'. The translation manual simply tells us which pairs of expressions have the same meaning; it does not tell us what they mean.

Some philosophers aspire to a theory which offers more than this; it should *explain* the meanings of expressions and show how they relate to the world. For each expression of the language under study, the theory would provide a statement of what it means:

'Rouge', in French, means red

'Bachelor' means unmarried male

and so on. One could not understand such a statement without coming to understand the quoted expression. As we shall shortly see, such a theory is likely to talk about the circumstances in which a sentence is true, about what names and predicates refer to, and to use other semantical concepts.

Evans shares this aspiration, and he holds that Quine's arguments are philosophically important only if they point towards an indeterminacy in the theory of meaning. He denies that they do this. Whereas the translator can divide a sentence or phrase into parts in any way which he finds convenient for his practical task of setting up a mapping between expressions, the theorist of meaning 'aims to uncover a structure in the language that mirrors the competence speakers of the language have actually acquired' (pp. 25–6). The theorist of meaning, or semanticist, wants to explain how the meanings of sentences depend upon the semantic properties of their parts. The most important point is that a theory of meaning – unlike a translation manual – is an *explanatory theory*. The demand that we provide good explanations of semantic competence rules out theories which entail that the aliens are talking about rabbit stages or undetached rabbit parts, in the cases which we have been discussing.

I shall sketch what a theory of this sort might look like, before introducing Evans's objection to Quine's argument. The general pattern of explanation will be familiar from earlier chapters. Suppose a simple language contains two predicates F and G, and two names a and b, as well as a negation operator '~' and a conjunction operator '&'. The meanings of the names and predicates can be given through axioms such as

a denotes Ceasar

b denotes Brutus

(x) x satisfies F (or 'F is true of (or applies to) x') if and only if x is brave

(x) x satisfies G if and only if x is tall

The semantic significance of the simplest mode of sentence formation can be captured by an axiom like

T^w is true if and only if the denotation of w satisfies T

With the aid of this theory, we can prove

Fa is true if, and only if, Caesar is brave.

A statement of the truth conditions of a sentence which is derived, in this way, from the axioms of the semantic theory is taken to give the meaning of the sentence in question. Axioms for our operators might take the following form:

~S is true if and only if S is not true

S & T is true if and only if S and T are both true

It is hoped that the construction of theory of this sort, which will do justice to the complexity of a natural language, will provide revealing insights into the underlying logical structure of our language and into our ontological commitments.

I hope that this conveys the general idea of such a theory. In fact an adequate theory will be much more complex than this simple model suggests. For example, in order to account for our competence with tense and indexical expressions, it is likely that the theorems will state when sentences are true only relative to a context:

'I was here yesterday' is true (when uttered by u at time t and at place p) if and only if u was at p one day before t.

But we shall ignore these complexities.

Compare the following axioms for an alien predicate H:

(x)(x satisfies H if, and only if, H is a rabbit)

(x)(x satisfies H if and only if H is an undetached part of a rabbit)

Evans criticizes the claim that if there is an adequate theory of meaning for a language incorporating the first axiom, then there will be another such theory, incorporating the second, which is cognitively (if not pragmatically) equivalent to the first. Unless this claim is true, Quine's argument does not prove that there is indeterminacy in the theory of meaning.

The claim is false, according to Evans, because use of the second axiom will leave us unable to give a correct account of the truth conditions of some complex sentences in which H occurs. I can only illustrate the kind of argument that he uses. The term H, he points out, will also occur together with other predicates, like W, which is naturally translated 'white'. Our theory will tell us, on the basis of its axioms for W and H, that

(x) (x satisfies W^H if and only if x is a white rabbit).

What axiom for W will enable us to attach the right sort of meaning to W^H, if we adopt the second axiom for H?

The problem is that the meaning of W^H appears to be sensitive to the boundaries of rabbits. The theorem

(x) (x satisfies W^H if, and only if, x is a white undetached rabbit part)

would get stimulus meanings wrong: it allows W^H to be satisfied by a white foot on an otherwise brown rabbit, while, we assume, W^H is assented to only in the resence of a wholly white rabbit. Hence, it looks as though our axiom for W must be

(x)(x satisfies W if and only if x is a part of a white animal).

But that will prevent our making good sense of statements about white pieces of paper or white handkerchiefs.

Our discussion in the previous section suggests a response that Evans does not consider. As no more than a first approximation to a satisfactory response, we could consider:

> (x)(x satisfies W if, and only if, either
> (a) W occurs 'together with' H and x is a part of a white animal

or

> (b) W occurs in some other context and x is white).

The vague 'occurs together with' would have to be made more precise, and it is possible that the attempt to develop this proposal consistently would run into technical dificulties. However, it is not obvious that such *ad hoc* manoeuvres could not be employed to overcome the difficulties that Evans raises.

We shall obviously prefer a theory which incorporates a simpler axiom, like:

> (x)(x satisfies W if and only if x is white).

The crucial question, taken up in the next section, concerns our grounds for this preference. Are they 'factual' or simply pragmatic? We shall find that the underlying difference between Quine and Evans surfaces in their contrasting responses to this question. Evans conception of a 'theory of meaning' – which is as a kind of explanatory theory – imposes requirements which would rule out such proposals. Quine's defence of the indeterminacy of translation depends upon a rejection of that conception.

9.4 PSYCHOLOGICAL THEORY AND THE THEORY OF MEANING

Evans relies upons two fundamental claims. Firstly, attempting to understand a language by constructing a theory of meaning is a very different activity from developing a translation manual. He thinks that it is a deeper, more fundamental inquiry, and that translation manuals should be answerable to the kinds of facts uncovered by theories of meaning. A semanticist is looking for an *explanation* of linguistic behaviour, and the structure he finds in phrases and sentences is understood in terms of its role in these explanations. The translator is not engaged in explanation at all: he simply wants a useful manual which will facilitate communication.

Secondly, Evans holds that once we turn to the construction of a theory of meaning for a language, we should prefer theories like the 'natural' one to the *ad hoc* variant on the grounds that they provide better explanations of verbal behaviour. Furthermore, if one theory provides better explanations than a second, then the second is false: explanatory power is an indication of truth.

I shall argue that Quine would reject both of these views. He may agree that approaching a problem of radical translation by trying to construct a 'truth theory' for the alien language is an important and good idea. He will also agree that we would be crazy not to prefer the 'natural' theory to the *ad hoc* one. But he would not attach any 'cognitive' significance to these judgments. The different approaches fit the *facts* equally well. The preferred choices are justified on pragmatic grounds.

Before defending these claims, let us look at how Evans would defend the 'natural' theory of meaning. In the background lies a point familiar to philosophers. The construction of a meaning theory or translation manual for a language alludes to regularities in the linguistic behaviour of its speakers. Our natural and *ad hoc* theories characterize the same regularities in dispositions to assent to or dissent from sentences: they simply describe those regularities in more or less complex ways. If speakers self-consciously reflected upon explicit rules in deciding what to say – so that a set of semantic rules could reveal the mechanisms involved in linguistic competence – then a substantive question of fact would lie behind our choice of theory. Although both characterize regularities to which linguistic behaviour conforms, only the natural theory (let us suppose) gives us the rules that actually *guide* or govern linguistic behaviour. We prefer the theory which reveals the 'mechanisms' of linguistic competence. The preferred theory reveals the 'knowledge' which explains linguistic behaviour.

The suggestion that language use rests upon the conscious application of rules has no plausibility. However, some people retain the view that semantic theories reveal rules which 'govern' linguistic behaviour: they claim that the theories formulate rules which are 'implicitly' or 'tacitly' or 'unconsciously' known to speakers. Quine holds that talk of unconscious or tacit knowledge, of our behaviour being *governed* by rules of which we are not consciously aware, is – at best – suggestive metaphor. In 'Semantic competence and tacit knowledge', Evans dissents from this view. He proposes that 'we construe the claim that someone tacitly knows a theory of meaning as ascribing to that person a set of dispositions – one corresponding to each of the expressions for which the theory provides a distinct axiom' (1985, p. 328). This talk of dispositions is to be taken in a 'full blooded sense', so that claims about tacit knowledge are more than 'simple statements of regularity' (p. 329). To each disposition corresponds 'a single state of the subject which figures in a causal explanation of why he reacts in a regular way to all the sentences containing' the expression in question (p. 330).

In other words, theories of meaning point towards a system of dispositions which will provide *psychological explanations* of linguistic behaviour: we are moving towards a form of cognitive psychology. While the natural theory hypothesizes a single dispositional state underlying all uses of the term W, the more *ad hoc* theory finds two underlying states: one is introduced to explain linguistic behaviour when the subject is talking of rabbit stages, and the other is introduced to explain other cases. If that is correct, we can choose between the two theories by noting which provides the best explanation of the subject's linguistic behaviour and which fits best into all the other things we know about his psychology. For example, if we find that initial training in how to use W equips an alien child to do so in all contexts – there is no need for separate training in how to use the term in connection with rabbit stages and how to use it for other purposes – then we shall conclude that the natural theory will fit best into a general psychological theory which accounts for language learning and colour perception in a satisfying way. The child acquires a single disposition which is responsible for all its uses of the term W.

This kind of point seems so obvious, and seems to undermine Quine's argument so effectively, that we may wonder how Quine was convinced by his rabbit example. It is surprising, too, that he has never seriously addressed this challenge: it is as if he thinks it so obviously ineffective that it does not merit serious attention. Before looking at why he might think this, let us remind ourselves of two elements in the response. The first is that a theory of meaning should be looked upon as an *explanatory* theory of linguistic behaviour rather than as recording regularities useful in translation. Secondly, it achieves this explanatory function by identifying dispositions which are further clarified in a psychology of the cognitive processes: an explanatory theory of the mechanics of mind tells us more about the dispositions which are introduced by the axioms of a theory of meaning. Why should Quine be uneasy about these?

It seems that Quine's argument must rest upon rejecting the demand that a translation manual or theory of meaning should contribute to a satisfying psychological explanation of speakers' verbal behaviour. It is sufficient that it accurately describes their verbal dispositions. There are other ways of illustrating this point. Suppose we accept a translation manual which leads us to regard 'gavagai' as referring to undetached rabbit parts. It is very likely that, according to such a manual, the aliens will have no term which refers specifically to rabbits at all. We can make sense of this only by ascribing to them a very curious psychology: they are perceptually sensitive to undetached rabbit parts without being perceptually sensitive to rabbits; they go to the market to buy undetached rabbit parts because they desire to eat undetached rabbit part pie. Unger makes this point clearly:

> Suppose you want a rabbit for a pet. In that your thoughts connect with language, your desires should be most clearly expressed in your own words. If I translate your 'gavagai' as indicated, I will describe to you some such desire as wanting to have undetached rabbit parts around to fondle. But this makes your thinking, which is, in fact, sane and commonplace, seem either mad or else exceptionally complex, like the technical thought of a metaphysician.
>
> (1984, p. 18)

Some of Quine's suggested translations lead us to attribute desires and beliefs to people which are psychologically absurd. And the problem does not vanish if our translation manual views another word, perhaps used less frequently, as applying to rabbits.

In the same spirit, it has been suggested by Putnam and others that according to many of the more bizarre translation manuals which are deemed to 'fit the facts', agents will emerge as employing arguments and relying upon deliberations which we will find crazy (Putnam 1975, p. 169). Quine's conception of the facts which are relevant to translation fails to account for the role of such considerations in choice of translation manual. Our understanding of human perceptual capacities, of the nature of human desire, and of the psychology of reasoning and deliberation – as well as sociological and anthropological information – all seem relevant to choice of translation manual. The arguments for translational indeterminacy depend upon ignoring all of these factors. It is almost as if Quine had moved from the obvious truth that the evidence for translation consists solely of behaviour to the far more questionable claim that a translation manual is correct so long as it 'fits' the behaviour. It seems plain that among the manuals which fit behaviour, some will serve better than others as a means to finding satisfying explanations of behaviour.

9.5 PHYSICALISM AND PSYCHOLOGICAL EXPLANATION

Evans's position incorporates three distinct elements.

(1) Cognitive psychology and semantic theory enjoy a kind of *explanatory autonomy*. Hence, we will prefer theories of meaning for languages when they offer better explanations of linguistic behaviour than their rivals.
(2) These explanations offer *causal* accounts of the underlying processes involved in human behaviour.
(3) These autonomous causal explanations are properly understood as revealing to us some aspect of *reality*.

While Quine would agree that true causal explanations of behaviour are to be interpreted realistically, he denies the possibility of an autonomous intentional psychological theory. Recall our discussion at the end of chapter 4. We saw that Quine believed that all facts were physical facts, and all explanation was physical explanation. Explanations in non-basic sciences, like economics, do not reveal facets of reality: they gesture towards little understood physical mechanisms; or they organize physical facts according to subjective criteria that reflect our interests. Hence, unless psychological explanations simply allude to physical mechanisms, they do not enhance our knowledge of (physical) reality. This is the key to his arguments for the indeterminacy of translation. The criteria which suggest that one translation manual offers 'better explanations' of linguistic behaviour than another reflect subjective (or 'pragmatic') concerns: they reflect the uses to which we put translations rather than pointing us towards translation manuals which offer a better insight into underlying physical mechanisms.

In this, as we have seen, Quine is close to the outlook of traditional behaviourism, which held that the only scientifically respectable descriptions and explanations of behaviour are cast in a vocabulary reducible to the terms of physics. Indeed, it is easy to view Quine's position as a combination of two claims. First, the metaphysical assumptions of traditional behaviourism are unassailable. Secondly, the behaviourist outlook cannot do justice to the kinds of discourse about meaning and the mind which are familiar from ordinary language and the work of more adventurous cognitive psychologists. Chomsky and those who have been influenced by him find Quine's behaviourist-sounding stress upon stimulus meaning unmotivated: 'It is obvious and uninteresting that, given an arbitrary restriction on permissible evidence, there will be incompatible hypotheses compatible with the evidence. It is less obvious that there are incompatible hypotheses such that no imaginable evidence can bear on the choice between them' (Chomsky and Katz 1974, fn. 7).

A related frustration at the Quinean spoiling of the wells of vernacular psychological explanation and apparently prospering research programmes in cognitive science is evident from many complaints by Fodor. For example, in his paper 'Banish disContent', we read that it is a '*grotesque* proposal' that we should abandon propositional attitude psychology: we can't do without it 'because, on the one hand, propositional attitude psychology works and, on the other hand, nothing else does' (1986, p. 1). If Quine's arguments threaten the integrity of cognitive sciences that make use of notions of propositional content, then they are best seen as a *reductio ad absurdum* of one or other of his premisses. So, if the indeterminacy of translation (in its Quinean form) follows from the Quinean version of behaviourism, all that this shows is that something is wrong with that behaviourism.

Quine, of course, would not see it that way. Roger Gibson has correctly remarked that his 'naturalistic behaviourist' account of language is one of the last things he would be prepared to give up (1982, *passim*). We are already in a position to see that Quine's stress upon stimulus meanings is not unmotivated – it is not simply an 'arbitrary' restriction. It is important to stress that he does not rely upon any straightforward identification of the mental with the behavioural, and anticipates explanations of linguistic behaviour in terms of inner states. The following passage, from 'Facts of the matter', is helpful here:

> Mental states and events do not reduce to behavior, nor are they explained by behavior. They are explained by neurology, when they are explained. But their behavioral adjuncts serve to specify them objectively. When we

> talk of mental states or events subject to behavioral criteria, we can rest assured that we are not just bandying words; there is a physical fact of the matter, a fact ultimately of elementary physical states. (p. 167)

We are brought back to Quine's physicalism and its relation to psychological talk and explanation. It seems to me that this is a vital premiss for his conclusions about meaning and translation.

In chapter 5, we attributed two views to Quine. The first was that the role of dispositional talk was to gesture towards underlying structure. We talk happily of solubility because we believe that there is 'a hidden trait of some sort, structural or otherwise, that inhered in the substance, and accounted for its dissolving on immersion' (WO, p. 223). Sometimes such talk alludes confidently to a known explanatory trait; sometimes it usefully enables us to attend to a range of phenomena which will eventually receive a common explanation which is currently not well understood.

This could remind the reader of Evans's claims about the dispositions which correspond to axioms in a theory of meaning. The difference between the two emerges when we notice the second Quinean thesis: at root, all explanation is physical explanation. Non-basic sciences usefully collect phenomena with analogous physical explanations. They also help to point us towards the explananda for physics. But, as we saw, Quine denies that they have explanatory autonomy. The search for them must be motivated by 'an earnest quest for an eventual explanatory model, integrated with our overall physical system of the world' (cited in Gibson 1982, p. 204).

So far, we might suppose, the theory of meaning and cognitive science are not distinguished from other non-basic sciences like chemistry and physiology. But it is apparent that Quine does see a difference. In the closing paragraphs of 'Facts of the matter', he reminds us that ordinary language (including ordinary psychological talk) is, for all its merits, 'only loosely factual' (p. 168). For purposes of 'scientific understanding' it must be replaced by a suitable regimented form of talk:

> [It] needs to be variously regimented when our purpose is scientific understanding. The regimentation is . . . not a matter of eliciting a latent content. It . . . is free creation. We withdraw to a language which, though not limited to the assigning of elementary physical states to regions, is visibly directed to factual distinctions – distinctions that are

> unquestionably underlain by differences, however inscrutable, in elementary physical states. This demand is apt to be met by stressing the behavioral and the physiological.
>
> (FM, p. 168)

The best regimentation will employ concepts 'that promise to play a leading role in causal explanation': 'causal explanations of psychology are to be sought in physiology, of physiology in biology, of biology in chemistry, and of chemistry in physics – in the elementary physical states'.

Somehow, it is these explanatory connections, together with Quine's physicalism, which ground his assurance that behaviouristic or physiological terms should be employed for describing the mind 'when our purpose is scientific understanding'. Intentionality and talk of meaning are a reminder of how ordinary talk is only 'loosely factual'. Quine has commented that if holism was false – if each statement was assented to in a distinct set of circumstances – there would be no translational indeterminacy. To a word or sentence would correspond a disposition which would probably receive a definite physiological explanation. It is the truth of holism that raises the problem – it is because all terms are more or less theoretical that translation is indeterminate. But these connections are currently not very clear.

9.6 SOME QUESTIONS

As well as the pressing issue of the defensibility of Quine's version of physicalism, several other questions now call for attention. For example, critics may object that the relation which ordinary psychological talk bears to physics does not differ significantly from that of non-intentional basic sciences like chemistry and neurophysiology to physics. They may also complain that Quine has failed to take account of all of the physical facts that are relevant to matters of meaning and mind. Quine's moderate holism appears to be relevant here, and in the following chapter we shall look more closely at the bearing of this upon the indeterminacy of translation. We have to establish why the holistic character of language entails that ordinary psychological terms do not classify events in ways that are relevant to causal (physical) explanation.

It would be natural to think of our psychological theories in terms of Neurath's familiar metaphor. We possess a more or less structured set of views about human psychology: these guide us in attributing beliefs and desires to people, and in explaining their actions. Gradually, we add to this body of knowledge, criticizing some of our beliefs, qualifying others, extending our grasp of the unconscious and conscious mechanisms which constrain our thought and action. Any of these beliefs may come into question. When one of them is questioned, our investigation is guided by the others which, at the moment, it does not occur to us to doubt. Thus, our 'folk psychology' and the scientific psychology which grows out of it develop just like the ship which Neurath describes. They evolve through piecemeal adjustments; and those beliefs which, at any time, are not being questioned, keep the ship afloat.

If we hold this picture of our evolving corpus of psychological beliefs, then it would surely be inappropriate to claim that the situation of *radical* translation provides a model for all attempts to understand someone's linguistic behaviour. We should make use of all of the laws that enter into our fallible model of human psychology, and we are likely to have more information available to guide us in attempting to understand members of our families or colleagues than we have available for entering the minds of people who inhabit very different forms of life.

Somebody who liked this picture could find Evans's (or Fodor's) view of psychological explanation congenial, as just suggested, the Quinean approach would have less appeal. In view of Quine's liking for Neurath's model, it is initially surprising that he does not accept such a picture. We may feel that the role he assigns to physics fits rather poorly with these epistemological views. In order to explore these points further, we shall turn, in the following chapter, to the views of a philosopher who subtly transforms Quine's philosophical outlook. Like Quine, Donald Davidson is no friend of cognitive science, and he agrees that radical translation provides a suitable model for all attempts to make sense of the language of another. But he allows for the autonomy of our ordinary patterns of psychological explanation, appealing to beliefs, desires and other intentional states. Although he is sympathetic to materialism, he is critical of Quine's conception of reality. He will have nothing to do with stimulus meanings and sees Quine's talk of stimulations as a last vestige of empiricism. Once empiricism is abandoned, he is ready to take a comfortably realist attitude towards all areas of discourse. Our examination of some of Davidson's arguments will help us to come to terms with what is of lasting importance in Quine's position.

10

Holism, Interpretation and the Autonomy of Psychology

10.1 HOLISM AND THE THEORY OF MEANING

As we have noticed several times, it appears to be a consequence of Quine's physicalism that all explanation is physical explanation. Hence, he is committed to denying that there can be a non-basic science (such as psychology) which is *autonomous* of physics, its explanations not serving simply as allusions to physical mechanisms. With this clearly in mind, we can understand the general pattern of argument we are looking for. Quine must hold that if 'holism' is correct, then any cognitive psychology or theory of meaning which explains behaviour by reference to beliefs and desires or other states with a propositional content *would* be autonomous of physics. The link between holism and the indeterminacy of translation may be that the former undercuts the explanatory pretensions of the sort of psychological theory which could be used to reduce the latter.

It also undercuts the explanatory pretensions of the sort of theory of meaning which, according to Michael Dummett, is the primary concern of 'analytic philosophers'. Such theories attempt to articulate what is known by someone who 'understands' (sc. 'knows the meaning of') different expressions and constructions. Like Evans, Dummett thinks that there is something that our mastery of an expression 'consists in', and that philosophers seek reflective accounts of the tacit or implicit knowledge manifested in their language use. Dummett is emphatic that the theory of meaning should not be understood as a part of psychology, so it would be wrong to include this as part of 'cognitive psychology'. However, it is equally the target of the Quinean argument. If Quine is right, there cannot be a theory of meaning which explores the cognitive underpinnings of language use.

Our concern is with the conditional claim:

If meaning is holistic, then there can be no cognitive psychology or theory of meaning of the sort we have described.

The antecedent 'Meaning is holistic' is vague, and requires further discussion. The issue is whether the conditional claim is true. In fact, it appears to be common ground among Quine, Davidson and those like Dummett who oppose them. The difference is that while Quine and Davidson (and possibly Putnam) exploit it in order to argue against the claims of cognitive science and the theory of meaning, Dummett contraposes. Persuaded that the construction of a theory of meaning is an article of faith for analytical philosophers, he denies that meaning has a holistic character.

10.2 SOME HOLISTIC THESES

We must distinguish two sorts of holism – holism with respect to the impact of *evidence* upon systems of beliefs, and holism with respect to *meaning*.

The first of these is easily described. Observations do not bear upon relatively theoretical claims directly. Rather, what is being tested is always some larger body of theory. So, when one of our predictions turns out to be false, we can accommodate this by revising our beliefs in different ways. This – the 'Duhem thesis' – was discussed in chapter 2.

This epistemological holism has semantic implications, for what holds about the nature of evidence generally will apply to the testing of manuals of translation or theories of meaning. Behavioural evidence does not bear directly upon single proposals for translations or statements about what expressions mean. Rather, we are justified in accepting particular translations because evidence as a whole supports the translation manuals which produce them. However, when philosophers talk of 'meaning holism' or 'semantic holism', they often have a more arcane doctrine in mind.

It is easier to produce neat slogans expressing this doctrine than it is to find a clear formulation of it. 'The unit of meaning is not the word, nor the sentence, but rather the theory – or the whole of science'; 'the meaning of a sentence is determined by the meanings of all the other sentences in the language.' As Fodor neatly puts it: 'Roughly, epistemic (sc. evidential) holism is the view that whole theories are units of *confirmation*; by contrast, semantic holism is the doctrine that whole theories are units of *meaning*'. Fodor himself sees semantic holism as a 'dubious doctrine of sceptical import' and conjectures that it 'gets some of its reflected glamour from *epistemic* holism, a much more plausible doctrine' (Fodor 1986, p. 12 n. 6).

The oddity of semantic holism emerges when we ask just what is involved in thinking of a theory as a unit of meaning. It is not something with which any linguistic action can be performed: we use sentences to say things; we don't use theories in the same sort of way. Moreover, the slogan threatens to leave us powerless to say anything about the use or understanding of particular sentences at all.

However, that is not the end of the matter. Somebody who is already committed to an empiricist theory of meaning, claiming that the meaning of a sentence is constituted by what would count as evidence for or against it, will not see much difference between evidential and semantic holism. If nothing much can be said about what confirms particular sentences, then there is nothing much to be said about what they mean. To develop this thought, imagine a philosopher whose sense of the philosophical role of the concept of meaning has been determined by the reductive empiricism of the early Carnap and other logical empiricists and by the use they made of the analytic/synthetic distinction. It is a natural thought that if evidential holism is correct, then there is little prospect of rescuing *that* notion of meaning as a philosophically interesting one. Hence, as Fodor states, semantic holism is a sceptical doctrine: it suggests that nothing very systematic or interesting can be said about meanings at all.

I wish to suggest that Quine's position is close to the one that we have just imagined. When we abandon the two dogmas of empiricism, it is important that we are left with 'empiricism without the dogmas'; the paper that we used to structure Part I of this volume heralded different themes as stages in the development of empiricism; the notion of stimulus meaning plausibly captures all that remains of *that* notion of meaning when evidential holism is acknowledged. Hence (*pace* Dummett), what is in prospect is not a 'holistic theory or model of meaning', but rather the denial that there is much to say about meaning at all.

We have identified two fundamental Quinean assumptions: his physicalism and his empiricism. If we find his finishing point unappealing, and his arguments appear sound, we can interpret it as a *reductio ad absurdum* of one or both of those positions. The remaining chapters attempt to evaluate these fundamental commitments. We start by considering the views of Donald Davidson, a philosopher who sees himself as working within the Quinean tradition: he calls himself 'Quine's faithful student' (1986a, p. 313). He accepts the indeterminacy of translation and the inscrutability of reference; like Quine, he is suspicious of logical frameworks that are not extensional; and he writes, in 'A coherence theory of truth and knowledge', that Quine's achievement in 'erasing the line between the analytic and synthetic saved philosophy of language as a serious subject by showing how it could be pursued without what there cannot be: determinate meanings' (ibid.). However, there is a difference. Davidson repudiates empiricism, and he clearly believes that he has a better sense than his teacher of where Quine's contribution was leading all along. Talk of observation sentences and stimulus meanings is to be abandoned; along with the assumption – shared by Dummett, Quine and many others – that 'whatever there is to meaning must be traced back somehow to experience' (ibid.).

Our examination of how the Quinean framework is transformed in Davidson's hands will help us to understand how it can be challenged. Since our primary concern is with Quine, I shall ignore many of the details of Davidson's approach, concentrating upon its broadest and most distinctive features.

10.3 RADICAL INTERPRETATION

Where Quine talks of radical translation, Davidson talks of radical interpretation (Davidson 1984, ch. 9). Once again, we are trying to break into the world of the speaker of a hitherto unknown language; and, once again, we have nothing to go on apart from observations of the aliens' behaviour. But there are also differences.

First, Davidson seeks a theory which tells us what the alien sentences mean, in particular, a theory which states what their truth conditions are. Our translations will be derived from a theory which delivers theorems like

> 'Es regnet' is a True German sentence uttered by S at time t if, and only if, it is raining near S at t.

If the theory as a whole is adequate, then the theorem tells us what the German sentence 'Es regnet' means. Similarly with an example like

> 'Gavagai' is a True alien sentence uttered by S at time t if, and only if, there is a rabbit near S at t.

Like Evans, Davidson seeks a theory of meaning rather than a straightforward linking of synonyms. In 'Radical interpretation' (1984, ch. 9), he makes the point that someone who knew these truths would thereby know what 'Es regnet' and 'gavagai' meant, while someone could know that

> 'Es regnet' means the same as 'It is raining'

and not thereby know what 'Es regnet' meant. This is because we could understand it without actually understanding the mentioned sentence 'It is raining'. A translation manual need not give us access to the alien language.

Although Davidson is thus allied with Evans – and the sketch of a theory of meaning provided in the last chapter illustrates the sort of theory Davidson wants too – there is an important difference between them. Evans's project opened the way for what I have called cognitive science because he claimed that his theory provided a theoretical representation of what was implicitly known by the speaker. He claimed that the axioms of his theory corresponded to psychological dispositions which can be appealed to in order to explain a speaker's linguistic behaviour. Although Davidson links his theory of meaning with the notion of knowledge, he does so in a significantly different way. A theory of meaning is adequate, he claims, if knowledge of it *would* enable someone to speak the language successfully.

It is important to be clear about what is at stake here. Evans claims:

> Competent speakers of the language implicitly know the theory.

But Davidson insists:

> Someone who knew the theory would be able to speak the language competently.

No claim is made about the tacit knowledge of normal competent speakers: the claim is just that grasping such a theory would suffice for radical interpretation. There is no suggestion that the axioms of the theory correspond to psychological dispositions which enter into the explanation of ordinary linguistic behaviour.

A second difference between Davidson and Quine is that the former is happy to continue using psychological terms like belief and desire. He views the construction of a theory of meaning for an alien language as part of a larger enterprise. The task of radical interpretation is to arrive at an account of the truth conditions of sentences of the alien language, a specification of the beliefs of the alien speakers we are studying, and an account of their desires. He sees this as a unified exercise in interpretation, and denies that it is possible to carry out one of these tasks without, at the same time, carrying out the others. Interpretations of individual sentences are ultimately justified through being a part of a more general interpretative theory which makes sense of all of the aliens' behaviour in terms of their beliefs, desires and utterances.

I have already mentioned the form that a theory of meaning for a language is to take. It is a systematic theory of the truth conditions of sentences which owes a lot to the theory developed by Alfred Tarski in the 1930s. My concern here is with how Davidson departs from Quine's account of how theories of interpretation are empirically tested. How are we to establish whether a theory of meaning is empirically adequate?

This raises what Davidson sees as a deep problem in interpretation: the interdependence of belief and meaning. What someone says at any time depends both on what his words mean and what beliefs he holds. Our evidence for people's beliefs includes what they say; and our way into understanding their language will reflect our view of what they believe. Perhaps a sentence containing 'gavagai' expresses the true belief that there is a rabbit present; perhaps it expresses the confused false belief that there is a dog present. Unless there is a limit upon how much confusion or false belief we can credit people with, there appears to be nothing that will constrain interpretation and prevent our saying whatever we like. If we knew what the words meant, we could make a good guess at the aliens' beliefs. If we knew what they believed, that would help us to break into their language. When we try simultaneously to identify beliefs and meanings, then we seem to lack any secure foundation for fixing either.

As I mentioned above, stimulus meanings and the like have no role in Davidson's solution to this problem, although he agrees with Quine that all we have to go on is what speakers assent to in what circumstances.

The theory is to be tested through theorems of the form:

T S is true if and only if p.

It is hard to see how such claims can be tested. We may be able to establish in what circumstances speakers *think* that S is true. But since they may be mistaken about this, we may have difficulty telling whether a given T-sentence is correct. The interdependence of belief and meaning threatens to leave the theory of meaning without any empirical content.

Corresponding to any T-sentence is a statement for which this problem does not arise – I shall refer to it as an 'H-sentence':

H S is held to be true if, and only if, p.

Davidson holds that we can establish empirically which sentences are held true by speakers, and then claims that we test theories of interpretation according to the principle that

P That a speaker holds S to be true is *prima facie* reason for thinking that it is true.

A theory of meaning is empirically confirmed if most of the H-sentences corresponding to its theorems are true: it is better confirmed than a rival if its H-sentences corresponding to its theorems are better confirmed than those of the rival. So, to return to the interdependence of belief and meaning, Davidson proposes to provide a solid basis for interpretation by making an assumption about belief: we assume that most of the aliens' utterances express *true* beliefs.

A major difference between Davidson and Quine emerges immediately. Recall that Quine suggests that we adopt a principle of charity as a regulative maxim in choosing between alternative empirically adequate translation manuals: we should prefer a manual which reveals the alien utterances to be largely true (by our lights) to one which shows them to have many false beliefs. The pragmatic benefits of such advice are clear. Davidson transforms the principle of charity from a regulative maxim which enables us to live with translational indeterminacy into a principle which determines which theories of meaning are empirically adequate. Charity becomes constitutive of correctness rather than a regulative maxim. Unless a theory of meaning shows that the aliens' beliefs are largely true, it is inadequate.

The picture is more complex than this suggests. Presumably, we should not expect people to have true beliefs about things with which they have had no contact – it would hardly support a theory of meaning for the language of a previously unknown Amazon tribe that it revealed them to have true beliefs about the dates of the Kings and Queens of England. There are circumstances in which we expect people to be mistaken, and the principle would have to be qualified to allow for this. The point survives that interpretation is possible at all only on the assumption that the subjects' beliefs are overwhelmingly correct. Our 'bridgehead for interpretation' is secured by assuming that the aliens' world view is substantially like ours – at least with respect to ordinary mundane matters

10.4 NORMATIVE PRINCIPLES AND THE HOLISTIC CHARACTER OF INTERPRETATION

The principle of charity has a *normative* dimension. Truth is what we aim at in our inquiries: it is a notion that is used in evaluating beliefs and assertions; once we see that one of our beliefs is not true, we cannot hold on to it as a full-blooded, conscious belief. Davidson's position suggests that standards used in evaluating beliefs also have a role in evaluating belief ascriptions. If one set of interpretations shows a subject to be more successful in acquiring true beliefs than another, then the first interpretation is, *ceteris paribus*, better supported by the evidence. Other normative standards are involved in interpretation, too. We should prefer interpretations which enable us to ascribe consistent systems of beliefs to agents: it counts against an interpretation that, according to it, someone fails to believe an obvious logical consequence of his beliefs. Similarly, the standards we use in evaluating people's desires have a role in evaluating views about what they desire.

In ascribing beliefs and desires to people, and in deciding on the meanings of their words, we *rationalize* their behaviour. The principles that are constitutive of this procedure are also employed in the evaluation and criticism of reasoning and action. The reader may detect a tension here. If we find irrationality in people's sets of beliefs, why should we take this as a basis for criticizing their cognitive performance rather than as refuting the interpretation we have made of their behaviour? How *can* standards serve this dual role: as principles that serve a constitutive function for the activity of identifying someone's meanings, beliefs and desires; and as normative standards that can be used to criticize those very beliefs and desires? How are we to resist the conclusion that any interpretation that shows its subject to be other than optimally truthful and rational is simply mistaken?

This raises complex issues which cannot be discussed fully here. Davidson's position involves the following two claims:

> An interpretation is not successful at all unless it reveals the subject's behaviour to issue from beliefs which are reasonably truthful and rational
>
> The fact that one system of interpretations reveals its subject to be more truthful (or rational) than another provides a *prima facie* reason for preferring it

Both leave room for interpretations which reveal an agent to have some false beliefs, and to be irrational in some of them.

First, interpretation rests upon a number of normative standards. We are constrained to look for true beliefs, to look for rationally coherent bodies of belief, to avoid ascribing inexplicable ignorance, to look for reasonable desires, to look for coherent patterns of preferences, and so on. Interpretations which do well according to some of these standards will probably do less well according to others. A trade-off is required, and an interpretation which does reasonably well according to each is likely to be optimal with respect to none.

Second, discussions of radical interpretation can encourage a distorted picture of what goes on when we attempt to enter the beliefs and meanings of another person. The object of interpretation is to be able to understand other people. This understanding is required for learning from them, for carrying out co-operative ventures with them, for responding to them as persons. Discussions of radical interpretation often suggest that we observe the aliens in a dispassionate, uninvolved spirit, and that it is not until we have confirmed a complete set of interpretations that we risk conversation and co-operation. This is absurd.

Once we have effected a bridgehead of a few obvious interpretations, we effectively move beyond radical interpretation. A limited translation manual is established, and shared forms of activity are established which exploit those translation manuals. Once this point is reached, one of the standards of adequacy for extending our interpretations and revising those we have arrived at will be that of minimal revision in the practices which sustain these shared activities. Interpretations which maximize truthfulness or rationality by claiming that the aliens are always talking about rabbit time slices, or areas of space one mile to the left of rabbits, are likely to undermine the basis of this co-operation.

A further observation upon how we use interpretations in understanding other people and co-operating with them introduces the third point. How do claims about beliefs and desires, constrained by normative principle in this fashion, enable us to understand our fellows? How do they enable us to predict how they will act? How do they enable us to learn from their testimony? How do they enable us to collaborate with them spontaneously and successfully?

Obviously, we do not do this by expecting them to be optimally truthful, rational and so on. It is hard work to establish what is optimal in these respects, and beyond our capacities to find out exactly what an optimally truthful believer would believe. What we can rely on is our view of what one should believe, if placed as the subject is, and how one should reason . . . All we can establish is what seems true and rational *by our lights*, and, if someone's beliefs meet those standards, this provides us with a basis for easy prediction and collaboration. We use ourselves as measuring instruments in establishing how far interpretations meet the normative conditions: the interpretations record and explain how far the beliefs and capacities of the subject differ from our own. Hence, our own cognitive limitations serve as a kind of benchmark in arriving at an interpretation of others. We are satisfied when we can render intelligible to ourselves their actions, including their linguistic actions.

The normative principles we have been discussing are often described as holistic constraints upon interpretation. We can understand the force of doing so by looking at the bearing of an unsophisticated principle of charity upon the testing of a theory of meaning. Suppose we are trying to construct a theory of meaning for German. One of its theorems is

> 'Es regnet' is a true sentence of German, when spoken by S at t, if, and only if, it is raining near S at t.

Its corresponding H-sentence is

> 'Es regnet' is held to be true by a German speaker at t if, and only if, it is raining near that speaker at t.

What supports the claim that this theorem gives the meaning of the

German sentence 'Es regnet' is not the truth of the H-sentence. Rather, it receives its support from the fact that it is a theorem of a theory of meaning most of whose T-sentences correspond to true H-sentences. The empirical test supports the theory as a whole; we accept the statement about what 'Es regnet' means because the theorem follows from an empirically adequate theory of meaning. Statements of truth conditions cannot be verified singly: utterances and actions always reflect the influence of many of an agent's beliefs and desires – there are no straightforward links between belief and behaviour.

Similar remarks can be made about the other normative standards employed in testing interpretations. Particular interpretations are justified if they form part of an overall pattern of interpretations which make the behaviour of speakers intelligible to us.

10.5 INTERPRETATION AND COGNITIVE SCIENCE

We must be clear about the significance of this stress upon the role of normative standards in interpretation. The point is not just epistemological or methodological; there is more to it than the suggestion that charity is more likely than any alternative to arrive at a subject's real beliefs. Rather, Davidson claims that psychology seeks a style of explanation which differs in principle from what is sought in the natural sciences. While the physicist or chemist attempts to make sense of phenomena by showing how they conform to natural law or by searching for hidden mechanisms, our aim, when we try to explain human action, is to render it intelligible by showing it to be a reasonable thing to do. The normative standards are *constitutive* of our concept of mind: it is a deep feature of our talk of beliefs and desires that it provides explanations which have an essential normative dimension. Psychological explanation is rationalization.

Thus, Davidson claims that psychological explanation has a *sui generis* character, employing a structure of concepts which has 'no echo in physical theory' (1980, p. 231. McDowell neatly contrasts the two styles of explanation:

> Propositional attitudes have their proper home in explanations in which things are made intelligible by being revealed to be, or to approximate to being, as they rationally ought to be. This is to be contrasted with a style of explanation in which things are made intelligible by representing their

> coming into being as a particular instance of how things generally tend to happen.
>
> (McDowell 1986, p. 389)

The physical and the psychological require different styles of explanation: talk about them is subject to contrasting constitutive ideals of intelligiblity. This introduces, according to Davidson, a kind of incommensurability between physical and psychological talk.

In order to describe this incommensurability, Davidson defends two theses which, together, capture the 'anomalous' character of the mental.

I There are are no strict laws connecting the psychological and the physical realms.
II There are no strict psychological laws.

If these claims are correct, then there is a lack of fit between intentional talk and the non-intentional sciences which will remind us of the views underlying the indeterminacy of translation. Before returning to indeterminacy in the following section, we shall look (very briefly) at why I and II might follow from the constitutive role of normative standards in interpretation and psychological explanation.

The anomalist view does not deny the existence of true generalizations linking the physical and the mental. Rather, it denies that any such generalizations function as strict *laws*. Laws are distinguished from other generalizations because they support counterfactual claims and other subjunctives (see section 6.4), and because they are confirmed by their instances – the more instances fitting the law we discover, the more confident we are that it is true. Instances do not confirm accidental generalizations: finding a few instances of these does not render it any more unlikely that we shall subsequently find counter-instances. Davidson thus denies that we have good reason to think that psychological generalizations, or psycho-physical generalizations, sustain counterfactuals, or that they are confirmed by their instances. He could probably allow that there are some rough and ready psychological 'laws'. But these would be 'heteronomic': they would be prone to exceptions, heavily guarded by *ceteris paribus* clauses, and could only be turned into 'strict laws' by abandoning psychological vocabulary, and turning to physics, neurophysiology or biology. Strict laws cannot be formulated in intentional terms. In contrast, physics is 'homonomic': the physical world is a closed system; its generalizations serve as laws; and any qualification required by sketches of physical laws can be provided employing physical terms. Physical 'laws', unlike psychological ones, do not gesture towards generalizations which can only be formulated 'outside' the discipline itself.

Although Davidson has defended the anomalous character of the mental on several occasions, it is still difficult to see exactly how the arguments are meant to work. In his paper 'Mental events' (reprinted in Davidson 1980), he offers some suggestive hints and sketches a more rigorous argument. For example, we are told that 'to allow the possibility [of laws linking the mental and physical] would amount to changing the subject. By changing the subject I mean here: deciding not to accept the criterion of the mental in terms of the vocabulary of the propositional attitudes' (p. 216). And we subsequently read that the 'holism of the mental realm' (the fact that 'beliefs and desires issue in behaviour only as modified by further beliefs and desires, attitudes and attendings, without limit') is a clue both to the autonomy and to the anomolous character of the mental' (p. 217). It is hard to see how these themes are related.

Central to the argument sketch is the view that within any area of theory is a set of postulates or laws which are constitutive or 'synthetic *a priori*' laws. Davidson discusses an example. Our measurements of length are governed by a postulate of transitivity: if one distance is longer than a second, which, in turn, is longer than a third, then the first distance is longer than the third. They are also guided by procedures which, we allow, establish empirically that one length is greater than another. Although there is no need to insist that these principles are *analytic*, and they may indeed be revisable in odd circumstances, Davidson holds that our talk of length is governed by a number of such commitments: indeed, it is hard to see what use or application the concept of length could have if these postulates were abandoned. He wishes to say that 'the whole set of axioms, laws, or postulates for the measurement of length is partly constitutive of a system of macroscopic, rigid physical objects'. From this, he concludes that the existence of strict laws in physical science depends upon a variety of conceptual commitments of the sort just described. These are deeply embedded commitments which are held to in arriving at precise formulations of empirical laws.

If there were strict laws linking the mental and the physical, then, Davidson seems to argue, there would have to be similar synthetic *a priori* constitutive elements to constrain us in the search for them. The existence of such constitutive postulates would undermine our familiar concept of the mental, for it would introduce constraints upon interpretation which would conflict with the normative standards which, in fact, guide our ascriptions of beliefs, meanings and desires. Our normal practice is to revise our belief ascriptions because they cannot be made to fit coherently with what we take to be the other attitudes of the subject. If there were psycho-physical laws, grounded in constitutive nomological principles, then it is not out of the question that we would be constrained to prefer an interpretation which shows an agent to be highly unreasonable to another which fitted much better the normative constraints which govern interpretation. According to Davidson, this would radically transform our mental concepts. The differences between the constitutive commitments of the two realms do not allow for synthetic *a priori* laws which would make possible strict laws linking the mental and the physical.

These arguments are suggestive and controversial. It is plausible that, if they are correct, then there cannot be strict psychological laws either. It is much too large a task for the present volume to attempt to resolve the debate: my aim is to use the argument in order to come to terms with Quine's position. They are related to the indeterminacy of translation. As Kim has noticed (1986), both the anomalous character of the mental and the indeterminacy of translation point to a lack of fit between the physical and the intentional; and, in 'Mental events', Davidson tells us that his thesis traces back to the 'central role of translation in the description of all propositional attitudes, and to the indeterminacy of translation' (1980, p. 222). In his slightly later paper, 'Belief and the basis of meaning', however, we read that the fact that mental concepts are not reducible 'in a fundamental way' to physical, behavioural or neurophysiological terms is 'not due . . . to the indeterminacy of meaning or translation' (1984, p. 154). This raises some interesting issues about Davidson's attitude towards the indeterminacy thesis, and we turn to these in the following section.

10.6 INDETERMINACY: QUINE AND DAVIDSON

Davidson often returns to the indeterminacy of translation: 'Quine is right, I think, in holding that an important degree of indeterminacy will remain after all the evidence is in; a number of significantly different theories of truth will fit the evidence equally well' (1984, p. 62). In 'Reality without reference' we learn that he doesn't 'for a moment imagine' that a unique correct account of the truth conditions of the sentences of a language will emerge. Since the principle of charity now enters into what it is for an interpretation to be correct – rather than being a regulative principle guiding choice among equally correct translations – there will be *less* indeterminacy than Quine allows. The fact that we are looking for a theory of truth conditions rather than a translation manual will restrict indeterminacy too. But Davidson expects to find – to a lesser degree – all the kinds of indeterminacy that Quine speaks of (1984, pp. 224–5, 228).

We must not lose sight of the fact that Quine and Davidson argue for the indeterminacy thesis in very different ways. Quine's argument rests upon his view of which physical facts are relevant to the correctness of a translation manual. He distinguishes cases where our preference for one manual over another results from our seeing that only the first fits the facts, from cases where, on pragmatic grounds, we prefer one manual to another when both fit the facts equally well. There could be alternative manuals each of which fits the facts perfectly. He allows for two distinct kinds of basis for choice between translation manuals: whether manuals respect the truths about stimulus meanings; and how far they meet pragmatic standards of charity and the like.

Davidson's picture is more complex. A range of normative standards contribute to our understanding of correct translation: charity, rationality and so on. David Lewis has offered a fuller account of some of the standards we use, and Davidson refers approvingly to his contribution (Lewis 1983, p. 112–5; Davidson 1984, p. 152n). It is hard to see that he has any basis for dismissing any standard we use for choosing between interpretations as of merely pragmatic significance. Hence, his position is *not* that many interpretations may meet all the normative requirements perfectly, choice between them being reasonably made on the basis of other sorts of considerations. If, among alternative possible interpretations, one seems to us to be obviously the best, then our judgement must reflect some normative standard or other. In that case, it is hard to avoid concluding that we do not have an instance of the indeterminacy of translation, for the standard we make use of can be admitted as one of the normative standards that helps to constitute our concepts of mind and interpretation.

In view of this, it is unsurprising that in an early paper, 'Truth and meaning', Davidson traces indeterminacy to the fact that there is a variety of standards used in evaluating interpretations: 'No single principle of optimum charity emerges; the constraints therefore determine no single theory' (1984, p. 27). Employing the fantasy that we actually have a number of competing interpretations available, we might find that they are differently ordered according to our different standards. One may allow us to attribute fewer false beliefs to our subject, but at the cost of convicting him of irrationality or inconsistency; another finds him to be consistent, but with more false beliefs; yet another finds him more truthful and reasonable, albeit at the cost of ascribing to him some desires we find it hard to understand; yet another meets some of these standards only by suggesting that he employs eccentric systems of classification; another meets many of our desiderata, but employs relatively *ad hoc* assignments of reference like those considered in the previous chapter, when we discussed 'gavagai'. Lacking any hard and fast rule about the priority relations among the different normative standards, we have no firm basis for choice among theories that meet the different standards reasonably well, but imperfectly. Indeterminacy issues from the need for trade-off between the different standards that constitute our practice of interpretation. Unless one translation perfectly satisfies all of the requirements (and that is very unlikely) indeterminacy looks inevitable (cf. Lewis 1983, p. 118 for similar remarks).

As we should expect from this, most of Davidson's examples of indeterminacy seem fairly innocuous. He considers an example of someone who says 'That's a whale' of an object that looks like a whale. We know that this object is not, in fact, a mammal. Should we translate his utterance homophonically, and thus attribute to him the false belief that this animal is a whale? Or should we decide that he is misusing the word 'whale' and attribute to him a belief which reflects that? The problem is that there is no sharp set of criteria which capture the meaning of 'whale'; so even if we know that he is aware that this animal is not a mammal, the question is not necessarily settled.

> Fortunately for the purposes of communication, there is no need to force a decision. Having a language and knowing a good deal about the world are only partially separable attainments, but interpretation can proceed because we can accept any of a number of theories of what a man means, provided we make compensating adjustments in the beliefs we attribute to him.
>
> (1980, p. 257; cf. 1984, pp. 100–1)

We can choose to describe the agent's beliefs as about whales, or as about a slightly different kind, which does not correspond to one that we recognize. Nothing is at stake in how we do this: as Davidson says, the choice is analogous to the one we make when we decide to measure temperatures in Fahrenheit or Celsius; we can use our beliefs to model the subject's beliefs in different ways.

However, Davidson also endorses more significant indeterminacies, as when he accepts the inscrutability of reference. For, shouldn't we expect theories which interpret 'gavagai' as involving reference to rabbits to be preferred to ones that interpret it as referring to rabbit parts? If so, surely we have normative standards available that will enable us to reduce the indeterminacy.

Let us consider an example. Suppose we interpret a fellow 'English' speaker as employing a deviant dialect whereby 'rabbit' is interpreted as meaning 'is a volume of space one mile to the north of a rabbit', and compensating adjustments are made to our interpretations of other terms. Systematic adjustments are made, so that the resulting theory gets the truth conditions of sentences right. Davidson's discussion of a similar example (1984, p. 230) suggests that he thinks that this interpretation would meet all possible evidence. It is not a system of interpretation that we would use, and presumably we have some basis for being uneasy with it. On some basis, Davidson must claim that these normative standards are not among those that are constitutive of interpretation. I find it hard to see how this is established.

He seems to argue that while there are normative standards of interpretation which bear upon our understanding of concepts like meaning, truth, belief, desire, reason and the like, there are none that bear directly upon concepts like reference and satisfaction. This is because we have no pre-theoretic concept of reference. The other concepts have a role in our ordinary practice of interpretation, so they function as points of anchorage for Davidson's philosophical reconstruction of that practice. We are constructing theories of truth, meaning, belief and so on; and like all theories, these grow through clarification and refinement of our familiar concepts. We understand Davidson's theory of interpretation largely because we already have some sort of understanding of truth, meaning, belief etc. Davidson's view is that reference is a theoretical notion that is wholly *internal* to his philosophical analysis of interpretation. Our claims about reference are defensible if, and only if, they contribute to an adequate account of truth, meaning and belief. There are no untutored intuitions about reference to which they are answerable. In consequence of this, there are no normative standards, constitutive of the practice of interpretation, which bear directly upon the concept of reference (1984, chs 15–16). If this claim can be sustained, it *may* follow that there are no constitutive normative standards that rule out the sort of disjunctive axioms that we have previously offered in developing Quine's argument for the inscrutability of reference (p. 151 above).

But the claim is highly controversial. It may also seem too weak to answer an argument based upon the observation that we obviously do have some basis for preferring the 'natural' interpretation. If this does not reflect our grasp of reference, it has some source, and seems to have a role in guiding interpretation. Davidson's liking for such examples of the inscrutability of reference remains questionable.

Another argument may be involved. When assessing interpretations, two standards can be employed. First, we can establish whether a given theory of meaning *can* be used as part of an interpretation of a subject's behaviour. It fails this test if we are left unable to respond to the subject as a intelligible agent at all. Secondly, we can establish whether it is the best among those theories which can be used to provide an interpretations. A theory might fail because others are better; but it can also fail because it leads us to assign such an outlandish set of beliefs and desires that we can make no sense of the subject as an agent at all. There are passages which suggest Davidson thinks that a theory is correct if it avoids this second kind of failure. Evaluations directed towards finding the best correct theory are choosing among acceptable interpretations: they are pragmatic rather than evidential choices.

This would make sense of some of Davidson's views, although I doubt that it is his considered position. It may fit with his talk of constitutive principles: these are standards that must be met if something is to serve as an intepretation at all. But it is not very satisfactory. In fact, Davidson and Quine share a picture of reality as, fundamentally, physical. Psychological terms represent a kind of framework we find it useful to use to talk about things which are really physical. This encourages an anti-realist view of the mental, and predisposes one to accept the indeterminacy of psychological and semantical talk. Once one has this 'interpretative' picture, the view outlined in the previous paragraph may seem attractive. But no one who is unsympathetic to such an anti-realism about the mental can then be argued out of his position through the argument for indeterminacy. Anyone unsympathetic to this picture will simply see all the standards employed in arriving at a settled consensus about interpretation as on a par. Unless the argument (like Quine's) tries to establish a distinction between evidential and pragmatic standards, its rhetorical force against doubters will be limited.

These remarks may be unfair to Davidson. He would disown an anti-realist picture of the mental, although a number of commentators have questioned his right to do so (e.g. Rosenberg 1986). Moreover, in developing his own positive views, he attaches more importance to the 'disparate conceptual commitments' of physics and psychology than to the indeterminacy thesis. In order to resolve some of the problems we have stirred up, we must turn to a more detailed examination of Quine's views about truth and reality.

Part IV

Knowledge and Reality

11

Nature and Experience

11.1 EPISTEMOLOGY: THE CARTESIAN PARADIGM

We have noticed several underlying commitments which influence the development of Quine's thought. We must now examine these more directly, and try to evaluate them. One of these commitments is to physicalism. Quine's own version of physicalism is quite radical: it denies that non-basic sciences, such as biology and economics, can describe ranges of facts which are (partly) autonomous of the truths of physics. A further commitment is connected to this. When we show that a form of discourse reflects human interests and concerns, we demonstrate that it is not properly descriptive. 'The facts' are as they are, independent of the subjective responses or pragmatic concerns of agents. Finally, Quine holds to a very restricted view of which physical facts are relevant to translation and interpretation. His empiricist claim that only stimulus meanings are relevant to translation shapes many of his views.

Many critics have sensed a tension between his austere physicalism and empiricism and other themes in Quine's epistemology. His liking for Neurath's ship metaphor encourages a more relaxed conception of how knowledge grows: perhaps any practice of inquiry which allows for ordered revision of opinions should be tolerated as revealing a facet of reality. Furthermore, Quine's occasional allusions to pragmatism suggest the more tolerant outlook defended by Nelson Goodman. As a first step towards evaluating Quine's physicalism and his conception of reality, we shall now examine his naturalistic approach to epistemology in more detail.

For many twentieth-century philosophers, the tasks of epistemology are fixed by their reading of Descartes. We reflect upon our beliefs, with a view to distinguishing those which are actually knowledge from prejudice and error. In the course of this reflection, we formulate sceptical challenges: evidence of illusion and delusion suggests that we could be wrong about what seems most certain. The most radical challenge proposes that our experience could be exactly as it is even if none of it was trustworthy. Unless we can rule out the hypothesis that all of our experience is a dream – or that we are manipulated by a deceitful spirit, or that an evil scientist has kidnapped us, removed our brains from our bodies and stimulated them to have 'experiences' by artificial means – our confidence that we have access to the *truth* seems misplaced. The task for philosophy, then, is either to acquiesce in scepticism – 'We don't know whether we can have knowledge of reality' – or to respond to this challenge. No one considers it a serious possibility that all is a dream. But responding to these sceptical challenges clarifies the nature of truth and justification. We try to work out what is involved in a belief being true, and to show how the considerations we take to justify beliefs actually do support them.

The sceptical challenges generally point out that our opinions often reflect subjective distortions. The state of our visual apparatus, our alertness, whether we are drunk or sober, features of the surrounding environment: all of these things can prevent our experiences and beliefs having the sort of normal causal history required for them to provide reliable information about our surroundings. From an experience or belief itself, we cannot tell whether its causal origin is of the normal, veridical, sort, or whether it is a distorting one. This raises a problem when we attempt to defeat scepticism through argument or reasoning. It is hard to see how we can satisfy ourselves that the premisses we use do not express beliefs that were acquired in an abnormal or distorting way. If that requires further argument, we face a damaging infinite regress of reasonings. If it does not require further argument, then these premisses must be somehow self-evident; they must wear their truth on their sleeves. But it is hard to see how any belief can be *so* secure that we cannot conceive that our confidence in it is due to the manipulations of the spirit or scientist. The sceptical challenges appear unanswerable.

We may think that these are *scientific* problems. We could carry out a psychological investigation of perception and reasoning, and discover that, for the most part, our everyday beliefs about everyday objects are correct. But that response appears to miss the point. If our everyday beliefs are all a dream, then so are our psychological beliefs. The sceptical challenge threatens all of science; if we take it seriously, we cannot use our scientific beliefs to defend other beliefs against these sceptical challenges. After all, if the wicked scientist is efficient, he will provide us with a set of psychological views which will conceal his activities from us. Rather than the achievement undermining scepticism, the various sceptical hypotheses *predict* that we will construct a non-sceptical scientific psychology. As Quine reminds us in 'Epistemology naturalized', the 'surrender of the epistemological burden to psychology . . . was disallowed in earlier times as circular reasoning'. If our goal is 'validation of the grounds of empirical science', we 'defeat our purpose' by employing scientific results in our reasoning (OR, pp. 75–6).

If this is right, the epistemologist appears to have two options. He can claim that philosophy has sources of knowledge which are more secure that those of science. Sceptic-proof philosophical reasoning can provide the self-evident beliefs which can be used to ground the rest of science: this is the discipline which Quine terms 'first philosophy'. Alternatively, we resign ourselves to the predicament forced upon us by the sceptical arguments. We cannot meet the challenge: all that we can do is to provide a scientific explanation of our practices, while under no illusion that this is a genuine answer to scepticism. We may even call this the theory of knowledge, but we must be aware that we have changed the subject; we have given up on the Cartesian challenge.

Of course, the matter is more complex than this sketch suggests. However, it does help us to understand the puzzlement prompted by Quine's epistemological views. He denies the possibility of first philosophy, and 'surrenders the epistemological burden to psychology', thereby 'naturalizing' epistemology. But he denies that he is simply changing the subject. His work is continuous with what he calls 'traditional epistemology'; and he undertakes to take seriously, and respond to, sceptical challenges.

11.2 POSITIVISM AND EPISTEMOLOGY

I shall approach these issues historically. Quine's links with the logical positivists have been mentioned on several occasions. Positivists, or logical empiricists, were unified by a number of doctrines. The first was scientism, the view that scientific knowledge serves as a paradigm for all knowledge. Physics and the other respectable sciences provide us with secure knowledge of truths. Areas of discourse which do not conform to this paradigm – theology, much philosophy, ethics – have no claim to knowledge. They either yield gibberish posing as truth or, at best, make expressive, poetic claims. The second was empiricism, the view that all meaning and knowledge has its source in sensory experience.

During the 1930s, those in the positivist movement faced a number of problems about truth and experience which suggested that their doctrines were themselves meaningless metaphysics. They had difficulty in formulating and defending these central claims. The positivists spurned concepts whose content could not be explained by reference to experience. For several years, Carnap believed that *semantic* notions failed this test. He thought that concepts like truth, reference, denotation and extension, which appear to relate language to an external reality, should be dismissed as metaphysical. The only framework available for use in studying the structure of language was that of *syntax*. Syntax studies only the forms and relations of expressions themselves; it does not study their relations to external things. When he wrote *The Logical Syntax of Language* (1937), Carnap thought that philosophy was restricted in its subject matter to syntactic analysis. We saw (p. 32 above), that the responsible inquirer, in constructing his linguistic frameworks, was subject to only one moral rule: to lay down explicitly the syntactic rules governing his practice.

Why should semantic notions be problematic? Let us consider just one semantic notion: *truth*. (For a fuller discussion of some of these themes, see Romanos 1983, pp. 130ff; and Davidson 1986b.) One reason for suspicion of truth comes from paradoxes like the Liar. Suppose I utter the sentence:

This sentence is not true.

If it is true, then it is false; on the other hand, if it is false, then it is true. On the reasonable assumption that it is a grammatical sentence of English, then the presence of the word 'true' introduces absurdities into the language.

It is natural to explain the notion of truth by saying that a sentence or proposition is true if, and only if, it corresponds to some fact. In this spirit Wittgenstein, in the *Tractatus*, wrote that sentences are logical pictures. They contain names that stand for objects, and a sentence is true if the arrangement of names in the sentence mirrors, corresponds to, or 'pictures', the arrangement of the corresponding objects in the world. Correspondence gives rise to problems of several kinds. For example, it was objected that the explanation is circular: in order to establish that one proposition P is true, we would first have to establish that it was true that it corresponds to the facts; and in order to do this, we must first establish that it is true that the proposition that P corresponds to the facts corresponds to the facts; etc.

Moreover, the relation between names and objects (and the correspondence relation itself) looked suspiciously metaphysical. How do we verify that some proposition stands for a fact? What is involved in comparing such disparate things as facts and propositions? How do names relate to the objects they stand for? Once the positivists tried to talk about how words and sentences relate to reality or to experience, they feared that they succumbed to indefensible metaphysical excess. This can be illustrated through the debates between Schlick, Neurath and others during the 1930s, over the nature of protocol sentences (see the writings in section D of Hanfling 1981).

'Protocol sentence' refers to sentences used to express the content of experience. Utterances of them served as the observation reports which were used in testing theories. They correspond, more or less, to Quine's observation sentences. Some such notion was required by the positivists' commitment to empiricism, which held:

(1) The meaning of any non-observational term is fixed by the logical links between the sentences in which it occurs and protocol sentences.
(2) Whether acceptance of a sentence is justified depends upon the truth or falsity of the protocol sentences which can be derived from it.

This formulation leaves two problems open. First, what is a protocol sentence; and how do we decide whether a given sentence is, in fact, a protocol sentence? Second, how do terms that occur in protocol sentences acquire their meanings? Unless an answer to these questions can be given – which does not smack of unacceptable traditional metaphysics – the positivists' claim that they have liberated philosophy from its past, and transformed it into a science, will fail.

One response is associated with Schlick and Ayer. Protocol sentences describe immediate experiences: they employ terms whose meanings can only be learned ostensively through confrontation with the features of experience they describe. It then becomes a matter for debate whether our immediate experience is of public physical objects, or whether it is of a two-dimensional array of sense data. It is equally controversial whether utterances of protocol sentences are fallible, or absolutely indubitable. According to Neurath, talk of ostensive definition of these protocol terms simply posits an ineffable relation. It fails to explain how these relations are set up. Moreover, debates about what we 'immediately' experience seem to be just the sort of unanswerable issues which positivists were eager to ban from philosophy. They had hoped to turn philosophical issues into issues of language: they now discover that they have to solve substantive philosophical problems before they can theorize about language.

The alternative, according to Neurath, was to characterize protocol sentences formally in syntactic terms. That such sentences should have the decisive role in testing theories is explained as due to a conventional decision. This accords with Carnap's subsequent defence of empiricism as a proposal, defended on pragmatic grounds. We decide to search for a coherent body of beliefs while assigning a stronger weighting to these protocol sentences in the course of doing so. Hempel, at one point, suggested that the way to establish which sentences were protocols was to observe which sentences were treated as protocols by the best scientists. This approach does not require us to make curious comparisons between sentences and 'reality'. All we compare are sentences and other sentences. The problem, according to Schlick, was that it left inquiry wholly free-floating. It smelled of the idealist outlook: we pursue coherent sets of beliefs or sentences, with no grounds for thinking that the coherent set we come up with will actually be true – unless we say that truth simply is coherence. That offended the tough-minded empiricist sensibilities of Schlick and Ayer: why should the coherent set of beliefs produced by the physicist be any better than non-scientific ones? As Schlick famously complained, the coherence theory makes 'any fabricated tale to be no less true than a historical report . . . so long as the tale is well enough fashioned to harbour no contradictions anywhere': we can arrive at 'as many internally non-contradictory proposition-systems' as we please (Hanfling 1981, pp. 184–5).

So, the positivist movement faced a predicament. Philosophy was to be replaced by the scientific study of language, and was to provide a vindication of science and of empiricism. But the positivist framework appeared to lack the materials for saying anything systematic about experience and truth. The unpalatable alternatives appeared to be: either a genuine commitment to science and empiricism, defended by metaphysical arguments; or a genuinely scientific philosophy which was powerless to explain what was so important about science and experience.

11.3 EPISTEMOLOGY NATURALIZED

For Quine, epistemology 'or something like it, simply falls into place as a chapter of psychology and hence of natural science', it 'goes on, though in a new setting, and a clarified status'. It studies a human subject who

> is accorded a certain experimentally controlled input – certain patterns of irradiation in assorted frequencies, for instance – and in the fullness of time the subject delivers as output a description of the three dimensional external world and its history. The relation between the meager input and the torrential output is a relation that we are prompted to study for somewhat the same reasons that always prompted epistemology; namely in order to see how evidence relates to theory, and in what ways one's theory of nature transcends any available evidence.
>
> (OR, pp. 82–3)

As well as the firm commitment to naturalism – the repudiation of first philosophy and the insistance that epistemology can be pursued as a science – note here the influence of Quine's physicalism. His canon of acceptable sciences is operative: it is natural science that he speaks of, and this excludes social sciences and disciplines like cognitive psychology which make use of intentional notions. Naturalized epistemology is theory of knowledge carried out within *natural* science.

There is an obvious relation between Quine's views and the problems for positivism just described. He is able to offer a naturalistic account of a notion of 'experience', and of an observation report. The latter is defined behaviourally, through his account of observation sentences as occasion sentences which all observers assent to in the same circumstances. His surrogate for experience is his notion of a stimulation. This lacks the traditional suggestion of awareness, but describes the uninterpreted impact of external things upon our cognitive apparatus. Our scientific beliefs are tested against observation sentences and understood as a response to stimulations.

No one will dispute the possibility of the kind of scientific study of cognition which Quine describes. Doubtless, it could issue in interesting perspectives upon our relations to our environment. Our problem is: why is it epistemology? More precisely: why does it inherit the mantle provided by the Cartesian paradigm rather than merely changing the subject? Despite occasional uncertainty about how much continuity there is, Quine has arguments to show that he is not just changing the subject. For example, there is the suggestion, noted above, that both traditional and naturalized epistemology are motivated by a desire to know 'how evidence relates to theory, and in what way one's theory of nature transcends any possible evidence'. Whether this is enough to establish that the subject has not been changed is unclear – so far, there is no explanation of why we can forget 'scruples about circularity'.

Quine's holism is crucial at this point. The substantive conception of reality which we employ in evaluating our opinions and methods is taken from the natural sciences. Science provides the planks of the boat which keep us afloat when we ask whether we have an accurate picture of reality at all: the question is reformulated as one about whether our methods will take us to the truth about the world of sticks, stones, protons, neutrons and so on. Quine announces that Berkeley and Hume were equally drawing on scientific information in their epistemological writings, and suggests that it was only an unwarranted 'timidity' that led to the worries about circularity (see e.g. RR, pp. 1–3). He thinks that 'traditional' sceptical arguments can emerge within his approach as easily as they do for those who respect the Cartesian paradigm. Moreover, he claims, he has a clearer understanding of just how sceptical challenges work: they arise within science, and there is no obstacle to our using science in responding to them.

Many readers find this material unsettling. Even those generally sympathetic to naturalism can sense an almost wilful refusal to see the point of the kind of epistemology that belongs to the 'tradition'. We can come to terms with this response best by examining in more detail Quine's analyses of sceptical arguments.

11.4 SCEPTICAL ARGUMENTS

In *The Significance of Philosophical Scepticism* (1984), Barry Stroud has forcefully challenged Quine's right to describe his work as epistemology. He emphasizes two differences between Quine's naturalized epistemology and what he calls 'traditional epistemology'. Firstly, he suspects that that it would be circular to use scientific knowledge in order to answer the questions that trouble the tradition, while Quine has no such scruples. And, secondly, Quine ignores the radical sceptical arguments based on the thought that we might be dreaming or the victims of a deceitful spirit or wicked scientist which provide the impetus for the traditional inquiries. Perhaps Quine is not responding to the deep insecurities about knowledge which have troubled the 'Cartesian tradition'. The differences are probably related: these sceptical arguments may be required to inspire the radical doubts about our methods of inquiry which cannot be resolved scientifically.

In *The Roots of Reference* Quine amplifies his remarks about the goal of epistemology in a style designed to emphasize continuities. Like ancient epistemology, Quine's successor responds to a sceptical challenge:

> The challenge runs as follows. Science itself teaches that there is no clairvoyance; that the only information that can reach our sensory surfaces from external objects must be limited to two-dimensional optical projections and various impacts of air waves on the eardrums and some gaseous reactions in the nasal passages and a few kindred odds and ends. How, the challenge proceeds, could one hope to find out about the external world from such meager traces? In short, if our science were true, how could we know it?
>
> (RR, p. 2)

'Doubt prompts the theory of knowledge' we are told (NNK, p. 67). But, 'the crucial logical point', to which Quine returns again and again, is that the challenge arises from *within* natural science. If we did not take natural science seriously, we should not have the information about the 'meager traces' which lead us to wonder how science is possible at all.

This was true of traditional epistemology too. 'Berkeley was bent on deriving depth from two-dimensional data for no other reason than the physical fact that the surface of the eye is two-dimensional' (RR, p. 2). The same holds of the ancient Greek sceptics, who appealed to familiar illusions to question the reliability of the senses: 'but this concept of illusion itself rested on natural science, since the quality of illusion consisted simply in deviation from external scientific reality' (RR, p. 3). The crucial difference between Quine's epistemologist and his more scrupulous forebears is that Berkeley 'and the other old epistemologists would have resisted this statement of the matter' (RR, p. 2), while their successor 'is enlightened in recognizing that the sceptical challenge springs from science itself' (RR, p. 3). Quine's view is that the 'fear of circularity is a case of needless logical timidity': once we see that 'the sceptical challenge springs from science itself', we shall grant that 'in coping with it we are free to use scientific knowledge' (RR, p. 3).

Quine is not claiming that since sceptical arguments arise within science, they cannot be used to question our scientific knowledge as a whole. Sceptics could use science in order to overthrow or refute science: 'this, if carried out, would be a straightforward argument by *reductio ad absurdum*' (NNK, p. 68). If our psychological study of cognition suggested that it was impossible that we could learn the scientific facts and theories which we make use of in that study, then this might shake our confidence in our scientific discoveries as a whole. Conflicts between our science and our account of how science is carried out *could* lead to doubt about science as a whole. It is Quine's view that this is how sceptical arguments generally work: science suggests that science is impossible. Of course, Quine himself is not *convinced* by the sceptical arguments. The important point is that the adoption of a naturalized epistemology does not prevent a serious sceptical challenge being mounted against the claims of science.

According to Quine, this diagnosis of the structure of sceptical arguments deprives us of any reason not to use scientific results in responding to them. Stroud disagrees, affirming that 'Quine's concession that the sceptic can be understood as arguing by *reductio ad absurdum*' strongly supports 'the traditional epistemologist's understanding of his question' (Stroud 1984, p. 229). He denies that scruples about circularity can be dismissed as easily as this. At first sight, Quine appears to be on solid ground. If a sceptic offers a scientific argument which appears to show that science is impossible, our best response is to find a mistake in the scientific argument. All we can do is to show that a better scientific theory removes the *appearance* of a scientific *reductio ad absurdum* of science. So, if we respond by correcting the scientific theory which supports the sceptical argument, we respond by doing science.

Stroud imagines us asking, like Descartes, 'whether we know anything about the world around us, and how any such knowledge is possible', and then finding that our physical knowledge of the processes of perception make our questions difficult to answer:

> If we then reasoned as Descartes reasons and arrived by *reductio ad absurdum* at the conclusion that we know nothing about the physical world, and we found ourselves dissatisfied with that conclusion, clearly we could not go blithely on to satisfy ourselves and explain how knowledge is nevertheless possible by appealing to those very beliefs about the external world that we have just consigned to the realm of what is not known. By our own arguments, despite their scientific origin, we

would find ourselves precluded from using as independently reliable any part of what we had previously accepted as knowledge of the world around us.

(Stroud 1984, p. 229)

He concludes that the scientific *origin* of our doubts does not guarantee that we can respond to them scientifically.

Is anything going on beyond an exchange of contrary intuitions? Compare two ways in which we could respond to sceptical arguments. The Quinean philosopher begins with a strong predisposition to accept science. When presented with sceptical challenges, his immediate reaction is that something is wrong with the theories used by the sceptic: his confidence in science is not shaken at all, but he entertains doubts about the sceptic's scientific capacities. Stroud finds the arguments devastating: he loses confidence in science and has to claw his way back without scientific aid. Quine thinks that Stroud is 'overreacting'; Stroud thinks Quine is blind to the force of the argument. If that is all that is going on, then there may not be much to say about who is right, beyond pointing out, with Peirce, that none of us are really devastated by sceptical arguments – we retain our confidence in our beliefs for all practical purposes and only pretend to doubt them.

This is not all that is going on. Stroud's comment contains two crucial references to Descartes. First, we ask Descartes' question:

Do we know anything about the world at all?

and second, the *reductio* results from our employing Descartes' argument. The question already raises the point alluded to in the last paragraph. For Quine, the question is:

How do we know as much as we do?

Until a challenge actually arises, the Quinean epistemologist finds scepticism unthinkable: the satisfactory character of our physical knowledge is one of the planks that keeps the boat afloat. Stroud thinks that there is something disingenuous about this attitude: it does not take scepticism seriously.

The reference to Descartes' argument provides the background to this. Quine's sceptical arguments rest upon discoveries about the physiology of the eye and brain: Descartes' rest upon a hypothetical possibility – that all is a dream, or due to the machinations of the evil scientist. It is plausible that sceptical doubts of *this* sort cannot be met scientifically. Any scientific discovery is compatible with the sceptical hypothesis, so none can be employed to refute it. According to Descartes, an affirmative answer to *his* question is impossible unless these possibilities can be refuted. Stroud's view appears to be that once science teaches us that our knowledge of external things is mediated through the experiences which those things cause in us, we have to take seriously the possibility that those experiences may be caused in abnormal fashion. Hence, worries about wicked scientists or the possibility that all is a dream have a role in a sceptical *reductio* whose *origin* is in science, but which cannot be resolved scientifically.

Quine does not consider these possibilities. He sees no need to eliminate the possibility that his 'stimulations' were caused in his disembodied brain by a scientist using a computer to stimulate his nerve endings directly. Although he takes sceptical arguments seriously, he only considers challenges that are weaker than those that impress Stroud. This is one source of the worry that he has changed the subject. At this point, we may wonder whether we are not wasting time over a minor verbal matter of classification. Especially if we are impressed by the thought that 'traditional epistemology' is a philosopher's fiction which imposes an unrealistic straitjacket upon a wide variety of philosophical investigations of knowledge, we may feel that it does not matter whether we call Quine's work 'epistemology'. This would be a mistake. For there is an underlying issue: does Quine's philosophical position allow him to deny that there is any philosophical interest in considering the Cartesian arguments at all? Has he managed to escape from a philosophical illusion which is the source of the apparent force of the more radical sceptical arguments?

Quine describes the new epistemologist as 'a defender or protector'. 'He no longer dreams of a first philosophy, firmer than science, on which science can be based; he is out to defend science from within, against its self doubts' (RR, p. 3). This is compatible with a sceptical resignation from the Cartesian issue, and a decision to restrict our attention to more manageable challenges to science. This interpretation may be strengthened by his acknowledgement of the 'Humean predicament' – the scientific method is fallible and any of the beliefs we acquire through using it may subsequently be abandoned. However, I think that something can be said to support the view that Quine does not simply turn his back on important questions. Why does he think that 'Cartesian doubt is not the way to begin' (NNK, p. 68)?

Sometimes he suggests that a straightforward mistake grounds the older approach. Scientific theories cannot be *proved* from observation claims. A variety of theories will always be compatible with the available evidence. Moreover general laws can never be established conclusively: however sure we may be that all ravens are black, there is no *proof* that we shall not find one of a different colour in the future. Quine complains that only an unreasonable desire for absolute certainty or security leads epistemologists to try to ground science 'from the outside'. Science does not work like that, and we need not view this with especial alarm. We may have to revise beliefs that now seem wholly certain to us; but why should that be disturbing? Since we are certain that science does work – and can offer scientific explanations of why it does – why do we need more? Just as the bare possibility that our favourite theories may be refuted in the future need not alienate us from them, so it is neurotic to lose confidence in science in response to the bare possibility that it might let us down.

This may be effective against the sceptical suggestion that we may some day recognize error where we are currently most certain. 'Cartesian' worries go deeper however, suggesting the possibility of error that could *never* become apparent to us. This is why scientific responses appear to miss the point. Once we pose the issue in this way, Quine's approach seems less adequate. Sceptical arguments question whether our beliefs correspond to *reality*. This requires that we have some sort of conception of 'reality', which we use to pose this question. Descartes did: his first concern was not with a science which would make sense of human experience, giving us predictive control over our surroundings. Rather, he wanted his science to tell him how things were for God – he sought an account of how reality *really* was, independent of human practices and human cognitive processes. This provides him with a conception of reality which allows that our science may be wholly wrong, concealing from us this 'absolute' character of reality. It is clear how, for example, the possibility that we may be dreaming can challenge the claim that we have insight into how reality is for God. To rely upon science to answer this challenge plainly would be to beg the question. (For development of a similar point, see Craig 1983.)

In a secular world, our science is not driven by this ambition; nor do we possess this conception of reality. The only conception of reality we have, according to Quine, is derived from the sciences: it is given by the planks that currently keep our ship afloat. When we ask what knowledge we have of reality, we gloss this as: how much do we know about stones, sticks, human beings, protons, neurons and so on. We cannot step off the boat, abandoning our scientific picture of the world while retaining a grip on 'reality' which can be used to raise epistemological questions. In that case, Quine could defend himself by saying that the naturalizing of epistemology is an inevitable consequence of the secularization of our conception of reality. We have abandoned the metaphysical framework which gave the Cartesian challenges their philosophical force. We need not consider these more radical sceptical arguments. Normative issues about how we should investigate our surroundings, and about when beliefs are justified, arise against the background of our conception of physical reality.

There is a natural riposte to this. When we read the first *Meditation*, we respond to the arguments: we feel the force of the possibility that all might be a dream; and students in their first weeks of philosophy are readily convinced of the need to reply to Descartes' challenge. Perhaps this shows that we still do have the conception of reality which Descartes exploits; perhaps it shows that 'traditional epistemology' does not require that conception: either way it is a response that cannot be ignored. However, we can question the significance of this phenomenon (cf. Rorty 1982, pp. 180ff). Philosophers and students are no less impressionable than others. We enjoy thinking through these possibilities, and they may make vivid to us the tenuous and contingent character of our relations to our surroundings. But, since they do not actually induce doubt in anyone, it is more plausible to see the response as a complex kind of pretence than as anything of epistemological importance. How are we to choose between these attitudes?

I suspect that Quine is guided by an attitude, which is typical of positivism, and which has been neatly captured by Carnap:

> the experience in our investigations and discussions led us to the following practical attitude. We regarded terms of the traditional philosophical language with suspicion . . . and accepted them only when they have passed a careful examination; in contrast, we regarded terms of mathematics and physics as innocent . . . unless cogent reasons had shown them to be untenable.
>
> (Schilpp 1963, pp. 65–6)

Science is innocent unless proved guilty, while philosophy is guilty unless proved innocent. Unless forced by science to take sceptical worries seriously, the sceptic's arguments can be set aside as enjoyable but unconvincing anomalies. While this may explain and even justify Quine's response to scepticism, it will be insufficient to persuade Stroud that the Cartesian challenge is of no philosophical importance.

11.5 A SCIENTIFIC REFUTATION OF SCIENCE?

According to Quine, a sceptical outlook is an overreaction to some common-place facts about the fallibility of human inquirers. We shall now consider whether Quine's own views about inquiry do not support scepticism. If he is right, isn't it a miracle that science is successful? Shouldn't he conclude that science vindicates scepticism rather than undermining it? Some readers suspect that an argument for scepticism lurks within his writings.

In a passage quoted early in section 11.4, we saw how 'meager' Quine takes the evidential basis for science to be. Prompted only by stimulations of sensory surfaces, we construct a complex, sophisticated account of the physical character of reality. Another speaker, subject to exactly the same stimulations, could have come to assent to a very different set of sentences. Even all possible evidence would not determine that one of us was correct and the other mistaken. Theory is underdetermined by data.

If I look on my current theories as knowledge, I have to believe that I hold them because they are true: if my account of the world were not correct, then (most probably) I would have some different account of the world. But if all of these theories fit all possible evidence, my experience would have been unchanged if another one was true. So I have no reason to think that I would not hold my own theory even if it were false. It is quite possible that one of these other theories is correct and nothing in my experience could reveal that to me. If I have hit upon the truth, this can only be because I have been very lucky: it is a miracle that we are on the right track at all (if we are).

Quine has a response to this argument. If theories fit all the same data, they are 'empirically equivalent'. We can then treat them as notational variants. If my colleague in the next laboratory defends one of these formulations while I prefer a different one, I can find an adequate translation manual for his language which shows him to defend the same 'theory' as me. In virtue of the indeterminacy of translation, there is no fact of the matter which 'theory' he holds, and thus no real semantic difference between the 'theories'. Quine illustrates this possibility by reference to the kind of example we discussed in chapter 8 (p. 143): if one of the alternative theories differs from mine only by using 'neutron' where I use 'proton' and vice versa, there is no real disagreement.

If this procedure is not readily available, Quine has another strategy. The alternative theories do not really compete: they are *all* true (TT, pp. 29–30). Our sense that there is a problem here rests upon the 'illusion of there being only one solution to the riddle of the universe' (NNK, p. 81). If choice of theory (of a set of sentences to accept as true) is empirically underdetermined, then there are many theory formulations which (as it were) say the same thing. Our sense that our way of putting it must be the right way to put it (the illusion mentioned above) is simply the result of 'tunnel vision', which (fortunately) prevents our being overwhelmed by all these alternatives in practice.

This account seems to solve our sceptical problem, and nicely illustrates the role of the indeterminacy of translation in removing philosophical illusions. But it seems to raise problems of its own. In 'The nature of natural knowledge', Quine announces that 'science is a linguistic structure that is keyed to observation at some points' (NNK, pp. 72). We have several times quoted his characterization of talk of the external world as 'just a conceptual apparatus that helps us to foresee and control the triggering of our sensory receptors in the light of previous triggering of our sensory receptors' (TT, p. 1). These statements suggest a view closer to anti-realism than to the scientific realism which Quine proclaims. The linguistic structure is a useful instrument whose only contact with reality is through these triggerings that prompt observation reports. Why should we take the scientific account of the world seriously as actually *true*?

There is an old-fashioned extreme empiricism that holds that all that we are directly aware of are our subjective experiences. Scientific theory and talk of ordinary physical objects both serve as useful instruments for predicting and controlling these experiences; but they do not pretend to tell us what there really is. Alternative theories are comparable in terms of how useful they are as instruments, but it is an error to worry about whether they are true or false. The picture we now find Quine defending seems like this view. But there is a difference: for the oldfashioned view, experiences were epistemologically prior to these other forms of discourse – we were immediately aware of them; the Quinean surrogates for experiences (stimulations) are themselves fabrications of scientific theory, and observation sentences themselves involve theoretical elaboration.

Quine clearly believes that this makes all the difference, enabling him to be a realist. It is easy to feel that, on the contrary, it makes things much worse. Scientific theories are looked upon as instruments which enable us to anticipate the future run of stimuli, which are described in theories which are instruments which enable us to make sense of . . . what?

Stroud clearly thinks that there are problems here, and insists that, while it is possible to think of another person in these terms, we cannot use this framework to make sense of our own cognitive activities. I cannot look upon my own beliefs merely as instruments which enable me to predict physiological states when I have no conscious access to the physiological states. If I only know that I have sensory surfaces as a kind of projection from empirical data, then the question of how I construct my empirical knowledge from stimulations of my sensory surfaces begins to seem very curious. It does not seem the right question to ask if my concern is with whether *I* can know anything at all (cf. Stroud 1984, pp. 234ff). It seems as if Quine's position defeats the sceptical argument mentioned earlier at the cost of making it impossible for us to accept his theory as true of the claims *we* make in doing epistemology.

We shall return to this issue in chapter 12. Quine has to show that his scientific explanation of science does not explain away the realist pretensions of science. If I look on my theories as such a 'linguistic structure', how can I view them as a true description of reality? How can we take our own theories seriously?

11.6 CONCLUSION

We will make no further progress with these issues until we understand Quine's views about truth and reality. These will be the topic of the following chapter. In concluding this one, I shall make some general observations.

First, it is important to distinguish the general project of a naturalized epistemology from the details of Quine's execution of the project. The difficulties discussed in section 11.5 reflect Quine's empiricist, physicalist account of science. People could share all our worries about that position while still maintaining that psychology has inherited the mantle of traditional epistemology. They could disagree about the kind of psychology that should be used, preferring the richer framework of mentalist cognitive psychology.

Second, there is a loose connection between these problems and others mentioned in section 11.4. Quine's philosophy is thoroughly in the third person. He is interested in how scientists, in general, know what they know. The question is conceived as an impersonal scientific one. It is important that Descartes raised his problem in the *first* person: do I know anything at all? If we state the problem for philosophy as that of making sense of, or coming to terms with, our own cognitive contact with reality, then the first-person perspective becomes appropriate. This is a very vague phrase, and for the present I shall not do much to clarify it. But, if this is the starting point, then the fact that we do find Descartes' sceptical hypotheses engaging becomes rather more prominent – and the fact that science does not worry about them fades into the background. Our worry from section 11.5 is related to this. For it suggests that Quine's epistemology does not provide a framework that we can use to make sense of ourselves and our relations to our experience.

I propose to leave this as a lurking worry for later discussion. Quine's philosophy may elucidate the concepts that are involved in physical and natural science, but it seems to say nothing about the concepts that we use to understand ourselves and our activities.

12

Physicalism and Reality

12.1. INTRODUCTION

As we have previously noticed, Quine claims to be a realist. In a review, he cites J. J. C. Smart's defence of 'an unashamedly realistic view of the fundamental particles of physics' and endorses his claim 'that the physicist's language gives us a *truer* picture of the world than does the language of common sense' (Smart 1964, pp. 18, 47; TT, pp. 92–3). He particularly approves of Smart's stress upon physics rather than science, and his denial that biology and psychology discover autonomous 'emergent' laws. Smart denies that biology and psychology study laws at all, their discoveries being at best 'local generalisations' 'on a par with natural history and geography, or with consumers' reports' (pp. 54–5). Quine agrees: 'Physics investigates the essential nature of the world, and biology describes a local bump. Psychology, human psychology, describes a bump on the bump' (TT, p. 93).

The closing pages of the previous chapter will have left us uncertain how Quine can be a realist at all. If science is just a 'linguistic structure that is keyed to observation at some points', whose utility lies in enabling us to anticipate the stimulations of our sensory surfaces, how can we take it as a true picture of the world? We are also uncertain of his grounds for insisting that physics tells the whole story: this looks like an impoverishment of our familiar world. Finally, we need to evaluate Quine's empiricism, which, we saw, shapes many of his views.

We shall not be able to make progress with these issues without looking at some abstract questions about truth and reality: just what is involved in treating an area of discourse as describing a facet of reality?

12.2 TRUTH

It is natural to suppose that the issues concern truth. Philosophers who wish to deny that a kind of statement is intended to describe reality sometimes try to do so by saying that the statement in question cannot be evaluated as true or false. For example, the judgement that mushrooms are delicious is neither true nor false, but simply expresses a preference; a moral judgement – that slander is evil, for example – expresses an attitude or commitment of the speaker's but is not intended to express a *truth*. In that case, perhaps Quine's physicalism could be expressed by saying that only statements from physics are genuine candidates for being true. When we evaluate or criticize other utterances, we do not do so by establishing whether they are true: other, weaker, evaluative notions are used. For example, we may complain that a moral judgement is insincere, or that it is inconsistent with other judgements made by the same person, or we may express moral disapproval of it, but the complaint that it is false is out of place.

Second thoughts may lead us to doubt whether this is the right way to state the issue. If truth were understood as correspondence to fact, then it may be the correct approach: physical statements correspond to facts while, it may be claimed, moral judgements do not. In the last chapter we described some of the difficulties facing this conception of truth. Confidence in it – and in use of the notion of truth in this area more generally – is further shaken when we remember that one of the consequences of the indeterminacy of translation is that theoretical sentences (including those from theoretical physics) do not have determinate truth values (see section 8.5). We shall see shortly that our suspicion is justified. However, although it is wrong to formulate the issue as about which statements can be properly said to be true, examining Quine's views about truth will help us to understand what is at issue.

We should begin by asking how our notion of truth actually works. In 1927, the Cambridge philosopher Frank Ramsey wrote that 'there really is no separate problem of truth but merely a linguistic muddle':

> [It] is evident that 'It is true that Caesar was murdered' means no more than that Caesar was murdered, and that 'It is false that Caesar was murdered' means that Caesar was not murdered. They are phrases that we

> sometimes use for emphasis or for stylistic reasons, or to indicate the position occupied by the statement in our argument.
>
> (Ramsey 1978, p. 44)

This is sometimes called the redundancy theory of truth: 'true' adds no conceptual element (like correspondence to fact) to a proposition. We could eliminate occurrences of it in statements like the one considered above without loss.

Quine makes similar remarks, although in a more explicitly linguistic vein: he describes 'true' as a device for *disquotation* (PoL, p. 12). When we put the sentence 'Caesar was murdered' into quotation marks, we obtain a name or description of the sentence. While we can use the original sentence to make an assertion, the quoted sentence cannot be used to make an assertion unaided: it is not a complete sentence, but just a name or description. The utility of the truth predicate is that by adding it to a quoted sentence we undo the influence of the quotation marks. So ' "Caesar was murdered" is true' can be used to make the same assertion as 'Caesar was murdered'.

> To say that the statement 'Brutus killed Caesar' is true, or that 'The atomic weight of sodium is 23' is true, is in effect simply to say that Brutus killed Caesar, or that the atomic weight of sodium is 23.
>
> (WO, p. 24)

In that case, we may wonder why we bother with the notion of truth at all: isn't it simpler to drop the quotation marks than to add a phrase? The value of the notion emerges most clearly when we want to formulate generalizations. For example:

> If all of the premisses of a valid argument are true, and the argument is valid, then the conclusion is true as well
>
> Every sentence the lecturer uttered this morning is true

It *may* be possible to find a way of saying such things without explicitly using the truth predicate, but we could not do so without using a very cumbersome sentence. For example, since we could understand the second of these without knowing which sentences the lecturer uttered, its paraphrase would be a very complex conjunction:

> If the lecturer said 'snow is white' then snow is white, and if the lecturer said 'snow is green' then snow is green, and . . .

Since there are indefinitely many English sentences, the paraphrase would have no determinate finite length.

This analysis makes talk of truth philosophically respectable while leaving it powerless to draw the sorts of philosophical distinction we are interested in here. For, if this is all there is to truth, there seems to be no reason not to accept instances of the disquotation such as:

> To say that 'Mushrooms are delicious' is true is simply to say that mushrooms are delicious
>
> To say that 'slander is evil' is true is simply to say that slander is evil.
> (TT, pp. 89–91)

If we are uneasy about these claims, it cannot be because we are unhappy about the role of 'true' in them – unless, of course, the disquotation approach is mistaken. We must find another way to express the anti-realist view that some sentences are not to be understood as describing the nature of reality, and the realist claim that some are.

Some philosophers claim that disquotation theories of truth miss a vital component of our concept of truth. Hilary Putnam and Simon Blackburn have both complained that without a more substantive understanding of truth, and of its role in *evaluating* judgements and assertions, we can make no sense of our thoughts and utterances being thoughts and utterances at all. Truth is what we aim for in our inquiries: we adopt theories because we think that they are true; the goal of assertion is to present a statement as true; standards of inference are justified by showing that they contribute to the search for the truth. Practices like thought and assertion are partly constituted by evaluative standards of justification and criticism. These standards are understood in terms of the notion of truth. So, there must be more to be said than the Quinean theory allows.

> Let us recognize that one of our fundamental 'self-descriptions', in Rorty's phrase, is that we are *thinkers*, and that *as* thinkers we are committed to there being *some* kind of truth, some kind of correctness which is substantial and not merely 'disquotational'.
> (Putnam 1983, p. 246)

This raises an important point, to which we will return. It challenges naturalized epistemology as much as the disquotational approach to truth, and links with the worries raised at the end of the previous chapter. If one of the tasks of philosophy is to help us to understand our 'self-descriptions', then it is natural to start from our first-person perspective upon these activities and to feel that Quine has missed something out. The challenge is that, in order to understand our own activities as speakers and reasoners, we must use concepts which are excluded by Quine's austere conception of reality.

12.3 TAKING OUR OWN PHYSICS SERIOUSLY

As we have seen, Quine denies that the issue of realism can be formulated in terms of truth. It is natural to object to this along the following lines. Quine appears to hold that the same sentence can be true according to one theory and false according to another, the theories being empirically equivalent. In that case, there seems to be no fact of the matter whether the sentence is true or false: it has a truth value only relative to a theory (and to a translation manual). 'Have we now so far lowered our sights as to settle for a relativistic doctrine of truth – rating the statements of each theory as true for that theory, and brooking no higher criticism?' (WO, p. 24). Realism requires that we answer (with Quine) 'Not so'. We regard our theories as (non-relativistically) true. We admit that our current best theories may be *mistaken*, but we evaluate them in terms of an absolute non-relativistic notion of truth.

According to Quine:

> The saving consideration is that we continue to take seriously our own particular aggregate science, our own particular world-theory or loose total fabric of quasi-theories, whatever it may be. Unlike Descartes, we own and use the beliefs of the moment, even in the midst of philosophizing, until by what is vaguely called scientific method we change them here or there for the better. Within our total evolving doctrine, we can judge truth as earnestly or absolutely as can be; subject to correction, but that goes without saying.
>
> (WO, pp. 24–5)

So, what is it to 'take seriously' our current theories, and how does that undermine the relativistic worries we have just stated?

Suppose that, according to my current theory, protons have positive charge. This is manifested in several ways: in the explanations I accept, in the inferences I draw, and in the assertions I make. Among these assertions will be the assertion that protons carry positive charge. It seems that my taking this as true 'absolutely' consists in the fact that I just *say* 'Protons carry positive charge'. Relativity to theory is not explicit or implicit in my speech act, nor is this relativity present in anything that I can offer as a reason for my assertion. I simply treat it as assertible. As the later sentences in the quotation suggest, I do not stand back and reflect upon how the assertion is justified, in philosophical terms. Rather, the fact that it is assertible serves as a kind of fixed point for philosophical and scientific reflection. This is the point we encountered in the previous chapter: my scientific view of the world provides the substantive conception of reality which is used to explain the success of my methods of inquiry.

However, the relativist or anti-realist tendencies have not disappeared. Suppose I consider another inquirer who has his own set of sentences which he 'seriously' assents to, taking them to be 'non-relativistically' true. Since I can only describe his theories by making use of a translation manual, and since alternative adequate translation manuals will assign different 'contents' to his assertions, I cannot look upon this inquirer's theories in the non-relative fashion I use for my own. His assertion has one content according to one manual, a different content according to another; it has different ontological commitments according to different manuals; and it may have different truth values according to different manuals. Although he confidently utters indicative sentences, and makes no relativities explicit in what he says, I seem to be forced to conclude that there is no fact about just what it was that he said. It seems to be much easier for me to be realist about my own theories than it is for me to be realist about those of others. Putnam cites a remark in which Quine admitted that he is 'asymmetrical', a realist with respect to his own language but not with respect to other languages (Putnam 1983, p. 242fn). This *seems* a very odd combination, but unless we see how it is plausible, we shall never understand the underlying forces at work in Quine's philosophy.

Let us go back to Carnap's pragmatism, discussed in chapter 2. Carnap held that we employ linguistic frameworks in order to make sense of our experience. Working within our framework, we make what seem to be objective discoveries: we answer internal questions employing criteria and standards which are provided by the framework. We can also step back and survey the framework as a whole, from what is often called the 'transcendental standpoint' – in Carnap's case, we employ a syntactic or semantic framework to carry out this transcendental exercise in a scientific way. From the transcendental standpoint, we discover that one framework is not to be preferred to another on the grounds that it is *objectively true*. The preference is justified on pragmatic grounds. We can express this combination of views by saying that when we are working within a framework, considering internal questions, we are 'internal realists': we look for the right answer to our questions. When we step back, we recognize the truth of 'transcendental pragmatism': our internal realism rests upon pragmatist (or anti-realist) foundations which can only be recognized from the transcendental standpoint. Cartesian epistemology, of the sort favoured by Stroud, rests upon the possibility of stepping back to take up a transcendental standpoint and thus question the adequacy of our means of obtaining knowledge of the world as a whole.

It should be clear that one element in Quine's rejection of the Carnapian framework is a denial that we *can* step back and take up a transcendental view of our knowledge. His 'realism' reflects the view that our cognitive position is always internal to a body of substantive theory: 'Whatever we affirm, after all, we affirm as a statement within our aggregate theory of nature as we now see it; and to call a statement true is just to reaffirm it' (EESW, p. 327). But there is a truth in anti-realism too, it seems.

The picture is becoming complex. The most important point is this. For Quine, when we can, so to speak, hold an area of discourse at arms' length, we can adopt an anti-realist attitude towards it. If, remaining secure upon the ship, we can look upon an area of talk as a separable unit, which can be surveyed from the solid timbers that remain, then we can treat that area of speech anti-realistically. Hence, secure within our own 'aggregate theory of nature', we can survey the assertions of another language user and appreciate that they have content only relative to a translation manual. Our aggregate theory provides a standpoint which is 'relatively transcendental': it is transcendental relative to the speech behaviour of other language users. There is no point which provides a secure foundation for stepping back and surveying our own theoretical activities: we remain *within* them, and hence can only construe them realistically. The question what I think is thus a Carnapian *internal* question; the question what some other individual thinks can become *external* because the relativity to a translation manual can be made explicit.

This observation bears upon a famous passage from *Word and Object*, in which Quine explains why we cannot conclude that 'translation synonymy at its worse is no worse off than truth in physics':

> To be thus reassured is to misjudge the parallel. In being able to speak of the truth of a sentence only within a more inclusive theory, one is not much hampered; for one is always working within some comfortably inclusive theory, however tentative . . . In short, the parameters of truth stay conveniently fixed most of the time. Not so the analytical hypotheses which constitute the parameter of translation. We are always ready to wonder about the meaning of some foreigner's remark without reference to any one set of analytical hypotheses, indeed even in the absence of any.
>
> (WO, pp. 75–6)

It is worth labouring this point, for it is easily misunderstood.

Suppose that, contrary to fact, we had arrived at many alternative theories, all compatible with all possible evidence. And suppose too that some sentence S is true in one of them, but false in another. Would the case then be different? Should we then take an anti-realist view of our own theories? I think that Quine's answer would be 'No'; and he would hold that the appearance of paradox about the truth value of S can be removed. We can either treat one theory as a notational variant of the other (recall our 'proton'/'neutron' example), or we treat *both* theories as true and recognize theoretical terms occurring in S as ambiguous. In the latter case, we may revise our terminology to remove the ambiguity, so that the sentence S no longer occurs in both theories. It is not a part of Quine's realism that a theory could fit all possible data yet not be true. (See TT, ch. 2 for an extended discussion of these matters.) We can live with the underdetermination of theory choice by evidence without being forced to acknowledge anti-realism or relativism explicitly.

Faced with a variety of translation manuals, all compatible with the physical facts, the situation is different. In line with the views alluded to in the previous paragraph, we could conclude that all are true or correct. The easiest way to eliminate paradox would be to claim that we have uncovered a kind of ambiguity in the concept of meaning, and we could revise our terminology to indicate this. We could do this by explicitly relativizing the notion of meaning to a translation manual. The following statements are all true:

'Gavagai' means-by-TM1 'rabbit'

'Gavagai' means-by-TM2 'undetached rabbit part'

'Gavagai' means-by-TM3 'rabbit stage', etc.

We could embed all of these in our 'aggregate theory'. The result of thus treating translation on a par with physical truth – on Quine's understanding of these matters – simply *is* the indeterminacy of translation. We ask what 'gavagai' means, and we take ourselves to be using a non-relativized notion of meaning; we seem to need such a notion, for we want our communication with the aliens to be based upon the translation manual which reflects what they actually *mean*. There is no basis for selecting one of these relativized notions of meaning as corresponding to the pre-theoretic non-relativized notion. We can only make the pragmatic decision to use one of these meaning notions for communicative purposes.

However, there is a further twist which means that Quine's anti-realism runs even deeper than we have suggested so far. When, secure within my 'aggregate theory', I begin to think about my own verbal behaviour in theoretical or semantical terms, I am forced to admit that, here too, indeterminacy reigns. Philosophical reflection upon my own verbal behaviour, concerned with hunting out semantic rules and ontological commitments, requires me to make use of translational notions. I then recognize that the intentional content of my own psychological states is subject to indeterminacy: semantical and intentional phenomena cannot be incorporated within the science of nature as I would wish. I can recognize, too, that others can be troubled by indeterminacy of translation when they attempt to understand my utterances and describe my thoughts. Hence, there seems to be a truth in anti-realism, even in the first-person case, which can be acknowledged, even if it cannot be stated explicitly through the use of a relativized notion of truth.

The most important point to notice here is this. When I communicate with other people, I have to use semantic or translational notions. My relations with other people are mediated through largely inchoate translation manuals. When I reflect philosophically upon my own thoughts and utterances – and when I try to construct an intentional study of the mind – I have to use semantic or translational notions in interpreting my own behaviour. Such semantic notions – rules and translation manuals – have no role in ordinary speech. In deciding whether to assent to a sentence, I respond 'blindly' with no sense of rules which force me to respond in one way rather than another. Philosophical reflection does not recover semantic facts which are unconsciously at work in normal speech behaviour. I don't employ semantic notions in deciding what to say on particular occasions. So, we can think of ordinary spontaneous speech about the physical world as pre-translational – unlike speech about the speech and thoughts of others and philosophical or scientific thought about our own speech and thoughts. Ordinary talk of truth and reference is not guided by sophisticated theory but rests simply upon disquotation principles. The embeddedness of such principles grounds everyday claims about what *must* exist for our theories to be true (see p. 25). This is why it is supposed that our ship can be securely afloat while we hold determinate translation relations at bay.

12.4 PHYSICALISM

For Quine, the physical facts are all the facts. The canonical notation is adequate if it can regiment all the claims made in a finished physical theory; translation is indeterminate if correctness of translation is not fixed by physics; and naturalized epistemology is best viewed as the physics of inquiry. We must now consider Goodman's question: why this special deference to physical theory? Goodman himself treats all 'versions' as on a par, with no favour for physics or even for science; Quine's refusal to do this has radical implications for the shape of his philosophy.

The Quinean response to Goodman itself reflects his scientistic outlook. Quine takes Goodman's point to be that, starting from physics, we can construct a continuous variety of worlds or versions, and we can find no principled basis for stopping short of admitting them all. He seems to think that Goodman would prefer to favour science or physics, but cannot see how to do so. It is far from clear that this is the correct way to view the matter. Goodman appears to revel in his pluralism and to show no embarrassment in what Quine sees as evident excesses. This outlook seems not to be one that Quine can comprehend.

There are several strands to this physicalism. Physics differs from other sciences. First, 'full coverage . . . is the very business of physics, and only of physics': 'nothing happens in the world, not the flutter of an eyelid, not the flicker of a thought, without some redistribution of physical states' (TT, p. 98). In consequence of this:

> Anyone who will say, 'Physics is all very well in its place' – and who will not – is then already committed to a physicalism of at least the

> nonreductive, nontranslational sort . . . Hence my special deference to physical theory as a world version . . .
>
> (TT, p. 198)

A related point is that physics studies the 'essential nature of the world' – the *fundamental* laws are physical laws. (These points are familiar from chapter 4.)

Related to this, Quine claims that sciences other than physics do not provide autonomous explanations, or study distinctive features of reality. Rather, their concern is to allude to physical features of reality in spite of ignorance of their physical nature. Alternatively, they may collect together wide ranges of physical facts in ways that reflect our practical interests and concerns. They describe physical facts in ways that are useful to us. Only physics is not compromised by the gaps of ignorance or 'subjective' distortion: only physics provides uncontaminated, complete scientific explanations.

It is possible to feel several kinds of unease about this, even granting Quine's point about 'full coverage'. The weakest of them surfaces in puzzlement about why philosophy should only be interested in the physicists' view of things. Quine's canonical notation enables us to capture the contents of finished physical theories, but does not serve as a useful instrument for understanding the practice of biologists, economists or cognitive psychologists. The move from the premiss that physics has full coverage to the conclusion that philosophy should concentrate upon making sense of physical theory, and should try to measure up to the standards of physical theory, needs more of an argument than Quine provides. The conclusion invites the response – suggested by remarks of Fodor – that it is grotesque for philosophers simply to dismiss or ignore fields of research which yield suggestive insights and appear to make progress.

The point can be strengthened. Human beings participate in a wide range of activities, from physics to painting, from cognitive psychology to politics. One thing we can look for from philosophy is a clarification of the concepts we use when participating in such activities: how do they enable us to understand our involvement in them? How do they guide the choices and evaluations we make when we vote, visit a gallery, or conduct an experiment? The vocabulary of physics seems wholly unsuited to this kind of self-understanding, and it can thus be argued that Quine ignores just those concepts and sentences that we use to describe and evaluate the activities we participate in as persons (cf. Putnam 1983, p. 246).

The first worry was that Quine has a narrow philosophical vision. There are philosophical exercises other than those that interest him. It would probably be unfair to claim that Quine was not aware of this, and there are papers where he makes initial attempts to explain or describe our ordinary practice in using concepts like belief or necessity. Even when he does this, he is hampered because he normally works within a physicalist framework, and thus insists that practices be described in rigorous, precise terms which are foreign to our ordinary practices of self-understanding. The second worry went beyond this in suggesting that what Quine misses may somehow be constitutive of human experience – of our ability to think of ourselves as persons. A level of explanation which provides the terms in which we understand our lives and activities has a kind of autonomous validity. For the logician, the task of constructing a calculus which we can use to reflect upon ordinary practices of reasoning is as important as the task of constructing a canonical notation for science.

This line of concern can be taken to a third stage, where it conflicts with Quinean theses. Why should we take the point about 'full coverage' to show that the physical facts exhaust the facts at all? If statements drawn from economics or cognitive psychology provide us with an understanding of phenomena which we could not obtain from physics, and if we have means for settling disagreements in these areas in a reasonably reliable fashion, why shouldn't we claim that they reveal a facet of reality which is not revealed to us by physics? In spite of full coverage, there are non-physical facts which we allude to in making sense of ourselves and our surroundings. That all change *involves* physical change does not entail that every fact *is* a physical fact.

Quine's resistance to this kind of view may be traced to assumptions shared with the positivist movement. The positivists generally wished to view all sciences as unified by a common method, and they claimed that all could be unified into a single structure of knowledge. The picture just described probably conflicts with this. But that does not count against it unless there are arguments which support the Quinean physicalist alternative. Can anything be said in its support? Let me mention two lines of argument which may be operative.

The first derives from Quine's empiricism. Quine distinguishes our sensory input (described in physical terms as patterns of stimulation at the surfaces of our perceptual organs) from the structures of sentences which provide our predictive control over them. Systems of explanation are satisfactory if they enhance our ability to anticipate the future run of stimulations. The distinction between input and interpretation, together with the claim that explanation consists in a kind of predictive control, are distinctive of an empiricist approach to human knowledge. Since stimulations are physical phenomena, they all have physical explanations. Moreover, physical theory will be as good as anything at enabling us to anticipate future patterns of stimulation. If other explanations are preferred, this can only be because they are more manageable: we find them easier to handle, even if they do not provide such accurate explanations or predictions. This fits with the Quinean picture that they allude to underlying physical explanations and have no independent explanatory force.

I shall return to this empiricist outlook in the following section. I think that much of Quine's position here can be traced to it. There is a problem about how far the conception of experience and knowledge which it involves results from Quine's physicalist naturalism rather than vice versa. Within the spirit of holism, I think that we can see them as mutually supporting elements of his overall position.

The second argument takes us back to another theme from chapter 4. Quine often explains away features of our usage by showing that they reflect subjective or expressive commitments. Our talk of necessity expresses our determination not to surrender a proposition too readily; many features of talk of belief reflect such a subjective element. In similar vein, we noticed, Hume denied the reality of causes by finding a subjective element in our causal judgements. Others have denied the reality of colours because they are dispositions to produce a subjective human response, or of values because they are to be understood by reference to human desire. All of these arguments rest upon the assumption that areas of discourse which are thus subjective or interest-relative do not describe reality. We are prone to a projectivist fallacy: if we claim that necessity, or colours, or values are real, we mistakenly project a subjective feature of our responses to things onto the world. We treat as *objective* what is really *subjective*.

Where non-basic disciplines apparently provide autonomous explanations, this is probably because they answer to distinctive human needs for understanding. The source of their value appears subjective or interest-relative. Perhaps only physical explanations are so remote from human concerns as to lack this interest-relativity. Failing that, other disciplines are *more* tainted by the subjective than physics is: the latter provides a benchmark against which we can measure the extent to which other disciplines reflect a compromise with human ignorance, frailty or interests. Physics describes the reality which other disciplines shape in various interest-related ways.

Somebody who is impressed by the sort of alternative to physicalism which I have described may look on the suggestion that reality lacks this sort of relativity to the subjective as mere scientistic prejudice. If talk of values, or beliefs, or meanings is necessary for us to understand our practices and our relations to them; and if there are means for progressing towards agreement on controversial issues about meanings, or values or beliefs – then values, beliefs and meanings are real. There may be room for a more relaxed realism which contrasts with Quine's austere conception of reality.

12.5 EMPIRICISM

Quine defends empiricism. When he criticizes the two dogmas of empiricism, he concludes by describing 'Empiricism without the dogmas'. Traditional empiricists tend to claim that we are 'given' uninterpreted sensations or experiences. These raw empirical data are then interpreted through a system of concepts and theories, the conceptual framework being meaningful – and the theories being justified – only if they 'fit' the raw data. The raw data serve as the 'source' of all knowledge and meaning. Although Quine denies that we are *conscious* of any raw data, his naturalized epistemology retains a similar dualism (WO, ch. 1, OR, ch. 3). Our knowledge of the external world is mediated through 'stimulations' at the surfaces of our perceptual organs, and our framework of sentences is tied down to reality only insofar as it enables us to anticipate these stimulations. This does not require that we can predict which stimulations will occur. Rather, stimulations cause us to assent to observation sentences (minimal theoretical interpretations), and we anticipate the future run of stimulations accurately if we correctly anticipate which observation sentences we will assent to. Our relation to our stimulations is indirect, and rarely conscious.

We have seen how Quine's empiricism shapes his account of the evidence for translation. If it did not do this, it could hardly have this central role in his views of meaning, justification and truth. I have also suggested that it has a role in supporting his austere physicalist conception of reality. We now have to ask how defensible it is.

Two claims must be distinguished:

(1) We know about external objects because of causal interactions with them – we see them, hear them, touch them and so on.
(2) Our knowledge of external objects is mediated through sensations or experiences (or stimulations), which receive conceptual interpretation through our activities of inquiry.

Claim 1 seems undeniable. Empiricism involves a commitment to (2), and this shapes its approach to issues of meaning and knowledge.

Davidson holds to (1) but not to (2). He denounces the dualism of 'data' and interpretation as the final indefensible dogma without which empiricism collapses. His argument is Quinean in spirit: like the analytic/synthetic distinction and various reductionist prejudices, the distinction does not help us to explain how we understand each other or how we enter an alien tongue through radical interpretation. The argument involves many issues that are not of immediate significance here and I shall ignore many of the details – the reader is advised to consult Davidson (1986a,b), as well as the work of a philosopher influenced by Davidson, Richard Rorty (e.g. 1986).

According to Davidson, the radical interpreter looks for an interpretation that makes his subject as truthful and rational as possible – although, of course he does not expect him to believe what he could not have learned, and he is not discouraged by explicable error. A consequence of this is that an acceptable interpretation will find its subject to hold largely true beliefs.

This means that scepticism is ruled out from the beginning. If our beliefs and utterances have interpretable content, they cannot be substantially false. The most important feature of the approach is that it ensures that the contents of beliefs and utterances are fixed by the external states of affairs that cause them, rather than by experiences, stimulations, or other intermediaries which could exist in the absence of the external object. Thus, suppose that 'Il pleut' is accepted by a Frenchman in the presence of rain. Our presumption is that his claim is about (and truly describes) the external state of affairs that appears to cause it. We shall abandon the translation 'It is raining' only if doing so is required to maximize truth and rationality elsewhere. The interpreter attends to the relations between the speaker and his environment, but sees no need to posit intermediaries, such as stimulations, in order to ground interpretations. Indeed, the 'diverse conceptual commitments' of physics and psychology suggest that it would be wrong to expect there to be such intermediaries.

The strategy is supposed to be applied quite generally. When we interpret people's moral discourse, we presume that they are describing 'our' moral world. To begin with, we look for (perhaps complex) intepretations cast in our own moral vocabulary for the moral evaluations we are trying to understand. If we can interpret their moral discourse at all – if we can recognize it *as* moral discourse – then there must be a substantial shared moral framework: we understand alien moral views by relating them to concepts of justice, cruelty, shame, honour, which we use in our evaluations; or we exploit our own moral sensibilities in order to enter an alien moral world. Of course, substantial differences of emphasis are possible against this background: we are not prevented from finding other people's moral outlooks crude, brutal, or a fascinating challenge to our own moral perceptions. Simply seeing them as moral outlooks at all – and being able to interpret them – requires a background of shared concepts. This shared background provides for objectivity. Disagreements can be understood and overcome, and disputed questions resolved by reference to it.

Once the Davidsonian approach to interpretation is accepted, there is no basis for distinguishing areas of discourse as Quine does. The notion of truth applies unproblematically to all, and the shared beliefs underlying interpretation in any area provide some basis for attempting to resolve differences and produce agreement. But if this shows how there might be an alternative to Quinean empiricism, it does not yet refute it. Which picture corresponds best to our ordinary practices of interpretation? The question seems unanswerable: both provide rigid codification for a practice which seems far more piecemeal and informal than either. Choice between them (or preference for a different story altogether) may ultimately rest upon the kinds of preferences that were mentioned at the end of the last section. Physicalism or scientism supports the empiricist view of intepretation as much as vice versa. There seem to be differences of philosophical mood or temperament, according to whether one finds the austere physicists' conception of reality all that is required for an account of what is 'really real', or whether one prefers one's philosophy to make sense of all facets of human experience and thought.

12.6 CONCLUSION

Over the last few chapters, we have contrasted Quine's views with an alternative outlook. His scientific conception of 'reality', with its denial that anything subjective or interest-relative could count as 'real', confronts a more relaxed conception which is happy to affirm the reality of a wider range of phenomena. Davidson's epistemology challenged Quine's extreme empiricism; and their contrasting views of the epistemology of interpretation, and translation, were juxtaposed. Finally, we have contrasted two ambitions for philosophy: the concern with the ultimate furniture of the world which appears to be Quine's guiding concern; and the interest in enabling us to come to a reflective sense of our experience of the world and our actions in it. At several points, we have seen connections between these contrasts. If our interest is the ultimate furniture of the world, we may favour a more austere conception of reality than if we wish to make sense of 'our own self-descriptions'. The contrasting views of interpretation may appeal, too, to these contrasting philosophical concerns and opposed conceptions of reality.

Insofar as these juxtapositions consitute a 'response' to Quine's position, this is by suggesting the possibility of an alternative philosophical perspective to his own. It is not clear that they reveal contradictions or evident errors in his reasoning, although we are apt to find it unsettling that he seems able to make no informed or sympathetic response to them. Indeed, it seems to me that the importance of Quine's work lies in the fact that he has worked through what is involved in a physicalist empiricism more thoroughly and rigorously than any other post-positivist philosopher. Many will feel that, in the course of doing so, he has helped us to see why it is unsatisfactory, but Quine's refusal to see it that way does not diminish his achievement. Most philosophers can feel the attraction of both physicalism and empiricism, and it is of the first importance to have these ideas worked out so fully.

How are we to choose between Quine's physicalist empiricism and the alternative? What sort of choice is it? If we concentrate upon the differing views of 'reality', knowledge and interpretation, we may suppose that the issue is a substantive one. Which conception of reality is correct? How does interpretation really proceed? But the concept of 'reality' is so abstract – so much a philosophical term of art – and the competing reconstructions of radical translation and radical interpretation are so remote from our ordinary experience of attempting to understand each other, that the apparently substantive issue seems impossible to resolve. This is especially so when we remember that Quine could agree with Davidson about how it is best to do interpretation while disagreeing about which of the standards involved are 'constitutive' and which 'regulative': once again the issue turns on questions about what is constitutive of 'reality'.

On the other hand, if we concentrate upon the alternative philosophical ambitions, the issue ceases to look substantive: we can contrast different philosophical concerns and admit the interest of both, while concluding that Quine's philosophical vision is rather narrow. Just as tunnel vision is required to sustain our confident scientific realism, something similar is needed to maintain Quine's confidence in the centrality of his philosophical concerns. But if our complaint is that there is philosophical interest in issues other than the search for the ultimate laws governing the universe, we may not be disagreeing with Quine in what he says about those topics which he does discuss. The appearance that there is a substantive disagreement depends upon formulating the issue in terms of the concept of reality. We assume that we have a pre-theoretical conception of reality, and we inquire which approach correctly elucidates that concept. But it is far from clear that we do have a pre-theoretical conception of reality which can actually carry that weight. And it is far from clear that debates over what is real do more than disguise the underlying nature of disagreements that rest ultimately upon upon disagreements about which issues are philosophically important and about the role of science in our thought. If we conclude that patterns of psychological explanation and moral judgement do not share the 'conceptual commitments' of physics, yet allow for reasoned argument and for resolving disputes in settled or reasoned ways, it is easy to conclude that it is only a physicalist or empiricist prejudice that justifies restricting our conception of the real in the way that Quine desires.

References

WORKS BY W. V. O. QUINE

Sources for quotations from these works employ the abbreviations given after the titles.

Books

Methods of Logic (ML). London: Routledge & Kegan Paul, 1952.

From a Logical Point of View (FLPV). Cambridge, Mass.: Harvard University Press, 1953.

Word and Object (WO). Cambridge, Mass.: MIT Press, 1960.

Ways of Paradox and Other Essays (WP) (revised edition). Cambridge, Mass.: Harvard University Press, 1976. (First edition, 1966.)

Ontological Relativity and Other Essays (OR). New York: Columbia University Press, 1969.

Philosophy of Logic (PoL). Englewood Cliffs, N.J.: Prentice-Hall, 1970.

The Roots of Reference (RR). La Salle, Ill.: Open Court, 1973.

Theories and Things (TT). Cambridge, Mass.: Harvard University Press, 1981.

The Web of Belief (WB) (with Joseph Ullian) (second edition). New York: Random House, 1978. (First edition, 1970.)

Articles which are not reprinted in any of the books

'On empirically equivalent systems of the world' (EESW), *Erkenntnis* 9, 1975, 313–28.

'The nature of natural knowledge' (NNK) in Guttenplan (ed.) 1975, pp. 57–81.

'Facts of the matter' (FM) in Shahan and Swoyer (eds) 1979, pp. 155–69.

'Replies to eleven essays' (SWP) *Southwestern Journal of Philosophy*, 11, 1981, 227–43.

OTHER REFERENCES

Alston, William. 1958. 'Ontological commitment', *Philosophical Studies*, 6, 8–17.

Averill, Edward. 1985. 'Color and the anthropocentric problem', *Journal of Philosophy*, 82, 281–304.

Blackburn, Simon. 1984. *Spreading the Word*. Oxford: Oxford University Press.

Block Ned (ed.). 1981. *Readings in Philosophy of Psychology*, vol. 2. Cambridge Mass.: Harvard University Press.

Butterfield, Jeremy (ed.). 1986. *Language, Mind and Logic*. Cambridge: Cambridge University Press.

Carnap, Rudolf. 1928. *The Logical Structure of the World*. Berkeley and Los Angeles: University of California Press, 1967.

Carnap, Rudolf. 1937. *The Logical Syntax of Language*. London: Routledge & Kegan Paul.

Carnap, Rudolf. 1955. 'Meaning and synonymy in natural languages', *Philosophical Studies*, 7, 33–47. Appendix D of Carnap 1956.

Carnap, Rudolf. 1956. *Meaning and Necessity* (second edition). Chicago: University of Chicago Press.

Chisholm, Roderick. 1967. 'Identity through possible worlds: some questions', *Nous*, 1, 1–8.

Chomsky, Noam. 1969. 'Quine's empirical assumptions' in Davidson and Hintikka (eds) 1969, pp. 53–68.

Chomsky, Noam, and Katz, Jerrold. 1974. 'What the linguist is talking about', *Journal of Philosophy*, 71, 347–67, and in Block (ed.) 1981, pp. 223–37.

Church, Alonzo. 1958. 'Ontological commitment', *Journal of Philosophy*, 55, 1008–14.

Craig, Edward. 1983. 'Philosophy and philosophies', *Philosophy*, 58, 189–201.

Craig, Edward. 1985. 'Arithmetic and imagination' in Hacking (ed.) 1985, pp. 89–112.

Davidson, Donald. 1980. *Essays on Actions and Events*. Oxford: Oxford University Press.

Davidson, Donald. 1984. *Inquiries into Truth and Interpretation*. Oxford: Oxford University Press.

Davidson, Donald. 1986a. 'A coherence theory of truth and knowledge' in Lepore (ed.) 1986, pp. 307–19.

Davidson, Donald. 1986b. 'Empirical content' in Lepore (ed.) 1986, pp. 320–32.

Davidson, Donald and Hintikka, Jaakko (eds). 1969. *Words and Objections*. Dordrecht: D. Reidel.

Evans, Gareth. 1985. *Collected Papers*. Oxford: Oxford University Press.

Fodor, Jerry. 1975. *The Language of Thought*. Hassocks: Harvester.

Fodor, Jerry. 1986. 'Banish disContent' in Butterfield (ed.) 1986, pp. 1–32.

Forbes, G. 1985. *The Metaphysics of Modality*. Oxford: Oxford University Press.

Gibson, Roger. 1982. *The Philosophy of W. V. Quine*. Tampa: University Presses of Florida.

Goodman, Nelson. 1951. *The Structure of Appearance*. Cambridge, Mass.: Harvard University Press.

Goodman, Nelson. 1972. *Problems and Projects*. Indianapolis: Hackett.

Goodman, Nelson. 1978. *Ways of Worldmaking*. Indianapolis: Hackett.

Grice, H. P. and Strawson, P. F. 1956. 'In defense of a dogma', *Philosophical Review*, 65, 141–58.

Guttenplan, Samuel (ed.). 1975. *Mind and Language*. Oxford: Oxford University Press.

Hacking, Ian (ed.). 1985. *Exercises in Analysis*. Cambridge: Cambridge University Press.

Hanfling, Oswald (ed.). 1981. *Essential Readings in Logical Positivism*. Oxford: Blackwell.

Healey, Richard. 1978. 'Physicalist imperialism', *Proceedings of the Aristotelian Society*, 79, 191–211.

Hookway, Christopher. 1978. 'Indeterminacy and interpretation' in Hookway and Pettit (eds) 1978, pp. 17–41.

Hookway, Christopher. 1985. *Peirce*. London: Routledge & Kegan Paul.

Hookway C. and Pettit P. (eds). 1978. *Action and Interpretation*. Cambridge: Cambridge University Press.

Hylton, Peter. 1982. 'Analyticity and the indeterminacy of translation', *Synthese*, 52, 167–84.

Kim, Jaegwon. 1986. 'Psychophysical laws' in Lepore and McLaughlin (eds) 1986, pp. 369–86.

Kirk, Robert. 1986. *Translation Determined*. Oxford: Oxford University Press.

Lepore, Ernest (ed.). 1986. *Truth and Interpretation*. Oxford: Blackwell.

Lepore, Ernest and McLaughlin, Brian (eds). 1986. *Action and Events*. Oxford: Blackwell.

Lewis, David. 1983. *Philosophical Papers*, vol. 1. Oxford: Oxford University Press.

Loux, Michael (ed.). 1979. *The Possible and the Actual*. Ithaca: Cornell University Press.

McDowell, John. 1986. 'Functionalism and anomolous monism' in Lepore and McLaughlin (eds) 1986, pp. 387–98.

Mellor, D. H. 1981. *Real Time*. Cambridge: Cambridge University Press.

Newton-Smith, W. 1980. *The Structure of Time*. London: Routledge & Kegan Paul.

Putnam, Hilary. 1975. *Mind, Language and Reality*. Cambridge: Cambridge University Press.

Putnam, Hilary. 1983. *Realism and Reason*. Cambridge: Cambridge University Press.

Ramsey, F. P. 1978. *Foundations* (ed. D. H. Mellor). London: Routledge & Kegan Paul.

Romanos, George. 1983. *Quine and Analytical Philosophy*. Cambridge, Mass.: MIT Press.

Rorty, Richard. 1972. 'Indeterminacy of translation and of truth', *Synthese*, 23, 443–62.

Rorty, Richard. 1982. *Consequences of Pragmatism*. Hassocks: Harvester.

Rorty, Richard. 1986. 'Pragmatism, Davidson and truth', in Lepore (ed.) 1986, pp. 333–55.

Rosenberg, Alexander. 1986. 'Davidson's unintended attack on psychology' in Lepore and McLaughlin (eds) 1986, pp. 399–407.

Russell, B. A. W. 1903. *Principles of Mathematics*. Cambridge: Cambridge University Press.

Russell, B. A. W. 1905. 'On denoting', *Mind*, 14, 479–93.

Schilpp, Paul (ed.). 1963. *The Philosophy of Rudolf Carnap*. La Salle, Ill.: Open Court.

Sellars, Wilfrid. 1963. *Science, Perception and Reality*. London: Routledge & Kegan Paul.

Shahan, R. W. and Swoyer, C. V. (eds). 1979. *Essays on the Philosophy of W. V. Quine*, Hassocks: Harvester.

Smart, J. J. C. 1964. *Philosophy and Scientific Realism*. London: Routledge & Kegan Paul.

Stroud, Barry. 1984. *The Significance of Philosophical Scepticism*. Oxford: Oxford University Press.

Suppes, Patrick. 1985. 'Davidson's views on psychology as a science' in Vermazen and Hintikka (eds) 1985, pp. 183–94.

Unger, Peter. 1984. *Philosophical Relativity*. Oxford: Blackwell.

Vermazen, Bruce, and Hintikka, Merrill, V. (eds). 1985. *Essays on Davidson: Action and Events*. Oxford: Oxford University Press.

Wittgenstein, L. 1921. *Tractatus Logico–Philosophicus*. London: Routledge & Kegan Paul, 1961.

Wittgenstein, L. 1953. *Philosophical Investigations*. Oxford: Blackwell.

Wright, Crispin. 1983. *Frege's Conception of Numbers as Objects*. Aberdeen: Aberdeen University Press.

Index